HYMNIC AFFIRMATION OF DIVINE JUSTICE:

THE DOXOLOGIES OF AMOS AND RELATED TEXTS IN THE OLD TESTAMENT

SOCIETY OF BIBLICAL LITERATURE

DISSERTATION SERIES

edited by

Howard C. Kee

and

Douglas A. Knight

Number 24

HYMNIC AFFIRMATION OF DIVINE JUSTICE:

THE DOXOLOGIES OF AMOS AND RELATED TEXTS IN THE OLD TESTAMENT

by

James L. Crenshaw

SCHOLARS PRESS
Missoula, Montana

HYMNIC AFFIRMATION OF DIVINE JUSTICE:

THE DOXOLOGIES OF AMOS AND RELATED TEXTS IN THE OLD TESTAMENT

by

James L. Crenshaw

Published by

SCHOLARS PRESS

for

The Society of Biblical Literature

Distributed by

SCHOLARS PRESS
University of Montana
Missoula, Montana   59801

HYMNIC AFFIRMATION OF DIVINE JUSTICE:

THE DOXOLOGIES OF AMOS AND RELATED TEXTS IN THE OLD TESTAMENT

by

James L. Crenshaw
3807 Brighton Rd.
Nashville, TN   37205

Ph.D., 1964   Advisor:
Vanderbilt University   J. Philip Hyatt

Library of Congress Cataloging in Publication Data

Crenshaw, James L
   Hymnic affirmation of divine justice.

   (Dissertation series ; no. 24)
   Originally presented as the author's thesis, Vanderbilt University, 1964.
   Bibliography: p.
   1. Bible. O. T. Amos--Criticism, interpretation,
etc. 2. Praise of God--Biblical teaching. 3. Doxology. I. Title. II. Series: Society of Biblical Literature. Dissertation series ; no. 24.
BS1585.2.C73 1975   224'.8'06   75-22349
ISBN 0-89130-016-3

Printed in the United States of America
1 2 3 4 5
Printing Department
University of Montana
Missoula, Montana   59801

To Martha

TABLE OF CONTENTS

ACKNOWLEDGEMENTS

Without the assistance of a great host of people, this thesis would neither have been attempted nor brought to its completion. Several of them deserve a special word of appreciation.

First, to the faculty of Vanderbilt Divinity School, especially to Professors Hyatt and Harrelson, whose suggestions and criticisms have opened new vistas along the way, I wish to extend my sincerest appreciation.

Second, a word of gratitude is in order for the assistance given me by the library staff of the Religion and Reserve sections of the Joint Universities Library of Vanderbilt University.

Last, but certainly not least, I wish to thank my mother, whose love for God and his Word is an inspiration to her son, and my wife, who has made this study both possible and pleasant.

ABBREVIATIONS

ANQ	*Andover Newton Quarterly*
AJSL	*American Journal of Semitic Languages and Literature*
ARW	*Archiv für Religionswissenschaft*
Bib	*Biblica*
BR	*Biblical Research*
BWANT	*Beiträge zur Wissenschaft vom Alten und Neuen Testament*
BZAW	*Beihefte zur Zeitschrift für die alttestamentliche Wissenschaft*
EvTh	*Evangelische Theologie*
HDBul	*Harvard Divinity Bulletin*
HTR	*Harvard Theological Review*
HUCA	*Hebrew Union College Annual*
IB	*The Interpreter's Bible*
IDB	*The Interpreter's Dictionary of the Bible*
JAOS	*Journal of the American Oriental Society*
JBL	*Journal of Biblical Literature*
JEOL	*Jaarbericht...Ex Oriente Lux*
JMEOS	*Journal of Manchester Egyptian Oriental Society*
JNES	*Journal of Near Eastern Studies*
JSS	*Journal of Semitic Studies*
JTS	*Journal of Theological Studies*
NKZ	*Neue Kirchliche Zeitschrift*
NRT	*Nouvelle Revue Théologique*
NTT	*Norsk Teologisk Tidsskrift*
OTS	*Oudtestamentische Studien*
RGG	*Die Religion in Geschichte und Gegenwart*
STU	*Schweizerische Theologische Umschau*

StTh	Studia Theologica
SVT	Supplement Vetus Testamentum
ThLZ	Theologische Literaturzeitung
ThR	Theologische Rundschau
ThuGl	Theologie und Glaube
ThZ	Theologische Zeitschrift
VT	Vetus Testamentum
VerbDom	Verbum Domini
ZAW	Zeitschrift für die alttestamentliche Wissenschaft
ZDPV	Zeitschrift des Deutschen Palästina-Vereins

INTRODUCTION

The problem to which this dissertation is addressed can be stated both negatively and positively. In the first place, the study is undertaken because of inadequate treatment of the doxologies within commentaries on Amos. On the one hand, the doxologies are uncritically accepted as authentic words of Amos, with little attempt to understand the vast implications and difficulties of such a view. On the other hand, they are rejected with little thought as to their appropriateness to the text of Amos even if spurious, and are labeled "liturgical additions" for the purpose of public reading without any recognition of the hidden assumptions of such a statement in regard to the nature of post-exilic Judaism and her use of what came to be Scripture. In addition, the doxologies are said to be influenced by Second Isaiah and certain Psalms, and to be of no value in a discussion of Amos' theological position.

While most of these observations are helpful, they do not penetrate to the heart of the matter. This becomes evident when one asks the fundamental questions concerning the function and form of the doxologies. In other words, why were the doxologies placed in their present position instead of somewhere else? Does their form indicate something of the function of the doxologies, and can a similar literary piece in other books throw light upon the text of Amos? Furthermore, it is a methodological mistake to ignore the message of the doxologies, even though pointing to Second Isaiah and certain Psalms for illumination or comparison. In short, the doxologies deserve to be examined on their own merit, which is considerable, both Second Isaiah and Psalms being used merely as background material. One further point may be made in this regard: the doxologies are not alien to the thought of Amos, so it is not quite correct to exclude them from consideration in a discussion of his theology. Perhaps it would be more accurate to indicate that Amos' thought ultimately leads to the view of God and man contained within the doxologies.

The positive reason for undertaking this study is two-fold: first, the formal similarity of the doxologies, and second, the advances made in recent research on literary types in prophetic literature. The formal similarity of the doxologies cries for literary analysis, and the use of a common refrain calls attention to other contexts where it is employed. In view of the contexts in which the doxologies appear, one would assume that conclusions drawn by recent scholars in regard to the prophetic lawsuit ($r\hat{\imath}b$) could be applied most fruitfully to a discussion of the doxologies of Amos.

The purpose of this thesis derives from the negative and positive observations above. Three objectives are paramount: (1) to discover the reason for the presence of the doxologies in their context; (2) to determine whether they were placed here by Amos or by another; and (3) to ascertain the setting in life of the doxologies. The ultimate objective is to give a theological exposition of the doxologies within their contexts on the basis of conclusions drawn in regard to each of the three objectives.

The method employed is form-critical; the work will comprise four stages. First, a history of research on the doxologies will be given, together with conclusions about the key to analysis of the doxologies. Second, a chapter will be devoted to an examination of the text of the doxologies. Attention will be given to textual problems, philological matters, metrical concerns and translation itself.

The third chapter will attempt to give an answer to the questions of the form and function of the doxologies. The key to such an endeavor will be discovered in the refrain that appears in each doxology. Consequently, its use elsewhere will be studied, specifically as to the different forms of the refrain and motifs connected with each literary type. From this examination of form will also appear some indication of the refrain's function and various motifs associated with it. On the basis of conclusions regarding the form and function of the refrain in texts outside Amos, a historical reconstruction of the life setting of the phenomena will be given and defended. Once this has been achieved, the refrain and doxologies of Amos will be examined to see if they fit into the place in life offered, that is, to discover whether their form and function are the same as those of the refrain and its contexts elsewhere.

The final step will be a theological exposition of the doxologies within their contexts; this will employ the results of the earlier research, and will serve as a kind of test of the thesis itself. In essence it will seek to overcome the negative treatment of the doxologies referred to above, and to make proper use of the materials mentioned in the positive reason for the endeavor. This exposition will be followed by a concluding chapter in which the results of the study will be given, its relevance for the understanding of other biblical texts pointed out, and areas of further study suggested by the thesis will be mentioned, together with some observations about directions such research should take.

CHAPTER I

A HISTORY OF THE INTERPRETATION OF THE DOXOLOGIES
WITHIN THEIR CONTEXTS

A. *Arguments for Interpolation*

The doxologies of Amos have been thought to be later additions because of four factors: interruption of context, elevated
theology, late language, and the presence of a parallel phenomenon in Hosea.[1] However, recent research has raised a question
about these reasons for considering the passages the product of
the exilic or post-exilic community; therefore, it is necessary
that these arguments be submitted to careful scrutiny.

1. *The Doxologies and their immediate Contexts*

The contextual question deserves primary consideration.
The first doxology is at the end of a series of divine chastisements that had the purpose of bringing Israel to repentance for
her sins, although the refrain at the end of each punishment
("Yet you did not return to me") reveals the failure of God's
purpose (4:6-11). The list of chastisements concludes with a
threat of final punishment (4:12), but the nature of the judgment is uncertain, perhaps intentionally so, since an unnamed
threat may be psychologically more ominous than a specified one,[2]

---

[1]These arguments are conveniently summarized by R. S. Cripps,
A Critical and Exegetical Commentary on the Book of Amos (London:
SPCK, 1929) 184-85, and E. A. Edghill, *The Book of Amos* (London:
Methuen and Co., 1914), 46-47. To these arguments another is
sometimes added, namely that the doxologies are not necessary to
the prophet's argument. The authenticity of the doxologies
was first challenged by Bernhard Duhm, *Die Theologie der Propheten*
(Bonn: Verlag von Adolph Marcus, 1875), 119. A. Neher, *Amos:
contribution à l'étude du prophetisme* (Paris: Librairie Philosophique J. Vrin, 1950), 66, writes that these are wrongly called
doxologies. This would follow, if one accepts E. Werner's two
criteria of a doxology; see "The Doxology in Synagogue and Church,
a Liturgico-Musical Study," *HUCA*, XIX (1945-46), 277, and *The
Sacred Bridge* (New York: Columbia University Press, 1959), 276.

[2]S. R. Driver, *Joel and Amos*, revised edition (Cambridge:
University Press, 1915), 176; Th. H. Robinson and F. Horst, *Die
zwölf Kleinen Propheten* (Tübingen: J.C.B. Mohr [P. Siebeck],
1954), 87.

or the original words of the prophet may be lost.[3]   In favor of
the latter hypothesis it has been urged that the somewhat cumbersome repetition of the phrase "therefore thus I will do to you,
O Israel" in the form of "because I will do this to you" indicates the activity of a later hand.[4]   The section concludes with
the threat, "Prepare to meet your God, O Israel," namely in judgment.[5]   There follows the first doxology, which praises Yahweh,
the God of Hosts, as the Former of mountains, the Creator of
wind, the Revealer to man of his (God's) intention, the One who
makes the morning darkness and treads upon the high places of
the earth.[6]   Chapter five opens with a dirge lamenting the fall
of the Virgin Israel; apparently, this lament has no connection
with the preceding list of chastisements or doxology, although
it could be argued that the lament is but the response to the
working out of the threat in 4:12.

It may be concluded that while the somewhat cumbersome repetition of the threat could indicate a later hand in 4:12b-13,
this conclusion is not demanded. Moreover, the doxology fits
neatly as a description of the greatness of the God to be confronted in judgment.

Those who deny to Amos the doxologies because of intrusion
into the context have emphasized the second doxological fragment
(5:8-9), there being almost unanimous agreement that two verses
belonging together (5:7,10) have been split asunder by the addition of the doxology.[7]   The theme of the verses immediately preceding the doxology is "Seek me [Yahweh] and live." This divine

---

[3]So most commentators, W. Nowack, *Die Kleinen Propheten
Übersetzt und Erklärt* (Göttingen: Vandenhoeck & Ruprecht, 1922),
140, and W. R. Harper, *Amos and Hosea* (Edinburgh: T. & T. Clark,
1905), 102, for example.

[4]John D. W. Watts, *Vision and Prophecy in Amos* (Leiden: E.
J. Brill, 1958), 67, Karl Cramer, "Amos: Versuch einer theologischen Interpretation," *BWANT*, LI (1930), 90-95, and W. S.
McCullough, "Some Suggestions about Amos," *JBL*, LXXII (1953),
248, do not think a later hand has been at work here.

[5]It is surprising that Cripps, *op. cit.*, 296-97, had to
deny that this passage sounds the gospel trumpet, for such a
call to repentance is inconceivable here.

[6]This is the traditional interpretation.

[7]Only Watts, *op. cit.*, 54-57, disagrees; he attempts to
include 5:6-7 in the doxology.

word then finds elaboration and substantiation in the prophetic word, although there is some question about the extent of the word of Yahweh; more particularly, as to whether the command not to seek Bethel, enter Gilgal, or cross over into Beersheba, along with the prediction of the fall of Bethel,[8] is the divine word or the prophetic elaboration of it. There seems to be no reason to reject the view that 5:6 comes from Amos ("Seek the Lord and live, lest he break out like fire in the house of Joseph, and it devour, with none to quench it for Bethel"). The real question concerns the relationship and sequence of 5:6,7, 10,14-15.[9] Wilhelm Rudolph has argued that 5:6 belongs closely with 5:14-15, which gives further expansion of the divine word, and in this view he has been followed by Franz Hesse.[10] It must be admitted that there is much to commend the suggestion, for just as 5:6 has explained the divine word and offered the reason for the demand, so 5:14-15 gives further elaboration. In fact these verses define what it means to "seek me and live": namely, to seek good and not evil, so that the ancient cry of the people, "God with us," may find substance; again "to seek me" means hatred of evil, love of good, and establishment of justice in the gate. The prophetic explanation of God's word ends with the ominous note that "it may be that the Lord, the God of Hosts, will be gracious to the remnant of Joseph"--ominous because of the uncertain assurance as over against the popular claim that God is with us, no evil can befall us. But, attractive as Rudolph's suggestion may be, one could wonder if verse seven should not have been included in the unit, first because of its presence after 5:6 where it belongs logically; second, because 5:15 returns to the theme of justice in explaining the divine word; and finally, because one expects to hear a word about what the people are doing instead of seeking Yahweh. Such a word would constitute the prophetic accusation.

---

[8]For a comprehensive discussion of these sanctuaries, see Hans-Joachim Kraus, *Gottesdienst in Israel* (München: Chr. Kaiser Verlag, 1962), 172-202 (*Worship in Israel* [Richmond, Va.: John Knox Press, 1965]).

[9]Artur Weiser, "Die Prophetie des Amos," *BZAW*, LIII (1929), 183, 185-86, rejects 5:6,14-15 as later.

[10]Wilhelm Rudolph, "Gott und Mensch bei Amos," *Imago Dei: Festschrift für Gustav Krüger* (Giessen, 1932), 19ff.; Franz Hesse, "Amos 5:4-6, 14f.," *ZAW*, LXVIII (1956), 1-17.

Against this interpretation it has been argued that 5:10 completes the oracle in 5:7 and belongs naturally and logically to it, despite the difference in person, that is, the shift from the vocative (second person) to the third person.[11] Admittedly, 5:11 returns to the second person, and textual arguments based solely on a shift in persons are highly questionable. In actual fact, most commentators have felt that 5:7,10 belong together, and have believed this so strongly that this fact alone proves for them the doxologies to be insertions.[12]

Even if 5:7 were connected with 5:14-15, this would not seriously alter the conclusions about the doxology, for the absence of a referent illustrated by the Targum ("They have left off fearing before....") constitutes a serious problem, while the aphorism in 5:13 may indicate that the entire passage (5:8-13) has been added by a later hand, at least part of which (10-12) may be genuine words of the prophet.[13]

The second doxology praises the Lord who made the constellations, controls the natural sequence of day and night, gives rain, and sends destruction upon the strong.[14] The extent of the fragment is uncertain, the problem being increased by the Septuagint's rendering of 5:7 as a part of the doxology, and the textual and philological problems in 5:9.[15]

Unlike the first, which belongs quite well to its context, but can be dispensed with, the second doxology does not seem to fit its context at all, interrupting either 5:7,10 or more probably 5:4-7,14-15, and together with 5:13, setting off a passage containing authentic words of Amos (5:1-12).

In the final chapter of Amos a third doxological fragment appears, and recalls a part of the second (5:8b; 9:6b) and 8:8 (9:5b; 8:8b). This time the doxology does no violence to the

---

[11]So most commentators.

[12]Even G. A. Smith, *The Book of the Twelve Prophets* (London: Hodder & Stoughton, 1928), 213-14, is convinced that this is the real difficulty of maintaining their authenticity.

[13]On the other hand, S. R. Driver, *op. cit.*, 182, has called attention to Isa. 40:22 where Yahweh is implicit in the writer's thought.

[14]This is the traditional view.

[15]See J.D.W. Watts, "Note on the Hebrew Text of Am. V:7," *VT*, IV (1954), 215-16.

context, but can be omitted without loss of the meaning of 9:1-
4,7-8a. The chapter opens with a vision of Yahweh standing beside the altar, and proceeds to describe the divine act of destruction. Those who escape the collapse of the sanctuary will
find no hiding place, in Sheol, heaven, Carmel, sea, or captivity. The vision concludes with a terrible threat that Yahweh
will set his eyes upon Israel for evil and not for good.

The doxology praises the Lord, the God of Hosts, as the One
who touches the earth, causing it to melt and its inhabitants to
mourn, and bringing about a rise and decline similar to that of
the Nile; it further extols him who builds his upper chambers in
the heavens and founds his vault upon the earth; finally, it repeats the emphasis of 5:8b to the effect that he gives rain upon
the earth.[16]

The doxology is followed by two verses that reject the claim
that Israel will receive special treatment from God; these verses
give the prophetic elaboration of the divine threat, as well as
the reasons for it.[17] The promise in 9:8b, which is thought to
contradict the whole tenor of Amos' preaching, is certainly late;
however, 9:9-10 may very well come from the prophet.

By way of summary, the following can be said about the argument as to the lateness of the doxologies based on their intrusion into the contexts. The first in no way intrudes; the most
that can be said is that the repetition of the threat is somewhat
awkward. But the doxology is appropriate to the context as a

---

[16]According to the traditional interpretation.

[17]In 5:4-7,14-15, the prophet takes up the divine word
("Seek me") and expands it, explaining the meaning. Likewise in
9:1-4,7-8a, Amos repeats a part of the divine word ("eyes of the
Lord"). Could it be that in 5:1-2 Amos does the same thing?
Did 4:12b speak of the fall of the nation as in 3:12? If so,
this would be a confirmation along form-critical lines of Sellin's
view, *Das Zwölfprophetenbuch*, I (Leipzig: A. Deichertsche Verlags-
buchhandlung D. Werner Scholl, 1929), 220, 225, attained through
literary criticism alone. Such an understanding would fit perfectly with 5:1-2. There would be a similar procedure in each
case, the divine word being softened by Amos: 3:12 stresses the
terrible catastrophe, 5:1-2 defines it, while 5:3 shows that a
few will survive; 5:4 gives the demand and threat, while 5:14-15
represents Amos' toning down of the divine message under certain
conditions; and 9:1-4 has God's judgment on the sanctuary and
people, while 9:7 justifies it and 9:9-10 softens it by means
of the phrase "all *sinners* shall die."

description of the God to be confronted in judgment, and it certainly can serve the purpose of explaining why Israel had better "prepare to meet" him. A similar purpose could be suggested for the second doxology, which could provide the basis for the assertion that God might break out like fire and consume Bethel; but it is difficult to get around the problem presented by the lack of a referent for "He who made," and the doxology probably should be viewed as an intrusion, interrupting either 5:7,10 or 5:7,14-15. On the other hand, the third fits just as neatly into its context as do any of the oracles in the last two chapters of Amos.[18] Moreover, if the melting of the earth and pouring out of waters is viewed as destructive, then once again the doxology serves as the prophetic "grounds" for the divine word. Hence in regard to the third doxology, one must be cautious in speaking of "intrusion" in the text.

2.   *Elevated Theology within the Doxologies*

Another reason for rejecting the doxologies has been the supposed elevated theology characteristic of the hymns, a view of God that is said to have originated in the exile with Second Isaiah and Job.[19] Furthermore, such ejaculations of praise are said to have originated in the exilic period, as was thought to have been confirmed by the Psalms especially. The doxologies depict God as Creator and Sustainer of the universe, yet one concerned about man enough to reveal oracles to him and to

---

[18]This is rightly emphasized by George Adam Smith, *op. cit.*, 213. One of the defenders of the doxologies, W. R. Smith, *The Prophets of Israel* (London: A. & C. Black, 1897), 399, concedes that the doxologies are not closely connected with their contexts in detail, but maintains that they are thoroughly appropriate to its general purport. In this entire discussion of intrusion into the contexts it must not be forgotten that the prophet Amos is not responsible for the final form of the book named after him. This means that the question of authenticity must not be settled on the basis of "intrusion" alone.

[19]Julius Wellhausen, *Geschichte Israels*, I (Berlin: G. Reimer, 1878), 349-350, note 2, compares these to lyrical intermezzi celebrating Jehovah as Lord of the universe, which characterizes Second Isaiah, and says that the all-creating power of God acquired a sudden prominence in the exile. W. R. Smith, *op. cit.*, 398, writes that the ejaculatory form is no surprise, in view of the general conditions of prophetic oratory, and in each case the appeal comes in to relieve the intense feeling at a critical point. But does it not rather intensify it?

punish the strong. The designation of Yahweh as Creator ($bh\bar{o}r\bar{e}$')
of the universe is the bone of contention, especially significant
since the Yahwistic creation account lacks a cosmogony. It is
said that Yahweh was not thought of as Creator of the cosmos until the time of Second Isaiah, who emphasizes the fact in a context of new creation.[20] Paul Humbert has given attention to
this matter, concluding that the doctrine of Yahweh as Creator
is probably earlier than the eighth century, certainly as old as
the seventh.[21] However, his conclusions must be accepted with
a great deal of reserve, especially since the only "eighth century" use of the word $b\bar{a}r\bar{a}$' is that of the first doxology.
Nevertheless, from a study of the ancient Near Eastern background, it would be strange indeed if Israel did not have a
cosmogony, though some might find it in poetic allusions to a
battle between Yahweh and the sea monster, one of two creation
traditions argued for by Eissfeldt.[22]

Nor is the case different when one considers Amos' preaching more carefully, for Yahweh is not only God of all nations,
but one whose power cannot be escaped in heaven or Sheol, and
whose command can send sea serpent, sword, or fire upon the
sinners. Victor Maag has emphasized the cosmic fire that is
central to Amos' message, rightly seeing in it something ap-
proaching the view of God as Lord of the universe.[23] When this
is coupled with that author's conclusions about the meaning of
the phrase, "Yahweh, the God of Hosts," it is no longer possible

---

[20]G. A. Smith, *op. cit.*, 212; W. Nowack, *op. cit.*, 140-41.

[21]"Emploi et portée du verbe $b\bar{a}r\bar{a}$' (créer) dans l'Ancien
Testament," *ThZ*, III (1947), 401-22.

[22]Otto Eissfeldt, "Gott und das Meer in der Bibel," *Studia
Orientalia Ioanni Pedersen* (Copenhagen: Einai Munksgaard, 1953),
76-84.

[23]Victor Maag, "Jahwäs Heerscharen," *Festschrift für L.
Köhler (Schweizerische Theologische Umschau*, 1950), 49. Compare
A. S. Kapelrud, "God as Destroyer in the Preaching of Amos and
in the Ancient Near East," *JBL*, LXXI (1952), 33-38. In *Central
Ideas in Amos* (Oslo: H. Aschehoug, 1956), 46, A. S. Kapelrud
thinks that the universalism of Amos was taken over from the
ancient God '$\bar{e}l$ $^c\bar{e}ly\hat{o}n$. In the work referred to above, Maag
lists the mythical influences in Amos: 1:4-7; 2:12; 4:7-11; 6:8;
7:1; 7:4; 8:8-9; 9:3.

to dismiss the doxologies so easily simply on the basis of the view of God depicted therein.[24]

However, there still remains an element of truth in the contention that while Amos describes God as Lord of the nations, the doxologies praise him as Lord of the universe in a sense finding its closest parallels in Second Isaiah and Job. This similarity is not only one of subject matter, but even of style and vocabulary, as seen most clearly in Job 9:1-12, and to a lesser degree in Isa. 40:12,22-23,28 and so on.

3. *Philological Considerations*

The third reason given for considering the doxologies later additions is philological. It is argued that the doxologies contain a style more appropriate to Job and Second Isaiah, as well as individual words and phrases that point to a later period than Amos' day.[25] In regard to the style, it must be admitted that such a series of participles without a governing verb is unusual in Amos' oracles,[26] while the use of the refrain "Yahweh, the God of Hosts, is his name" finds excellent formal parallels in the series of threats against the nations (1:3-2:8): "For three transgressions of...and for four I will not revoke the punishment," and in the list of chastisements (4:6-11): "Yet you did not return unto me."[27]

The use of *bhōrēʾ* has already been mentioned; many see in this word alone conclusive proof that the doxologies are from a period subsequent to Second Isaiah. On the other hand, Paul Humbert's searching analysis concludes that *bārāʾ* was a technical

---

[24]Maag's conclusions about Yahweh of Hosts will be discussed later. The antiquity of such an elevated view of God might find additional support in the ancient hymn embedded in Ps. 18 and II Sam. 22, where the theophany is described in similar terms to those of the doxologies. See R. Vuilleumier, *La tradition cultuelle d'Israël* (Neuchatel: Delachaux & Niestlé, 1960), 88-90.

[25]G. A. Smith, *op. cit.*, 214-215; R. S. Cripps, *op. cit.*, 184-185. Attention is usually called to the use of participles, the refrain "Yahweh, God of Hosts is his name," *bhōrēʾ*, *śēhô*, *ʾagudāthô*, *maʿălôthaw*.

[26]J. P. Hyatt, "Amos," *Peake's Commentary on the Bible*, M. Black and H. H. Rowley, eds. (New York: Thomas Nelson & Sons, 1962), 621.

[27]In the *use* of the refrain, not the content of it.

term employed in the cult during the eighth century.[28] Humbert's
conclusions must be studied carefully, for if he is right, one
of the most cogent reasons for rejecting the doxologies has been
removed.

However, even Humbert recognized the possibility that Am.
4:13 was an addition to the prophetic text, so that he guarded
himself by viewing the use of *bhōrē'* in Amos as "probably" genuine. Nevertheless, far-reaching conclusions were drawn from
the text in Amos, becoming stronger with frequent repetition.
Because of the nature of the doxology, Humbert thought that Amos
borrowed a cultic hymn, so that the word *bārā'* must be understood as a technical word even before Amos' day, for use in a
cult does not grow up overnight.[29] Victor Maag has recognized
this fact; calling attention to the use of *yāṣar* as a parallel
to *bārā'*, which he understood as strongly anthropomorphic, Maag
strengthens his argument by reference to the phrase "who treads
upon the heights of the earth."[30] On the basis of this stark
anthropomorphic language, Maag argued that Am. 4:13 stands in
the mid-point of the development of *bārā'* from an originally
secular term to a technical one relegated to the Israelite cult
and employed to describe Yahweh's creative work.

Neither the conclusion of Humbert nor that of Maag is justified. Because of the nature of the doxologies in Amos, no
conclusion so important should be based on them alone. To argue
that since the doxologies use *bhōrē'*, the word antedates Amos,
and because *bārā'* is used before Amos, the doxologies are genuine,
is circular reasoning that should convince no one. In brief,
Humbert should have excluded Am. 4:13 from his pre-exilic uses
of *bārā'*. Had he done so, a different picture would have emerged.
In such a procedure, Jer. 31:22 could have been given a natural
interpretation rather than the forced explanation that the prophet has borrowed a cultic phrase and given it new meaning; that
is, a word previously employed only in a cosmogonic sense is

---

[28]Humbert, *loc. cit.*

[29]Humbert, *loc. cit.*

[30]V. Maag, *Text, Wortschatz und Begriffswelt des Buches
Amos* (Leiden: E. J. Brill, 1951), 134.

used here with a soteriological connotation.[31]   Once Am. 4:13 is
excluded from consideration as a pre-exilic use of $b\bar{a}r\bar{a}$' and Jer.
31:22 is given its natural explanation, only one other text remains. In Dt. 4:32 Moses is made to require of the people: "For
ask now of the days that are past, which were before you, since
the day that God ($'^{ae}l\bar{o}h\hat{i}m$) created man upon the earth, and ask
...whether such a great thing...was ever heard of."[32]   While it
is true, as Humbert points out, that this use of $b\bar{a}r\bar{a}$' occurs
in Levitical parenesis, one must not conclude from this fact
alone that the word is a technical term so full of mana that no
one will use it outside the cult.[33]   From the perspective suggested above, only two reasonably certain pre-exilic uses of
$b\bar{a}r\bar{a}$' exist, one of which is non-cultic, the other an incidental
allusion within Levitical parenesis. Thus the most that one can
do is suggest that the word was known by Jeremiah and the author
of the special introduction to Deuteronomy, at least one of whom
uses the word in a soteriological sense, but no conclusions as
to the use of $b\bar{a}r\bar{a}$' before Amos are justified.

Maag's hypothesis, which rested upon the findings of Humbert, likewise has little to commend it. While it is true that
the Priestly writer uses $^{c}\bar{a}sah$ as the exclusive parallel of
$b\bar{a}r\bar{a}$', one cannot conclude that the use of $y\bar{a}sar$ is proof of
antiquity, as a glance at Second Isaiah immediately indicates,
45:7,18, for example.[34]   The same can be said about the phrase
"and treads upon the heights of the earth," for its occurrence
in Job 9:8 and Hab. 3:15 cannot be attributed to an earlier period of Israelite thought when strongly anthropomorphic language

---

[31]Humbert, *op. cit.*, 404. He emends the text to read: "The
woman [Israel] will love her husband." This verse in Jeremiah
may be both eschatological and soteriological, Israel being depicted as mother (or bride) who shelters her son (or husband).
On the other hand, it may be neither cosmogonic nor soteriological.

[32]The use of $'^{ae}l\bar{o}h\hat{i}m$ here is strange (cf. $'\bar{e}l$ in Mal.
2:10). Humbert, *ibid.*, 409-10 considers them generic.

[33]Humbert, *ibid.*, 403-404, 418-19.

[34]Humbert, *ibid.*, 408, 413, calls attention to the fact
that the Priestly writer uses $y\bar{a}sar$ for the exclusive parallel
of $b\bar{a}r\bar{a}$'.

was common, but must be considered an archaistic tendency within later thought.[35]

The use of an elevated style, participial phrases, and the term *bhōrē'* are not the only philological arguments given for the lateness of the doxologies. By far the most decisive for some commentators is the phrase, "Yahweh, God of Hosts is his name," which is thought to have come into frequent use with Second Isaiah, the doxologies showing dependence on this late expression.[36] In view of the significance attributed to the phrase, a closer examination is necessary.

The grammatical relationship of the short form is uncertain, although the longer form *YHWH 'ᵃᵉlōhē ṣᵉbhā'ôth* is certainly a genitive construct.[37] Two explanations of *YHWH ṣᵉbhā'ôth* are possible; *ṣᵉbhā'ôth* may be viewed either as a genitive relationship or in apposition with *YHWH*.[38] If the former, two translations may be given, depending upon whether one views *ṣᵉbhā'ôth* as a concrete or abstract term.[39] On the other hand, the appositional use of *ṣᵉbhā'ôth* would demand a translation of *ṣᵉbhā'ôth* as a proper name.[40] All three interpretations are vividly illustrated by the Septuagint, which renders the phrase by κύριος τῶν δυναμέων, κύριος παντοκράτωρ

---

[35]W. F. Albright, "The Psalm of Habakkuk," *Studies in Old Testament Prophecy*, H. H. Rowley, ed. (Edinburgh: T. & T. Clark, 1947), 1-18, especially p. 9.

[36]Cripps, *op. cit.*, 330-33; G. A. Smith, *op. cit.*, 215.

[37]B. W. Anderson, "Hosts, Host of Heaven, *IDB*, II (New York: Abingdon, 1962), 656; Otto Eissfeldt, "Jahwe Zebaoth," *Miscellanea Academica Berolinensia*, II, 2 (1950), 131; Victor Maag, "Jahwäs Heerscharen," 28-29.

[38]Eissfeldt, *ibid.*, 131-32. He thinks *ṣᵉbhā'ôth* can be a proper name. Consequently, Yahweh the Mighty One is not understood as a paraphrase.

[38a]See now the author's essay entitled, "*YHWH ṣᵉbā'ōt šᵉmô*: A Form-Critical Analysis," *ZAW*, 81 (1969), 156-75.

[39]*Ibid.* One would render the phrase by "Yahweh of hosts" if concrete, and by "Yahweh of Hosts" if abstract.

[40]W. R. Arnold, *The Ephod and the Ark* (Cambridge: Harvard University Press, 1917), 142-48, who translates "Yahweh the Warrior."

and κύριος ζαβαώθ.[41] The issue would be resolved if one could accept the longer form as original, but this is by no means certain.[42]

Since no satisfactory solution to the problem can be gained from a grammatical analysis of the phrase or from the versions, perhaps a study of syntax will be more fruitful. Once again two views are voiced. By far the majority of scholars understand the word $ṣ^ebhā'ôth$ in terms of I Sam. 17:45, interpreting the hosts as the armies of Israel.[43] On the other hand, it is argued just as strongly that $ṣ^ebhā'ôth$ refers to cosmic entities (stars,

---

[41]In view of Maag's conclusions (below), the first translation is correct from the point of view of the history of religions, while the second is theologically correct, and the third is accurate from both perspectives if Eissfeldt's view be accepted (below).

[42]As can be seen by E. Kautzsch's article "$ṣ^ebā'ôth$," *Realencyklopädia für protest. Theologie und Kirche*, 3. Aufl., XXI (1908), 620-27, and his shift in position from that presented in the twenty-seventh edition of his grammar to a different view in the next edition (see Eissfeldt, "Jahwe Zebaoth," 132). Those accepting the short form are B. N. Wambacq, *L'épithète divine Jahve $ṣ^ebā'ôt$* (Desclee: De Brouwer, 1947), 100; B. W. Anderson, "Lord of Hosts," *IDB*, III (New York: Abingdon, 1962), 151; G. von Rad, *Old Testament Theology* I, D.M.G. Stalker, trans. (London: Oliver & Boyd, 1962), 18-19; W. F. Albright, "Review. B. N. Wambacq, L'épithète divine Jahve ṣ^ebā'ôt," *JBL*, LXVII (1948), 380.
On the other hand, L. Köhler, *Old Testament Theology*, A. S. Todd, trans. (Philadelphia: Westminster Press, 1957), 50, and V. Maag, "Jahwäs Heerscharen," 28-29, argue for the antiquity of the long form. Otto Eissfeldt, "Jahwe Zebaoth," 138, gets out of the impasse by suggesting that both forms are early, each being independent of the other, the longer form representing "$ṣ^ebā'ôthheit$," the shorter "$ṣ^ebā'ôthhafte$."
Against the originality of the long form, it may be noted that its eighteen uses (as compared with 267 of the short form) are not in the early literature alone, but almost to the contrary. However, the use of $'^{ae}lōhîm ṣ^ebhā'ôth$ in Ps. 80:5,8,15,20; 59:6, which must be understood as an alternative for Yahweh of Hosts, would seem to point to the longer form as earlier, in Maag's opinion. See Maag, "Jahwäs Heerscharen," 28-29.

[43]W. F. Albright, "Review. B. N. Wambacq, L'épithète divine Jahve ṣ^ebā'ôt," 377-81; J. Obermann, "The Divine Name YHWH in the Light of Recent Discoveries," *JBL*, LXVIII (1949), 309-14; E. Kautzsch, *loc. cit.*; and D. N. Freedman, "The Name of the God of Moses," *JBL*, LXXIX (1960), 151-56 (especially 156). But W. Eichrodt, *Theology of the Old Testament* I, J. A. Baker, trans. (Philadelphia: Westminster Press, 1961), 192-93, rejects this view on several grounds. First, I Sam. 17:45 is fairly late; second, the mention of $ṣib'ôt yiśrā'ēl$ which usually refers to people in general, not soldiers in particular, is common to passages in the Deuteronomic, Priestly and Psalm literature as well; and third,

angels, elements of nature, demons, the whole universe).[44] Thus it would seem that neither grammar, versions nor syntax favors any single position, so that Gerhard von Rad's point may be well taken that an element of cultic *epiklesis* as old as this is not in all circumstances capable of rational explanation.[45]

---

this view does not explain the prophetic use of the phrase, since $ṣ^ebhā'ôth$ is never applied to the heavenly hosts and the prophets use the term as a matter of course without any explanation.

[44]See Wambacq, *op. cit.*, 17-45, where he discusses these views rather extensively. He lists:
1. God of stars (H. Ewald, L. Köhler)
2. God of angels (O. Borchert)
3. God of the elements of nature (J. G. von Herder, H. Gressmann, H. Gunkel, K. Marti)
4. God of demons (J. Wellhausen, K. Budde, E. Sellin)
5. Lord of the Universe (S. R. Driver, H. Cramer, W. Eichrodt).

E. Jacob, *Theology of the Old Testament*, A. W. Heathcote and P. J. Allcock, trans. (New York: Harper, 1958), 55, calls attention to the Assyrian title *šar kiššati* in defense of the view of $ṣ^ebhā'ôth$ as the totality of forces over which Yahweh rules (without giving credit to J. Hehn; see W. Eichrodt, *op. cit.*, 193, note 2). A version of the fourth view has recently been championed by V. Maag, "Jahwäs Heerscharen," who understands Yahweh $ṣ^ebhā'ôth$ as the numerous Canaanite spirits of the sky, earth, sea and underworld that have been de-potentialized and made servants of Yahweh. Maag writes, "Die $ṣ^ebā'ôth$ sind die depotenzierten mythischen Naturmächte Kanaans, und die Propagierung des Titels 'Gott der $ṣ^ebā'ôth$' war eine erste wichtige Waffe im diesbezüglichen geistigen Ringer des Jahwismus" ("Jahwäs Heerscharen," 50). The article by Eissfeldt opens a new door toward the interpretation of the phrase. He notices that Latin and Greek have a plural of intensity, and seeks to understand $ṣ^ebhā'ôth$ as such, translating "Yahweh the Mighty One"; Eissfeldt, *op. cit.*, 136-37. The point of departure for this view was provided by B. N. Wambacq, who has given the most exhaustive treatment of the phrase, concluding that the term means "the all-powerful God, or rather the irresistible God" (Wambacq, *op. cit.*, 200). G. von Rad, *op. cit.*, 19, apparently has accepted Eissfeldt's conclusions. On the other hand, this unique solution has been attacked by B. W. Anderson, "Hosts, Host of Heaven," *loc. cit.*, and Maag, "Jahwäs Heerscharen," 49 (implicitly), on the ground that such an understanding is an abstraction of thought not characteristic of the Hebrew mind, and by W. Eichrodt, *op. cit.*, 193, who points out that "there is no instance of such an extension of $ṣabā'$ in an intensive plural in the sense which he assigns to it." Finally, against the interpretation of $ṣ^ebhā'ôth$ as stars, Maag, "Jahwäs Heerscharen," 30, note 2, has pointed out that the lord of stars is designated by $ṣebā'$ *hashamayim*, never with the plural $ṣ^ebhā'ôth$.

[45]Von Rad, *op. cit.*, 19. He suggests that the meaning of the name changed with the circumstances, and in this he finds support from Wambacq, *passim*. The attempt to discover its meaning was abandoned by H. Gressmann, *Der Ursprung der israelitisch-jüdischen Eschatologie* (Göttingen: Vandenhoeck & Ruprecht, 1905), 71ff., and E. Kautzsch, *op. cit.*, 626.

The source of the phrase is likewise debatable, some seeing in it a special Israelite name,[46] others arguing for a borrowing from Canaanite religion,[47] still others refusing to make a decision.[48] Eissfeldt has argued cogently for a mixture of Israelite and Canaanite influences, concluding that there is no great difference between the views of a special Israelite expression and a Canaanite borrowing.[49]

Two firm conclusions about the phrase can be made. First, a connection with the ark at Shiloh as a palladium of war must be posited;[50] second, the prophets preferred the term to all other epithets.[51] The first conclusion raises the question of the term's origin, the second that of its use in Amos. W. F. Albright thinks that Yahweh $ṣ^ebhā'ôth$, which he understands to mean "He brings armies into existence," together with $'ehyeh$ $'^asher\ yihyeh$ (Ex. 3:14), were ancient litanies in which the God of the Fathers was praised as Creator of the universe.[52]

---

[46]Albright, "Review. B. N. Wambacq, L'épithète divine Jahve ṣ^{e}bā'ôth," 377-81.

[47]Maag, "Jahwäs Heerscharen," *passim*.

[48]Eichrodt, *op. cit.*, 194.

[49]Eissfeldt, "Jahwe Zebaoth," 146-48. He reasons as follows: E. Kautzsch is right that the phrase must be connected with the ark, but I Sam. 4:4 and II Sam. 6:2 include the concept of the One who sits on the cherub, a Canaanite motif which the Israelites could not have used prior to the settlement. However, it is highly probable that they reached the high point of religious development in the twelfth and early eleventh centuries B.C., and the creation of a new cultic name for God ($ṣ^ebhā'ôth$) is likely. Moreover, the temple at Shiloh was patterned after a Canaanite model, and the later Solomonic temple combines the Isrealite and Canaanite elements in wondrous fashion (ark and cherubim).

[50]Maag, "Jahwäs Heerscharen," 32; Eissfeldt, "Jahwe Zebaoth," 139-42; Anderson, "Hosts, Host of Heaven," 655; von Rad, *op. cit.*, 18.

[51]The prophetic literature has 247 of the 285 uses. However, one must take into consideration the fact that many of these are later insertions, as can be seen from the fact that the Masoretic text of Jeremiah has 62 uses, whereas the Septuagint has only 7 (6).

[52]Albright, "Review of B. N. Wambacq, L'épithète divine Jahve ṣ^{e}bā'ôth," 380-81. D. N. Freedman, *op. cit.*, 156, while accepting Albright's conclusions about the latter phrase, wants to view Yahweh $ṣ^ebhā'ôth$ as a secondary epithet from the time of the Judges. For a discussion of the phrase in Ex. 3:14, see Th. Vriezen, "'ehje 'asher 'ehje," *Festschrift für A. Bertholet* (Tübingen: J.C.B. Mohr [P. Siebeck], 1950), 498-512.

In contrast, Maag and Eissfeldt have put forth strong evidence for their contention that the origin of the phrase is to be seen in the time of Samuel at Shiloh.[53]

What about the prophetic use of the epithet? This is another way of considering the development of the phrase after the capture of the ark and destruction of the temple at Shiloh. From David's verbal exchange with Goliath one can perceive that veneration of Yahweh of Hosts is central to Davidic religion (I Sam. 17:45). This is confirmed by the narrative of the ark's removal to Jerusalem (II Sam. 6:2,18; cf. Ps. 24:7-10). Moreover, the Solomonic temple continues the twofold religious symbolism from Shiloh, namely the ark and the cherubim. Thus one should not be surprised to discover the epithet in the description of Isaiah's call, which must have taken place in the temple (Isa. 6). But the real question is raised by the prophetic use of *YHWH ṣᵉbhā'ôth*, namely "What does it mean for them?"

Eichrodt has pointed to the difficulty of explaining the prophetic use of *YHWH ṣᵉbhā'ôth* if one interprets it to mean the armies of Israel.[54] One would have to assume some kind of spiritualization of the term from the terrestrial to the celestial sphere.[55] Such a spiritualization could be discovered in the idea of the heavenly council over which Yahweh presides, as seen most clearly in the story of Micaiah ben Imlah and in the prologue to the book of Job.[56] On the other hand, if Eissfeldt were

---

[53] Maag, "Jahwäs Heerscharen," 32; Eissfeldt, "Jahwe Zebaoth," 139-42. Against Albright's view, Maag has pointed to the silence of the wilderness tradition in regard to the epithet and to the later reading back into the text of a theological stance (32-33).

[54] Eichrodt, *op. cit.*, 192-93.

[55] G. von Rad, *Der heilige Krieg im alten Israel* (Göttingen: Vandenhoeck & Ruprecht, 1958), 50-68. But it is surprising that only two of the passages to which he calls attention as containing the "holy war" concepts have the epithet *Yahweh ṣᵉbhā'ôth* (Isa. 31:4; Zech. 4:6).

[56] H. W. Robinson, "The Council of Yahweh," *JTS*, XLV (1944), 151-57; F. M. Cross, Jr., "The Council of Yahweh in Second Isaiah," *JNES*, XII (1943), 159-72; B. W. Anderson, "Hosts, Host of Heaven," 654-56. The last mentioned suggests that the historical dynamism of holy war or the sovereign decree of the holy council must be the key to the phrase *Yahweh ṣᵉbhā'ôth*. This is also maintained by A. Weiser, *The Psalms*, H. Hartwell, trans. (London: SCM Press, 1962), 41, who links this with the theophany and covenantal armies.

correct that *YHWH* $ṣ^ebhā'ôth$ should be translated "Yahweh the
Mighty One," then the prophetic usage would need no explanation,
for the prophetic emphasis on universalism and Yahweh's uniqueness is enhanced by the epithet. Perhaps the best explanation
of the prophetic use of *YHWH* $ṣ^ebhā'ôth$ has been given by Maag.
According to him, various powers previously attributed to Canaanite mythological beings were absorbed by Yahweh through a process
of identification, elimination and integration.[57] Then when Assyrian and Babylonian astral religion threatened to swallow

---

[57]Maag, "Jahwäs Heerscharen," 33-44. He writes that Yahweh
was very soon identified with *'ēl*, so that Israel's God took on
the traits of the God of Bethel. Maag calls attention to Ps. 50:
1 where *'ēl* *'ae͡lōhîm* occurs as an epithet for Yahweh, Ps. 82
which depicts Yahweh in the role of *'ēl* as judge of the gods, and
Jeroboam's golden calves which give the identification of the two
gods; rather it was made through the mediation of Habiru elements
that preceded the attraction, for Yahwism was able to identify
Yahweh and the God of the Fathers in the Genesis narratives (37-
38). Moreover, Maag thinks the equation of Yahweh and Baal,
brought to a halt by the prophetic-Deuteronomic reaction, was
initiated by this faith of the fathers, although only the control
of rain and fruitfulness was taken over by official Yahwism. Nevertheless, Maag admits that popular religion went further, as can
be observed in Ps. 16; I Sam. 28:7ff.; Gen. 32:22ff.; Azazel and
the *she'ērîm* (35, note 4; 38-39). When had Yahweh taken over the
powers of the spirits? Maag believes that the reign of Saul is
the *terminus ante quem*, since the official religion of his day
was opposed to consultation of the spirits and demons, which to
Maag must mean that Yahweh has taken over their role (41ff.).
Maag thinks of the conquest as the *terminus pro quem*, so that the
time from the conquest to the reign of Saul must mark the origin
of the phrase "Yahweh of Hosts" (43). In his opinion this view
can be substantiated by the texts. Omitting those from the conflict with Assyrian and Babylonian astral religions, he concen-
trates upon the early texts in which the phrase occurs. From an
analysis of I Sam. 4:1ff. and II Sam. 6:4ff. he concludes that
the God of Shiloh, who is connected with the ark and has taken
over three demonic categories (pestilence, mouse spirit, and
plague) is known as "Yahweh God of Hosts"(44ff.). In another
narrative about events at Shiloh, the story of Samuel's birth,
Maag notices that Hannah's prayer for a child is directed to Yahweh of Hosts. He rightly asks what this has to do with Yahweh as
God of war or stars (45). Rather, Hannah wishes that the power
over motherhood were in Yahweh's hand, so she turns to Yahweh of
Hosts. The doxologies of Amos come into consideration next. Here
Maag offers a very suggestive interpretation of a phrase usually
emended (4:13b). "He declares to man what is his thought" is
understood to mean that Yahweh rules the world from the giving of
oracles to the control over stars (5:8); thus there is no need to
consult conjured spirits for oracles (45-48). Needless to say,
Maag thinks the phrase "Yahweh God of Hosts is his name" in Amos
is genuine, and the doxologies constitute for him an ancient hymn
to Yahweh of Hosts, who has taken into himself the many Canaanite
powers, subordinating them to the status of servants.

Israel, the prophets had a weapon derived from an earlier battle
with a similar phenomenon, and this instrument, the understanding
of God as *YHWH $s^ebh\bar{a}'\hat{o}th$*, was taken up a second time and used
with particular force.[58]

Where do the doxologies fit into the picture that has emerged?
Both Maag and Wambacq think of the epithet as genuine, and view
the doxologies as an ancient hymn to Yahweh as Creator.[59] But
this conclusion is by no means demanded by their evidence. Wambacq's arguments are least convincing; he wants to include in the
ancient hymn similar passages from Jer. 10:12-16; 31:35; and Isa.
51:15, each of which contains the refrain *YHWH $s^ebh\bar{a}'\hat{o}th$ $sh^em\hat{o}$.*[60]
Maag has certainly shown the possibility of viewing the epithet
YHWH $'^{ae}l\bar{o}h\bar{e}$ $s^ebh\bar{a}'\hat{o}th$ as an ancient phrase, so that the doxologies must not be rejected because of its presence. But he has
also pointed to the struggle with Assyro-Babylonian astral religion as the setting for the use of the epithet, so that one may

---

[58]Maag, "Jahwäs Heerscharen," 44. Perhaps the most stimulating discussion of the problem raised by the silence of many
later works in regard to the title has been given by Werner Kessler, "Aus welchen Gründen wird die Bezeichnung 'Yahweh Zebaoth'
in der späteren Zeit gemieden?" *Gottes ist der Orient: Festschrift
für Otto Eissfeldt* (Berlin: Evangelische Verlagsanstalt, 1959),
79-83. Kessler argues that the rejection of the title by the
authors of Hos., Dt., Ez., III Isa., (to some extent II Isa.),
Ezr., Neh., Chr. and Priestly material stems from a theological
reason far more profound than the destruction of the ark (80).
The key is discovered in the meaning of the title itself: Kessler suggests that Maag's study shows that the title contained
both positive and negative value. Negatively, it destroyed the
immediateness of the presence of Yahweh (81). He further suggests that the intolerable situation brought about by Sennacher-
ib's invasion in 701 B.C. led to the devaluation of the title,
since many used the phrase to defend the worship of Assyrian
deities as "underlords" of the great God Yahweh. Kessler thus
thinks that such a danger was consciously overcome by the theological perception of Ez., II Isa., and III Isa., for whom Yahweh was the only God, and about whose immediateness there could
be no question (82-83). Kessler further observes that the integral connection of the title with the Temple in Jerusalem explains its use by Isa., Jer., Hag., Zech., and Mal. (79).

[59]Maag, *ibid.*, 45-48. He suggests that the hymn originated
at Shiloh in the time of the Judges (29, note 2). Wambacq, *op.
cit.*, 195-99. Both think that the hymn antedates Amos, but Wambacq does not venture a specific date or locality.

[60]Wambacq, *op. cit.*, 208-20. These will be examined in
detail later.

just as easily view the doxologies as products of this late conflict. Therefore, his explanation of the epithet in no way demands his conclusion in regard to the doxologies.[61] But another
observation must be made. Maag neglected the crucial element of
the refrain within the doxologies, namely the $sh^e m\hat{o}$. It is not
sufficient to show that YHWH $'^{ae}l\bar{o}h\bar{e}$ $s^e bh\bar{a}'\hat{o}th$ was used prior to
Amos; one must consider the entire refrain YHWH $'^{ae}l\bar{o}h\bar{e}$ $s^e bh\bar{a}'\hat{o}th$
$sh^e m\hat{o}$. Once this is done, a different picture emerges, and the
probability of lateness increases tremendously, despite Wambacq's
attempt to prove the opposite.[62]

   At this point it may be helpful to examine the use of YHWH
$s^e bh\bar{a}'\hat{o}th$ within the book of Amos.[63] According to the Masoretic
Text, Amos used the expression nine times: (1) $'^a dh\bar{o}nai$ YHWH
$'^{ae}l\bar{o}h\bar{e}$ $hass^e bh\bar{a}'\hat{o}th$ (3:13); (2) $'^a dh\bar{o}nai$ YHWH $hass^e bh\bar{a}'\hat{o}th$
(9:5); (3) YHWH $'^{ae}l\bar{o}h\bar{e}$ $hass^e bh\bar{a}'\hat{o}th$ (6:14); (4) YHWH $'^{ae}l\bar{o}h\bar{e}$
$s^e bh\bar{a}'\hat{o}th$ (4:13; 5:14,15,27; 6:8); and (5) YHWH $'^{ae}l\bar{o}h\bar{e}$ $s^e bh\bar{a}'\hat{o}th$
$'^a dh\bar{o}nai$ (5:16). All of these usages are rare: (1), (2) and (5)
appear only here; (3) occurs only two times (Hos. 12:6); and (4)
is found fourteen times (II Sam., I Kgs., Ps., Jer.).[64] If one
could prove that the longer form is earlier, then this might be
evidence that the doxologies come from a time prior to the crystallization of the epithet into the popular YHWH $s^e bh\bar{a}'\hat{o}th$. Until this important question is resolved, one must not conclude

---

[61]He understands the mythological allusions behind the
doxologies as live issues and dates them early, but it is hard
to tell at what stage mythological language loses its realistic
force.

[62]Wambacq, *op. cit.*, 208-20. This problem will be dealt
with more extensively in the next chapter.

[63]Wambacq's analysis (52-76) is very valuable.

[64]Wambacq, *op. cit.*, 55, thinks that the form in 9:5 originally had $'\bar{e}l\bar{o}h\bar{e}$ as in 3:13 and the LXX of 9:5. He also views
6:8b as a later gloss, chiefly because of its omission in the
LXX and the appearance of an asterisk beside it in the Syriac
Hexaplaric (73-74). Similarly in 6:14 the LXX (A,Q,W) omits the
epithet, as does the Bohairic, although B and V add it after the
nations (74-75). Moreover, Wambacq thinks that the long form is
original in 5:8 (following the LXX, except B and the Hexaplaric,
Peshitto, Targum Jonathan and Itala). Likewise in 9:6, he thinks
of the longer form as original on the basis of LXX (despite B,W,
c), Syriac Hexaplaric, Peshitto and Itala (75-76). Finally, Wambacq prefers the Masoretic Text of 9:14 (76).

anything about the date of the doxologies on the basis of the
long form, for this expansion could just as easily constitute an
attempt to explain an enigmatic expression.[65]

In short, there is no compelling reason to follow Maag and
Wambacq in viewing the phrase "Yahweh of Hosts" as evidence of
the antiquity of the doxologies, first, because of Maag's failure
to consider the entire refrain, and second, because of the conflict with Assyrian and Babylonian religion as a possible setting
for the use of the refrain. As a matter of fact, examination of
the contexts in which the entire refrain is found would seem to
indicate that the latter struggle is both possible and probable.

To the arguments of style and the use of *bhōrē'* and "Yahweh
God of Hosts is his name" has been added the occurrence of several
unusual words, two of which are thought to be examples of late
vocabulary.[66] Besides this, many commentators draw attention to
the use of star names in 5:8, and also in 5:9, if Georg Hoffmann's
interpretation of the verse is accepted.[67] Those who emphasize
this presence of star names seek to show the influence of Job 9:9
and 38:31 upon the doxologies. In both passages, the Pleiades or
Orion are mentioned. This will be considered more thoroughly at
a later time.

4. *The Doxology in the Septuagint at Hosea 13:4*

The fourth argument usually given for the lateness of the
doxologies is drawn from a parallel occurrence in the Septuagint
of Hos. 13:4, although George Adam Smith dismisses this argument
on the basis of comparing the content of the doxologies.[68] Smith
thinks that, while the doxology in Hosea is unsuited to the total
doctrine of Hosea and is inferior and flat, those in Amos are
"appropriate poetry to the desert nomad."[69] But it must be noted
that the actual fact that a doxology was inserted into the text

---

[65]Albright, "Review. B. N. Wambacq, L'épithète divine Jahve
ṣ^eḇā'ôth," 380-81; and B. W. Anderson, "Lord of Hosts," 151.

[66]*Šeḥo* and *'ᵃgudāthô.*

[67]Georg Hoffmann, "Versuche zu Amos," *ZAW*, III (1883), 110-
11. His view will be discussed later.

[68]G. A. Smith, *op. cit.*, 213.

[69]*Ibid.* In view of the light that has been thrown upon the
history of Israel from recent archaeological finds, it is no
longer correct to describe Amos as a "desert nomad."

of Hosea, regardless of its theological merit, means that such
an addition into the text of Amos is also possible.

5. *Summary*

The preceding has examined the four arguments usually given
in defense of the view that the doxologies are a later addition
to the text of Amos. It has been seen that in regard to arguments from intrusion into the contexts, the second doxology
(5:8-9) actually interrupts its context. The other two are
hardly essential to the argument of the text. As for the theology of the doxologies, it was concluded that there is a recognizable difference between Yahweh as Lord of the nations in the
text of Amos and Lord of the universe in the doxologies, although
the cosmic fire and mythological serpent, sword, and plague play
a major role in removing the gulf between the two pictures of
Yahweh. It has been further observed that little can be concluded from the use of $bh\bar{o}r\bar{e}$' in the doxologies, since there is
a remote possibility that the word was known as early as Amos.
Nor is the use of "Yahweh God of Hosts is his name" decisive,
since the phrase was frequently used before and after Amos' time,
although it seems to point to another period for the origin of
the doxologies. Similarly, the use of star names does not prove
that Amos could not have written the doxologies, especially if
Hoffmann is right about 5:9, but it raises grave doubts, which
are increased by the affinity with Job 9. Finally, the fact
that the Septuagint has an added doxology after Hos. 13:4 points
to a similar possibility in Amos, though perhaps at an earlier
period.[70] As a matter of fact, no single argument is conclusive,
but it must be admitted that the cumulative evidence favors, nay,
almost demands, the assumption that the doxologies do not come
from Amos, and, in fact, are from a much later time.[71]

B. *The Purpose for Inserting the Doxologies*

This raises the question of the purpose for the addition
of such doxologies, whether by Amos or by a later hand, which

---

[70]This is because they have found acceptance in the Hebrew
text of Amos.

[71]The only other thing that might argue for an early date
of the doxologies is the use of several different combinations
of the phrase Yahweh of Hosts, which could indicate a time before the crystallization of the form.

seems more probable. A number of suggestions have been made, ranging from the view that Amos himself used an ancient hymn to one that the later worshiping community added appropriate liturgical texts to the prophetic words.[72]

1. *Reasons for the Doxologies' Presence*

Perhaps the most conservative approach to the doxologies is that of K. Cramer, who wrote: "Ich entscheide mich also dafür, dass wir in den Doxologien echtes Gut des Amos haben können."[73] According to him, Amos sang his speeches, the doxologies often being the most essential part of the message.[74] At the other

---

[72]Watts, *Vision and Prophecy in Amos*, 67; Maag, "Jahwäs Heerscharen," 46-48, *Text, Wortschatz und Begriffswelt des Buches Amos*, 57; T. H. Gaster, "An Ancient Hymn in the Prophecies of Amos," *JMEOS*, XIX (1935), 24; K. Cramer, *op. cit.*, 90ff. Watts thinks of Amos as having inserted only the first strophe, while Maag attributes to the prophet 8:8 which is understood to be a quotation from an ancient hymn. On the other hand, Gaster thinks Amos used the entire hymn, and Cramer considers the doxologies authentic words of Amos. Other defenders of the doxologies have been A. Kuenen, who referred to Mic. 1:2-4 and Jer. 5:20-22; R. Vuilleumier, *op. cit.*, 88-90, who compares Ps. 18, Job 9, 38; and Th. Robinson, *op. cit.*, 87, 89-90, 105-106.

Among those who consider the doxologies later post-exilic additions are F. Horst, "Die Doxologien im Amosbuch," *ZAW*, XLVII (1929), 45-54; A. Weiser, "Die Prophetie des Amos," 173; R. H. Pfeiffer, *Introduction to the Old Testament* (New York: Harper, 1941), 583. Weiser's views in the reference above have been changed slightly in A. Weiser and K. Elliger, *Das Buch der zwölf Kleinen Propheten* (Göttingen: Vandenhoeck & Ruprecht, 1949), 156-67. He no longer limits the hymnic glosses to 4:13, 5:8, and 9:6. In the early work he thought that 8:8 had described the earthquake, while 9:5 was a prophecy of it. However, neither was attributed to Amos; Weiser wrote that several things argue against the authenticity of 9:5, namely the general use of the Nile, repetition of "like the Nile," change of subjects back and forth, use of 'ābhal rather than 'ābhadh, use of kulāh. Nor does 9:5 come from the same hand as the hymn, in his opinion, since its mood is threatening and gloomy. Its original place was thought to have been after 8:7. Moreover, 5:8 was considered an insertion because of the play on hāphakh and 5:9 was viewed as a later gloss to the preceding verse. Weiser wrote that there is some connection between the hymn which celebrates Yahweh's power over nature and the prediction of an earthquake, thinking such an association a better explanation for the insertion of the doxologies than Horst's attempt (below). Again 4:13 is said to be a pious gloss brought on by the prediction of an earthquake; while bhōrē' and śēḥô are considered late. Nor did Weiser think these verses were one hymn, in which view he is followed by Cripps, *op. cit.*, 185. See Weiser, "Die Prophetie des Amos, 30-32, 202-03, 173.

[73]Cramer, *op. cit.*, 92.

[74]*Ibid.*, 93.

extreme, Ernst Sellin attributed the doxologies to a post-exilic
redactor who added them wherever Amos made reference to the destruction of the idolatrous sanctuary in the North (Bethel).[75]
In order to hold such a view, Sellin had to argue that 3:14 belongs before 4:12a; confirmation of this theory was sought in
Hos. 12:6 and 13:4, which Sellin also attributed to the same
editor.

Using the composition of the Psalter as an analogy, K.
Guthe suggested that the doxologies originally formed the conclusions of brief collections of Amos' speeches, just as individual collections of the Psalter are concluded by doxologies.[76]
Thus Guthe would attribute the doxologies to collectors of the
individual speeches of Amos. Also using Psalms as the point of
departure, S. B. Frost argues that the doxologies constitute an
"asseveration by thanksgiving," the purpose of which is to affirm
that the fulfillment of the oracles is certain.[77] Frost points
to Jer. 20:7-13; Isa. 42:10-13; 44:23; 29:13; 12:1b-2, 4b-6; Hos.
13:4; Isa. 25:1-5 as further examples in prophetic literature,
the last two of which he thinks may be secondary.

Dissatisfied with any of the views before his time, Karl
Budde suggested that the doxologies were "fillers for lost
speeches of Amos," and characterized the hymn, first recognized
as such by Hans Schmidt, as a eulogy of Yahweh as Creator.[78] To
make sense of the various fragments, which Budde believed to comprise one strophe, he radically rearranged the individual parts
of the hymn. Budde rejected as inappropriate to a eulogy of Yahweh as Creator two passages describing destruction of strongholds
and human mourning.[79]

A somewhat similar view has been offered by Artur Weiser,
though without elaboration. He proposed that the hymn-like passages were inserted during the exile, perhaps to bring to a close

---

[75]Sellin, *op. cit.*, 193.

[76]K. Guthe, "Amos," *Die Heilige Schrift des Alten Testaments*,
II (Tübingen: J.C.B. Mohr [P. Siebeck], 1923), 37.

[77]S. B. Frost, "Asseveration by Thanksgiving," *VT*, VIII
(1958), 380-90. His examples from the Psalter are 22; 54:8-9;
57; 86:8-13; 116:5; 118:21.

[78]K. Budde, "Zu Text und Auslegung des Buches Amos," *JBL*,
XLIII (1924), 46-131; XLIV (1925), 63-122. See XLIV (1925), 106.

[79]Budde, *ibid.*, (SLIV), 107.

sections read during the liturgy and to show how men honored
prophetic oracles and submitted to God's judgment.[80] The following comment shows keen insight into the nature of the post-exilic
community that inserted these passages. He writes: "So sehen wir
in diesen hymnischen Stücken das Bekenntnis eines Glaubens der
nachexilischen Gemeinde, der ohne den Kampf der Propheten nicht
diese Früchte hatte reifen lassen können."[81] A similar observation is made by Susumu Jozaki.[82]

In this emphasis upon the judgment of God, Weiser reveals an
indebtedness to Friedrich Horst, who made the most stimulating
suggestion yet.[83] Combining the literary-critical and history-
of-religions approach, Horst suggested that the doxologies had
their proper setting in sacred law. His view merits careful consideration. The first problem to which he addresses himself is
that of the scope of the individual fragments, their relation to
one another and their actual meaning. Rejecting 8:8 as a later
gloss arising out of reflection upon 9:5, Horst limits himself to
4:13; 5:8; 9:5-6; all of which he thinks have no connection with
their contexts, while 5:8 is said to interrupt 5:7,10. Horst believes 5:9 to be a later gloss by a copyist who cited the place
from which 5:8 was taken.[84] Unlike Budde, Horst thinks of the
reference to the shaking of the earth as genuine, the Creator
also causing anxious tears.[85]

As for the strophic arrangement of the hymn, Horst thinks
of two strophes with concluding refrain and an identical conclusion ("Yahweh is his name" and "He calls for the waters of the
sea and pours them out upon the earth"). The first strophe is
said to have been broken apart through an unfortunate accident,
its original form including 4:13 and 5:8, and 4:13b having been

---

[80]A. Weiser, *Das Buch der zwölf Kleinen Propheten*, 156-57,
164, 189.

[81]*Ibid.*, 189.

[82]S. Jozaki, "The Secondary Passages of the Book of Amos,"
Kwansei Gakuin University Annual Studies, IV (1956), 25-100 (see
especially page 26).

[83]F. Horst, *op. cit.*, 45-54, with *Gottes Recht* (München: Chr.
Kaiser Verlag, 1961), 155-66.

[84]Horst, *op. cit.*, 45-46.

[85]*Ibid.*, 46-47.

added after the original unity was broken.[86] On the analogy of
Ps. 65:7ff., Horst thinks that the doxology must have concluded
with a reference to vegetation, and emends the text accordingly.[87]

After solving to his satisfaction the problems of scope, relation, and text, Horst attempts to discover the life setting for
such doxologies.[88] He calls attention to Josh. 7:19, where Achan
is asked to give glory to God and to confess his sins.[89] Here in
this passage, Horst discovers confession and doxology, which he
understands to be components of sacred law. Then he brings forward a number of parallels from the history of religions (Lydian
and Phrygian expiation inscriptions, Alexandrian literature, Israelite legal practice).[90]

Having discovered parallels to such a procedure of confession
and doxology in the history of religions, Horst returns to the Old
Testament in search of further examples. Especially significant
for him is Job 4-5; for 5:8 refers to a trial before God, while
5:9-16 has a doxology. Again these elements are found in Jer.
13:15f.; I Sam. 6:5; Ps. 118:17-21; I Chr. 30:8 (LXX).[91]

Horst concludes that the doxologies of Amos have their locus
in sacred law, 4:12b taking on new meaning.[92] In the words of
the prophet (4:6-11) the people heard about their sins: this

---

[86]Horst, *op. cit.*, 47. While accepting Horst's hypothesis
as to the reconstruction and the purpose of the doxologies as
quite satisfactory, Jozaki does not see the necessity to think
that 5:8 originally followed 4:13 (*op. cit.*, 77).

[87]*Ibid.*, 49.

[88]*Ibid.*, 49ff.

[89]The meaning of *tôdāh* and *hôdāh* was the subject of an article by Hubert Grimme, who sought to explain how in later thought
the idea of "confession" in the dogmatic sense arose. Perplexed
by the fact that the words sometimes mean "confess sin" and at
other times "confess praise, extol," Grimme suggested that in the
cult there is basis for the later dogmatic sense. He refers to
Josh. 7:19 and Ezr. 10:11 especially, and suggests that if Horst
is right about Josh. 7:19, then it might be a confession of the
essence of Yahweh, not a "*Lobpreisung*." H. Grimme, "Der Begriff
von hebräischen תודה und הודה," *ZAW*, LVIII (1940-41), 234-39.
Two New Testament passages add force to Horst's thesis (Jn. 9:24
and Acts 12:23).

[90]Horst, *op. cit.*, 51-52.

[91]*Ibid.*, 52-53.

[92]*Ibid.*, 53-54.

prophetic word expressed their confession, affirming the validity of the exile as a chastisement of God. Likewise in 9:5-6, even if the confession is missing, the chastisement is mentioned in 9:1-4. By means of these doxologies the worshiping community confesses its assurance that the punishment is over and that it cannot suffer any more for the sins of the fathers. Thus the ominous prophetic word has been given a luster, and to it has been added a deep understanding of the God to be confronted in judgment. For these doxologies Horst coins the name of the literary *Gattung* "Doxology of Judgment."[93]

The next major attempt to understand the doxologies was that of T. H. Gaster, who argued that the doxologies constitute an ancient hymn to Yahweh of Hosts.[94] Referring to the fact that the Old Testament contains many quotations and adaptations of early Palestinian literature (for example, Nah. 1 and many Psalms), Gaster thought it possible to view the doxologies as remnants of early Palestinian literature used by Amos.[95] According to him, the fragments intrude upon their contexts, but link together logically and have a single dominant theme, namely, universalism. Furthermore, the ancient song was thought to be present only in 4:13; 5:8; 9:6, each closing with the same refrain.[96]

Gaster focused his attention primarily upon textual problems of extent, relation to each fragment, and meaning. In 5:8 he suggested a mis-quotation of the original; here Amos is said to have repeated a line also appearing in the third passage, to the latter of which it belongs both logically and mythologically.[97] Because of this erroneous repetition, so Gaster argued, a line has been ousted, the lost sentence evidently referring to the heavenly bodies.[98] As for the suggested readings of difficult words, Gaster understood '^{a}gudāthô from Arabic 'ajd, the foundation

---

[93]Jozaki, who combines the views of Horst and Pfeiffer, suggests a date for the insertion of the doxologies between the late sixth and early fifth centuries (*op. cit.*, 77, 91).

[94]Gaster, *op. cit.*, 23-26.

[95]*Ibid.*, 23.

[96]*Ibid.*, 23-24.

[97]*Ibid.*, 24.

[98]*Ibid.*

of a building (9:6), while thinking that $^{ca}liyy\bar{a}th\hat{o}$ had been
corrupted to $ma^{ca}l\hat{o}th\bar{o}$ by dittography (9:6). On the analogy of
Ps. 104:3, Gaster wanted to read "in waters" rather than "in
the heavens" (9:6); this reading was in his opinion more in accord with Babylonian cosmogony.[99] In 4:13, Gaster made a major
change from the usually accepted meaning of the text; reading
$\hat{u}magd\hat{\imath}l\ la'^{a}dh\bar{a}m\bar{a}h\ \acute{s}i\hbar\bar{a}h$, Gaster translated "And maketh her foison [archaic - abundance] to grow unto the earth."[100]

Gaster thought that 5:9 might belong to the poem, although
isolated from its original context. On the basis of subject
matter, he proposed that 9:6 must logically have preceded it.
As for the difficulty in the text of 5:9, Gaster suggested an
emendation to $hammabhl\hat{\imath}g\ shebher\ ^{c}al\ ^{c}\hat{o}z$.[101]

The next important attempt to solve the problem presented
by the doxologies was that of Victor Maag, who followed his
teacher, Ludwig Köhler, in viewing 8:8 as a word of Amos overcome by the horror of God's wrath, but went farther by suggesting that this verse was a quotation from an ancient hymn.[102]
Maag thought that Amos, by means of a rhetorical question, played
on the word sequence of a hymn sung regularly by his contemporaries who were unaware that they sang of their own judgment.[103]
According to Maag, the ancient hymn was earlier than Amos, perhaps having originated at Shiloh during the time of the judges,
and embraces all the passages in Amos.[104] However, Maag did not
believe that Amos added these fragments; rather he thought it

---

[99]Gaster, *op. cit.*, 25.

[100]*Ibid.*, 24-25.

[101]*Ibid.*, 25-26.

[102]Maag, *Text, Wortschatz und Begriffswelt des Buches Amos*,
57.

[103]This view has a great deal of similarity to Weiser's emphasis upon ironic paradox, against which Würthwein and Hesse
have raised their pens. Weiser wrote that in the speech of Amos
preserved in 5:4-6 is the "Tragik aller echten Prophetie zum
Ausdruck, dass sie im Kampfesteht zwischen zwei religiösen
Welten, die durch eine unüberbruckbare Kluft voneinander getrennt
sind" (Weiser, "Die Prophetie des Amos," 194, note 1; Hesse, *op.
cit.*, 1-2, 8; Ernst Würthwein, "Amos-Studien," *ZAW*, LXII [1949-
50], 10-51).

[104]Maag, "Jahwäs Heerscharen," 29, note 2.

The final section of Watts' article deals with Amos' use of cultic materials, and in some ways this discussion is the most provocative.[120] Rejecting all earlier views about the reason for the presence of the hymn, Watts suggested that the prophetic word led up to a ritual in which a choir chanted the song in the appropriate place.[121] Much weight is laid upon the second strophe, where the prophetic word is said to be connected with the doxology at two points ("Seek me and live" in 5:4, and "Seek good and not evil, that you may live" in 5:14). In both, words from Amos vary the original hymnic phrase, "Seek Yahweh and live" (5:6); thus the hymnic portion indicates to Watts the original source of Amos' play on words.[122] In the third strophe, Watts could find no obvious contacts with the context, though according to his emendation a phrase in 9:4,8 is touched upon in 9:6a ("set his eye upon").[123] In this phrase, Watts understood a prophetic documentation of the work of God which was the basis for visions and messages; more precisely, Watts argued that Amos used a cultic motif (New Year's omen) and cultic language ("setting his eye upon one") as bases for his message of judgment. Watts thought that behind Amos' words lay the desire to call the people to repentance, but also ritual necessity; Amos has picked up a phrase from the liturgy and expanded it for the hour.[124]

Finally, Watts held that the first strophe was closely connected with the prophetic text, so that Amos may have quoted it.[125] But this was not thought possible in the second and third strophes. This raises the question as to the reason for the presence of other strophes in the text. In answer to this, Watts proposed that the hymn was included when the two books were collected, one in Israel, the other in Judah. From this redactional activity he argued that the hymn was well known in both places.[126]

---

[120]Watts, *Vision and Prophecy in Amos*, 64-67. This will be discussed more thoroughly at a later time.

[121]*Ibid.*, 65.

[122]*Ibid.*

[123]*Ibid.*, 66.

[124]*Ibid.*, 66-67.

[125]*Ibid.*, 67.

[126]This only accentuated the difficulty of accepting his view in regard to the composition of the book.

2. *Assessment of Theories about the Doxologies' Purpose*

As can be seen from the preceding discussion, the solutions to the problem presented by the doxologies have taken several different forms, there being little agreement among the commentators. Although the solution offered in this work will be discussed later, some evaluation of the main theories discussed above must now be made.

First, minor suggestions come under consideration. The weakness of Sellin's view that the doxologies are added where the destruction of the sanctuary at Bethel is spoken of arises out of his radical rearrangement of the text (5:8 before 5:7 and 3:14 before 4:12a), while the passages appealed to in Hosea prove nothing.[127] The judgment of Ludwig Köhler is valid, namely that Sellin reads too much into the text.[128]

Guthe's suggestion that the doxologies were added at the close of various collections of Amos' speeches, as in the Psalter, is impossible in view of what has been said above about the second doxology, that is, the close relationship between 5:4-7 and 5:14-15. One cannot ignore the fact that the second doxology actually interrupts an oracle. Another difficulty with this view, rightly seen by Horst, is the supposition that collectors of Amos' words, at different places and times, would have selected individual verses from the same hymn to serve as conclusions to each collection.[129]

The basic weakness of Frost's suggestion is the time factor. If he thinks of the doxologies as genuine words of Amos, as perhaps is intended since Hos. 13:4 and Isa. 25:1-5 are called "later insertions," then proof of this should have been supplied. But if these doxologies are thought to be a product of the post-exilic community, then what is the purpose of asserting that Amos' prophecies would be fulfilled? In fact, the people recognized that the prophecies had been actualized long before, and this is the real reason for the preservation of Amos' words.

Perhaps the conclusions of Cramer have least of all to commend them; he thinks of the doxologies as genuine words of Amos.

---

[127]Horst, *op. cit.*, 49.

[128]Köhler, "Amos Forschungen von 1917 bis 1932," *ThR*, IV (1932), 200.

[129]Horst, *loc. cit.*

In a caustic criticism of Cramer's assumptions, methodology and
conclusions, Köhler writes that "Gottes Drohworte, die Amos zu
verkünden hat, sind keine Arien für Bariton" and "Kurzum, man ist
mit diesem Hymnus auf einmal in einer ganz anderen Welt [from that
of Amos], und dasselbe wiederholt sich 5:8f. und 9:5f."[130] Köhler
objects to translation, meanings of words, and "spiritual" exegesis as they are found in Cramer's book. He points out that Cramer
goes to the text with preconceived notions about the speech and
behavior of prophets (by which Köhler means ideas different from
his own) and from them draws far-reaching conclusions: (1) by
speech forms, which must be either preceded or followed by God's
name, the prophet marked off new divisions in his message and ar-
rested the attention of the people, changing the forms of speech
to gain or keep attention; (2) the prophet, who sang his message,
could recognize signs of inattention, stubbornness and lack of
appreciation: to offset these he varied the meter of his address;
(3) the original message was changed according to the response of
the audience; and (4) the doxologies are therefore not to be denied
to Amos.[131] Köhler objects to the arbitrary treatment of the text
reflected in the first, the assumption about the mode of prophetic
address in the second, the extemporaneous character of the third,
which to him was incredible in view of his idea that the prophet
merely reported what God had told him to say, and finally, the
illogical statement in the fourth, which Köhler rightly sees as
a *non sequitur*.[132] Although Köhler was too severe in some of his
criticisms, especially in regard to the mode of prophetic delivery,
his judgment is certainly preferable to that of Cramer. In short,
Johannes Lindblom's basic criticism of Cramer that the latter
failed to study the prophets in their religio-historical context
appears correct.[133]

Budde's view that the doxologies were fillers for lost
speeches of Amos is unsatisfactory, first, because it fails to
explain the need for such "fillers," and second, because it cannot clarify how anyone could have happened to insert strophes

---

[130]Köhler, "Amos Forschungen von 1917 bis 1932," 199, 201-
213.

[131]*Ibid.*, 201-202.

[132]*Ibid.*

[133]Lindblom, *Prophecy in Ancient Israel* (Philadelphia:
Muhlenberg Press, 1962), 315.

from a single hymn in the place of a prophetic text.[134] Moreover, Budde's radical "scissors-and-paste" method of rearranging
the original hymn must be rejected, as well as his limitation of
the hymn to a eulogy of Yahweh as Creator, with no place for God's
judgment upon man.[135]

Criticisms of Gaster's conclusions are primarily philological, and are best reserved for a later time. However, one can
raise a question about the so-called dominant note of the hymn,
universalism, and Gaster's primarily theological criteria for
determining the scope of the hymn. In addition, it must be remarked that Gaster is certainly inaccurate in maintaining that
the doxologies intrude into their contexts but link together
logically and in ordered sequence. In actual fact, only the
second really intrudes into its context, while Gaster has to
omit various parts of the individual doxologies in order to arrive at a hymn that links together so smoothly. Gaster is also
in error when he asserts that in 5:8b Amos misquotes his original, seen in its correct context in 9:6b.[136]

Maag's hypothesis that the doxologies were introduced in
places where Amos presses towards the mighty power of God leaves
unanswered the basic question of the reason for their insertion.
Nor does his reference to fate as the cause for the position of
the doxologies satisfy the desire to find the reason for their
presence. But an evaluation of Maag's views must go deeper;
crucial to his solution is the affirmation that in 8:8 Amos
quotes a word from some hymn used by the people, giving it a
totally new meaning. This idea of ironical paradox, first accepted and developed in regard to Amos' total message by Weiser,
has been questioned by Ernst Würthwein and Franz Hesse who have
no sympathy with such an understanding of the method of prophecy.[137] However, Würthwein's arguments are not convincing at

---

[134]Maag, *Text, Wortschatz und Begriffswelt des Buches Amos*,
57-58. Horst points out that 9:7 disproves this, since a lost
text before it is inconceivable. Horst, *op. cit.*, 50.

[135]Horst, *op. cit.*, 46-47.

[136]Julian Morgenstern, *Amos Studies* (Cincinnati: H.U.C.
Press, 1941), 93, note 17, writes that Gaster's discussion is
interesting and suggestive though by no means convincing, and
views the doxologies as later liturgical insertions.

[137]See note 103.

this point, for they rest upon and seek to support a view of the
strophes against the nations that cannot be accepted, namely that
the oracles against foreign nations come from a period when Amos
was a prophet of salvation, while those against Israel and Judah
stem from the time after Amos' transition to a prophet of doom.[138]
Such a change Würthwein attempts to discover in the visions.
One other remark must be made about Maag's hypothesis; since he,
following his teacher, Ludwig Köhler, thinks of 8:8 as the original verse from the hymn quoted by Amos, the relationship of 8:8
and 9:5 becomes a crucial factor, especially in view of Horst's
contention that 8:8 originated in dependence upon 9:5.[139]

This brings the views of Horst into purview. His method
and conclusions are extremely valuable, so his basic approach to
the doxologies will be followed here. Horst has certainly given
the most illuminating analysis yet considered, and his view of
the setting in sacred law must be considered carefully. The real
weakness in his article stems from failure to examine similar
passages in the rest of the Old Testament, specifically Jer. 10:
12-16; 31:35; 51:15-19; Isa. 51:15; Job 9:5-10. Where Horst had
great difficulty in finding adequate parallels to such a suggested
procedure in sacred law, this situation is quite different now
because of growing knowledge of the ancient Near East. Consequently, a certain refinement of his views proves necessary. In
view of the hymnic portions mentioned above, it would seem that
one could connect the doxologies with the oath required in the
process of sacred law. The present work will seek to establish
this connection, showing how such an understanding of the doxologies reflects the profound theological insight of the post-exilic
guardians of prophetic oracles.

But there is another weakness in Horst's article, although
understandable at this early date. While discerning the significance of Am. 4:12b as the announcement of a theophany, Horst
failed to investigate implications of that discovery. Consequently, this work will attempt to trace the origin and development

---

[138]E. Würthwein, *op. cit.*, 28-35. It is difficult to understand how Amos could have reacted to a "benevolent" suggestion
of Amaziah in the manner reflected in Am. 7:16-17. Indeed,
Würthwein's view is not demanded at all by the materials at hand.

[139]Horst, *op. cit.*, 45.

of the "Theophany of Judgment" reflected in the doxologies. It
will also show that this tradition is integral to genuine words
of Amos, so that the doxologies, though post-exilic, are the
final product of a "theophanic tradition" within Israel.

If the work of Horst has escaped with minor criticism, the
same cannot be said of that by Watts, even though his treatment
is almost equally stimulating. One must object to Watts' attempt
to include 5:6-7 in the doxology, in spite of the use of an im-
perative in 5:6.[140] But this rejection of Watts' analysis of
5:6-7 carries with it far-reaching implications, first in regard
to the relation of the doxology to the context (of which Watts
makes a great deal), and second, in considering the place of
revelation of the divine name.[141] Actually the whole argument
about duplications of the prophetic word within the doxology falls
with this, as does the emendation in 9:5a that probably arose from
Watts' desire to relate the prophetic text to the doxology. This
means that some of the six themes discovered by Watts must be
dropped, and with that the entire setting may be called into question.[142] Again one must object to Watt's assumption that poor
transition always indicates a later hand; in fact, the entire
treatment makes improper use of duplications and transitions.
Watts has precipitated another basic question: does the polemic
in the doxologies have in mind Baalism as he supposes, or the
Assyro-Babylonian astral religion, if indeed there be polemic
here?[143] As for Watts' conclusions concerning theological implications of the doxologies, specifically that the idea of monotheism

---

[140]First, because of the subject matter and absence of a participle in 5:6; second, because of Watts' arbitrary exclusion of
references to Bethel and Judah in 5:6; and, third, because of his
weak arguments in regard to 5:7.

[141]The entire discussion about the play on "Seek Yahweh" falls
to the ground, as well as Watts' conclusions about the hymnic
source of Amos' words in 5:4f. Moreover, the progressive revelation of the divine name (from the closing refrain in 4:13, to the
opening line as object in 5:6, to the subject in 9:5) can no longer be held.

[142]Trial by ordeal (5:6); omen of fate (9:5a,6a); expectancy
of rain (5:9).

[143]Kapelrud, *Central Ideas in Amos*, 77, has certainly gone
too far in the opposite direction from Watts. Kapelrud concludes:
"Thus polemic against foreign gods is no main issue in the Book
of Amos."

antedates Amos, such an assertion must find confirmation in an undisputed early text before it commands acceptance, especially in view of Am. 5:26.

In the section on Amos' use of cultic materials, Watts asserts that the prophetic criticism came from within the cult; but such an opinion is certainly open to question. Finally, the real difficulty with Watts' view about the addition of the doxologies arises from his thesis in regard to the composition of the book. Watts argues that one book was composed in Israel, to which were added two strophes of a hymn, while the second book was compiled in Judah, with a third strophe from the same hymn inserted there. This view is indefensible; it also indicates the difficulty of Watts' idea of two-fold composition of the book. Although many of Watts' conclusions must be rejected, his basic approach is sound, particularly the attempt to discover the life setting of the doxologies. Furthermore, Watts' emendations of the text often show keen insight.

C. *Amos' Use of Cultic Materials*

Reference has been made above to Watts' discussion of Amos' use of cultic materials, and the matter was touched upon briefly in the evaluation of Maag's hypothesis about ironical paradox in 8:8. This question merits further discussion, inasmuch as the views of both Watts and Maag depend upon this factor in one way or another. Maag thinks that Amos took over a verse from a hymn of the liturgy and used it in the opposite sense from that usually understood by those singing it; on the other hand, Watts believes the prophet himself probably used one of the doxologies from an ancient hymn, while the choir chanted the entire hymn at the appropriate place in the liturgy. One interpreter thinks Amos broke with cultic aims, while the other sees him as serving a function within normal cultic worship, though declaring judgment. Which view is more nearly accurate?

Some light is thrown upon this question by the cultic phrase "I will never again pass by them" in 7:8 and 8:2, as well as "For I will pass through your midst" in 5:17. The cultic nature of this phrase is clear from Ex. 12:12 and the idea of a theophany that rests behind it, especially in the New Year Festival when this appearance of God brought with it promise of rain and fertility, destruction upon Israel's enemies, and judgment upon sinners within Israel.[144]

In 5:17 God warns the people that wailing will be in all squares and shouts of "Alas, Alas," in the streets, while farmers will be called to mourning, and those skilled in lamentation to wailing, and in all vineyards wailing will take place, for "I will pass through your midst." In other words, the promise of rain and fertility that accompanies God's epiphany has been changed to a threat of drought and defeat.

The other two uses change the emphasis from a positive threat of passing through to the solemn "I will never again pass by them." In 7:8 the vision of the plumb line precedes this assertion, which is followed by the announcement that the high places of Isaac will be desolate, the sanctuaries of Israel laid waste, and Yahweh will rise against the house of Jeroboam with a sword. Similarly, 8:2 describes a vision of a basket of summer fruit, which conveys to Amos the message that "the end has come upon my people Israel"; this awful announcement is made all the more terrible by the cultic phrase "I will never again pass by them." The meaning of this threat is expanded in the following manner: the songs of the temple shall become wailings in that day, the many dead bodies, cast out everywhere in silence.[145]

What is the meaning of the phrase in question? Perhaps some help can be gained from an examination of the prepositions with which the verb $^c\bar{a}bhar$ is used. The first (5:17) is followed by b^e, as in Ex. 12:12 where the meaning is destructive. In the other two passages (7:8 and 8:2) the preposition l^e occurs, and has been variously interpreted. Würthwein, following Sellin, thinks that the phrase means "I will never again forgive them"; likewise Harper and Cripps argue for this interpretation,

---

[144]A. Weiser, "Zur Frage nach den Beziehungen der Psalmen zum Kult: Die Darstellung der Theophanie in den Psalmen und im Festkult," *Festschrift für A. Bertholet*, 513-31; Hans Peter Müller, "Die kultische Darstellung der Theophanie," *VT*, XIV (1964), 183-91.

[145]Other uses of $^c\bar{a}bhar$ have as subject the people (5:5; 6:2) and the New Moon (8:5), while the nominative $^c ebr\bar{a}th\hat{o}$ attributed to God occurs in 1:11. From Dt. 29:12 (Heb. 11) it appears that $^c\bar{a}bhar$ is a covenant term, which Amos here uses of Yahweh's coming to punish the violators of the covenant (cf. Gen. 15:17).

comparing Mic. 7:18 which uses ^{c}al after $^{c}\bar{a}bhar$ ("Who is a God
like you, pardoning iniquity and passing over transgression for
the remnant of his inheritance?").[146] But one wonders if another
answer could not be given, specifically that God warns of a final
"Theophany for Judgment," after which He will cease to deal with
Israel.[147]

In brief, the phrase "For I will pass through your midst"
is a complete reversal in meaning of the cultic expression for
God's epiphany; the coming of God in judgment upon Israel has
replaced hope of destruction upon the enemies, as in Ex. 12:12,
and sinners within Israel. In like manner, the phrase "For I
will never again pass by them" implies that a final appearance
for destruction will mark a change in God's dealing with Israel:
the *deus revelatus* will become the *deus absconditus*.[148]

Further illumination upon the problem of Amos' use of cultic
materials comes from the occurrence of $d\bar{a}rash$ in Amos. This cultic expression for the consulting of oracles at the sanctuaries
occurs in a crucial passage for interpreting the doxologies (5:
14-15).[149] Verse four opens with the divine word, "Seek me and
live; but do not seek Bethel, and do not enter into Gilgal, or
cross over to Beersheba, for Gilgal shall surely go into exile,
and Bethel shall come to nought."[150] There follows the prophetic

---

[146]Würthwein, *op. cit.*, 30; Harper, *op. cit.*, 166; Cripps,
op. cit., 226; Lindblom, *op. cit.*, 338; and Morgenstern, *Amos
Studies*, 420, agree with this interpretation.

[147]A. Neher, *op. cit.*, 124, agrees with J. Halévy that $^{c}\bar{a}bhar$
in the sense of forgive is curious in Amos, especially in view of
the use of $\d{h}\bar{a}dhal$ and $s\bar{a}la\d{h}$ in the prayers associated with the
visions, and understands this threat as a "placing of Yahweh him-
self" in their midst for judgment.

[148]Hesse, *op. cit.*, 2. It does not follow that this change
in God marks a similar one in Amos "von Nabi zum Unheilspropheten,"
as Würthwein, *op. cit.*, 40, maintains.

[149]A number of questions emerge from this text; does Bethel
refer to a god? Is the reference to Beersheba later: Does this
refer to the practice of fleeing to an altar for safety?

[150]It is difficult to discern the exact place at which the
divine word leaves off and the prophetic word begins. H. W. Hertzberg, "Die prophetische Botschaft vom Heil," *NKZ*, XLIII (1932),
518, believes that neither Amos nor Isaiah makes it clear when the
speech of God ends and that of the prophet begins. "Es mache sach-
lich keinen Unterschied, ob sie von Jahwe in der 3. Person sprech-
en oder ihn in der 1. Person reden lassen." On the other hand,
Johannes Hempel and H. W. Wolff have attacked this view (see Hesse,
op. cit., 3-4, for a discussion and reference).

interpretation of the divine word; this assumes a three-fold
form: (1) "Seek the Lord and live" in 5:6; (2) "Seek good and
not evil that you may live" in 5:14; and (3) "Hate the evil and
love the good, and establish justice in the gate; it may be that
the Lord the God of Hosts will be gracious to the remnant of Joseph" in 5:15. Moreover, the prophetic exegesis of the threat
has three components: admonition, announcement of deliverance,
and threat (warning).[151] There is no reason to view 5:6,14f. as
late, or 5:4 as ironical paradox.[152] Rather, as Franz Hesse has
clearly shown, these so-called late passages are Amos' interpretation of the divine word.[153] Amos recognized that the καιρός
of grace had ended, yet he also knew that it was the very nature
of God to desire salvation for the people of the covenant. Rudolph has put it in the following manner: "Dass das letzte Ziel
der Wege Jahwes mit Israel das Heil sei, dessen ist auch Amos
gewiss."[154] In view of this, Hesse concludes that the tension
between Amos' knowledge of God's decision that the end had come
upon Israel and his conviction that God actually desired to deliver them is eased by the concept of the $sh^e{}'\bar{e}r\hat{i}th$ (5:15), although even this partial resolution of the problem stands under
the $'\hat{u}lai$ (perhaps) which softens the "surely" of 5:4.[155] However, Lindblom's thesis that $sh^e{}'\bar{e}r\hat{i}th$ in this verse means "descendants" seems to refute such an interpretation, the tension
remaining to the end.[156]

With this understanding of the crucial passage, what can be
said about the use of $d\bar{a}rash$? At least two observations can be

---

[151] Hesse, *op. cit.*, 4-7.

[152] As Weiser does in "Zu Amos 4:6-13," *ZAW*, XLVI (1928),
1-17.

[153] Hesse, *loc. cit.*

[154] Quoted from Hesse, *op. cit.*, 15, note 55.

[155] Hesse, *ibid.*, 13-17.

[156] Lindblom, *op. cit.*, 340, note 104; 350, note 124. His
view that $sh^e{}'\bar{e}r\hat{i}th$ means descendants (North Israel), not the
idea of a remnant spared as in Isaiah, is convincing. Thus 5:
15 refers to the descendants of the patriarch Joseph, as in II
Sam. 14:7 and Isa. 14:22, and the tension is unresolved. The
idea of election and imminent judgment stand side by side.

made. First, if Bethel actually refers to a god[157] and if Amos'
attack is upon religious syncretism, then Amos uses the verb in
its usual sense.[158] However, if Bethel is understood as a sanctuary, as the presence of Gilgal and Beersheba indicates, then
Amos has reversed the verb's meaning. The cultic word for seeking the sanctuary has been given its original meaning of consulting the God who chooses to remain without a special place of worship. Seek Yahweh, but do not seek the sanctuaries, for God has
nothing to do with them.[159] Behind this, one is able to formu-
late the real issue for Amos: cult or law.[160] Thus, as in the
case of the cultic phrase for theophany, so here Amos has used
the word *dārash* in a meaning opposite to the popular interpretation.

Within the latter passage occurs a reference to another
cultic expression from ancient times, the cry "With us is God"
(5:14). This cry of exultation, which probably goes back to the
period of the holy wars,[161] is obviously being used by the people
in the cult as an expression of assurance that no evil can befall
Israel (9:10).[162] Opposing this understanding of Yahweh's relation

---

[157]J. P. Hyatt, "The Deity Bethel and the Old Testament,"
JAOS, LIX (1939), 81-98; and O. Eissfeldt, "Der Gott Bethel," *ARW*,
XXVIII (1930), 1-30, should be consulted in regard to the possi-
bility that this verse refers to a deity.

[158]Würthwein, *op. cit.*, 51.

[159]Hesse, *op. cit.*, 5-6. But he is wrong that mention of the
sanctuaries is only incidental. See also Kapelrud, *Central Ideas
in Amos*, 36, who argues that *dārash* of 5:4,6 is used differently
from that of 5:5.

[160]Hesse, *op. cit.*, 12. The issue is neither cult nor ethics.
5:14-15 calls the people back to the old laws of the amphictyony.
See R. Bach, "Gottesrecht und weltliches Recht in der Verkündigung
des Propheten Amos," *Festschrift für Gunther Dehn* (Neukirchen:
Verlag der Buchhandlung des Erziehungsvereins, 1957), 23-34; Würthwein, *op. cit.*, 43-50; Hesse, *ibid.*, 12; and Julien Harvéy, "Le
'rîb-pattern,' réquisitoire prophétique sur la rupture de l'alliance ," *Bib*, XLIII (1962), 172-96. On the other hand, Kapelrud,
Central Ideas in Amos, 48, 67, thinks of cult or conduct as the
choice.

[161]For a discussion of holy war, see G. von Rad, *Der heilige
Krieg im alten Israel*.

[162]Compare Mic. 3:11; 2:6ff.; Hos. 8:2; Isa. 28:15; Jer. 5:
12; and the Immanuel passages in Isa. 7 and 8. Kapelrud, *Central
Ideas in Amos*, 45-46, makes a great deal of the fact that *Immanuel*
rather than *Immanujah* is mentioned in these texts.

to Israel, Amos leaves only a possibility that God will be with them, a possibility that is predicated upon the condition that Israel seeks Yahweh, who is the good. Only then will there be any substance to the ancient cultic cry of jubilation.

This leads to another expression dealing with the relationship between Yahweh and the covenant people. In 4:12 Amos uses the words "your God," a unique occurrence in Amos. But the context reveals that this phrase in no way connotes the usual idea; rather, what is meant is "prepare to meet your God" in judgment. Here the God of Israel is no longer thought of as a deity who must protect his devotées; the claim "my God" binds him in no way.[163] Although Yahweh calls Israel "my people" (7:8; 8:2; 9:14), he is also the God of Philistines and Syrians (9:7). Moreover, this God governs the affairs of all nations (1:3-2:8). Finally, this interpretation of the facts is confirmed by the well-known passage on Israel's election: "You only have I known [cared for] of all the families of the earth; therefore, I will punish you for all your iniquities" (3:2). Israel's election is to service and responsibility, the misuse of which leads to judgment. In brief, when Amos takes up the phrase "our God" that had come to imply special privilege, he gives it an opposite meaning: responsibility.

Such a radical reversal of cultic terminology is obvious in Amos' oracle on the Day of Yahweh (5:18-20). This reversal of the usual expectation has long been noted, and it needs no elaboration here.[164] The imagery is clear (darkness and not light, gloom with no brightness in it), while the illustrations reveal the real nature of the day: there will be no escape.

This tendency in the preaching of Amos to take up cultic expressions and give them opposite meanings is also seen in the words, "I will set my eyes upon them" (9:4,8). This phrase had always been used favorably (Gen. 44:21), as in the benediction

---

[163]Against Hesse, *op. cit.*, 10, who thinks that for Yahweh to give Israel up is to give himself up.

[164]G. von Rad, "The Origin of the Concept of the Day of Yahweh," *JSS*, IV (1956), 97-108; L. Černý, *The Day of Yahweh and Some Relevant Problems* (Prague: Sumptibus Facultatis Philosophicae Universitatis Carolinae, 1948); J.M.P. Smith, *The Day of Yahweh* (Chicago: University Press, 1901); and Kapelrud, *Central Ideas in Amos*, 71.

at Num. 6:25-26.[165] But Amos has changed the import of the
words to one of horror. God commands that the sanctuary be destroyed upon the people, so that none escapes--in Sheol, heaven,
Carmel, sea or captivity. The horror of this threat is made explicit by the addition of the words "for evil" (9:4) and "I will
destroy it [this sinful kingdom] from the surface of the ground"
(9:8).

Finally, the oracles against the nations (1:2-2:8) must be
considered in this context. Using the analogy of Egyptian exe-
cration texts, Aage Bentzen argues that Amos has taken over a
cultic act of cursing the enemies and leads up to a climax in
which he pronounces a curse upon Judah and Israel.[166] However,
Bentzen writes that this judgment upon Israel is not totally new,
since the ritual took place in the New Year Festival, a part of
which celebrated Yahweh's epiphany to destroy enemies and to
judge sinners within Israel. Thus Bentzen sees the new element
in Amos' emphasis, not in the threat itself; the former joy over
Yahweh's appearance has given way to dread.[167]

On the other hand, Ernst Würthwein has sought to defend the
thesis that the oracles against Judah and Israel come from a
different time than those against foreign nations.[168] He thinks
Amos spoke the latter when a cultic prophet, a *Nabi'*, whose task
it was to promote blessing; but the oracles against Judah and

---

[165]Cripps, *op. cit.*, 260; Weiser, *Das Buch der zwölf Kleinen
Propheten*, 201. G. von Rad's treatment of a phrase related to
this in subject matter is instructive. He observes that the activity of levitical preaching (cf. Neh. 8:7f.) can be discerned
in several passages within Chr. that cite earlier prophetic words.
This he discovers in II Chr. 16:7-9 in which the phrase, "Yahweh's
eyes sweep over the whole earth," is said to be a quotation of
Zech. 4:10b, and to form the high point of the sermon--the reminder that although men do not see Yahweh, he sees them and delivers
or punishes. Another quotation discovered by von Rad (II Chr.
15:2-7, "If you seek him, he will let himself be found by you,"
which comes from Jer. 29:13-14 and 31:16b) is strikingly like the
emphasis of Am. 5:4,6,14-15 (see "Die levitische Predigt in den
Büchern der Chronik," *Gesammelte Studien zum Alten Testament*
[München: Chr. Kaiser Verlag, 1961], 248-61, especially 250-51).

[166]Bentzen, "The Ritual Background of Amos 1:2-2:16," *OTS*,
VIII (1950), 85-99.

[167]*Ibid.*, 94-95. Kapelrud, *Central Ideas in Amos*, 20, thinks
that the new element is judgment upon *all* Israel.

[168]Würthwein, *op. cit.*, 35-40.

Israel are thought to come from the period after Amos' transition
to a prophet of destruction.[169] Against Weiser's view of the
rhetorical form of the oracles, which is similar to Bentzen's,
he raises two objections: (1) rhetoric is incredible in a world
where word is more than sound, but a power released (Isa. 55:11);
(2) the strophes against the nations, set off by "thus saith the
Lord," have independent life, shaping the future whether they
find believing hearers or not.[170] These arguments in no way refute either Weiser's or Bentzen's views since "rhetoric and preparation" do not exclude a realistic understanding of the oracles
against foreign nations. The nations are really cursed. Hesse
is certainly wise in doubting that the oracles against the nations come from an earlier period than those against Judah and
Israel.[171]

Once again the same conclusion has been reached: Amos takes
up a cultic expression or ritual and gives it new meaning, which
almost amounts to a reversal of the popular interpretation. A
ritual act that brought joy to the people through expected destruction of enemies and punishment of sinners within Israel has
been taken over and given a new emphasis, leaving no room for
jubilation in the face of the coming punishment of all Israel.

In view of these facts, what can be said about the question
from which this discussion of Amos' use of cultic materials pro-
ceeded? Which view is more nearly accurate? Did Amos borrow from
the cult, though exercising no function within it, and reverse the
meaning of cultic expressions, or did he serve a prophetic function within the liturgy, bestowing upon the expressions their normal meaning? The answer must be that Amos used cultic expressions
in a sense completely different from the popular understanding.

---

[169]Würthwein, *op. cit.*, 38.

[170]*Ibid.*, 36-38. But see E. von Waldow, "Der traditions-
geschichtliche Hintergrund der prophetischen Gerichtsreden,"
BZAW, LXXXV (1963), 49-50; J. Muilenburg, "A Study in Hebrew
Rhetoric," *SVT*, I (1953), 97-111; "The Linguistic and Rhetorical
Usages of the Particle כִּי in the Old Testament," *HUCA*, XXXII
(1961), 136-60.

[171]Hesse, *op. cit.*, 2. Weiser rightly accuses Würthwein of
breaking up the original continuity of the poem concerning the
nations and the series of visions (*The Old Testament: Its Formation and Development* [New York: Association Press, 1961], 242).

CHAPTER II

THE TEXT

The purpose of this chapter is to examine the text of the
doxologies, with special attention to strophic arrangement. It
also seeks to clarify meanings of difficult words, particularly
those often emended, and to discover semantic fields of key expressions. The goal of such considerations is, of course, to
provide an adequate translation of the doxologies that will become the basis for subsequent discussion.

A.   *Various Strophic Arrangements of the Doxologies*

The simplest division of the doxologies is that of K. Budde,
who thought in terms of a single strophe comprising 4:13; 5:8;
and 9:5-6.[1] According to him, "Sie sind aber so gleichartig,
dass man sie unbedingt der gleichen Hand zuweisen muss...."[2] On
the basis of what appeared to him to be the logical order, Budde
suggested that one might think of the following sequence:

הַבּוֹנֶה בַשָּׁמַיִם עֲלִיָּתוֹ וַאֲגֻדָּתוֹ עַל-אֶרֶץ יְסָדָהּ
עֹשֵׂה כִימָה וּכְסִיל וְהֹפֵךְ לַבֹּקֶר צַלְמָוֶת
וְיוֹם לַיְלָה הֶחְשִׁיךְ הַקּוֹרֵא לְמֵי-הַיָּם
וַיִּשְׁפְּכֵם עַל-פְּנֵי הָאָרֶץ
כִּי-הוּא יוֹצֵר הָרִים וּבֹרֵא רוּחַ
וּמַגִּיד לְאָדָם מַה-שֵּׂחוֹ
הַבּוֹלֵג בָּאָרֶץ וְתַמּוּג וְעָלְתָה כַיְאֹר כֻּלָּהּ
וְשָׁקְעָה כִּיאֹר מִצְרָיִם
עֹשֵׂה שַׁחַר וְעֵיפָה וְדֹרֵךְ עַל-בָּמֳתֵי אָרֶץ
יהוה אֱלֹהֵי צְבָאוֹת שְׁמוֹ.[3]

---

[1] K. Budde, *JBL*, XLIV (1925), 106, note 60. Budde is not
clear about the extent of the doxologies or the order of their
components. He refers to doxological insertion, mentioning 4:13;
5:8-9; 9:5-6; 8:8, but in his suggestion of the sequence only 9:
6a; 5:8; 4:13aac; 9:5aab; 4:13b are listed. Moreover, this list-
ing includes an error, for 4:13b is equated with 9:6bc. Obviously, 5:8b was meant instead of the former.

[2] Budde, *loc. cit.*

[3] He does not give the Hebrew in note 60, but this reconstruction is based on his entire discussion. Since his remarks
are incomplete, it is not certain whether 5:9 and 8:8 should be
included or not.

48

Noteworthy is his omission of 9:5ac based on the belief that reference to the mourning of earth's inhabitants is out of place in a hymn to the Creator.[4] Having radically rearranged the doxologies, which he thought might be considered a psalm or part of one as Hans Schmidt had suggested, Budde was confronted with the question of how the hymn became disjointed. Furthermore, Budde was convinced of the relative lateness of the doxologies; therefore, he had to find some reason for their subsequent insertion into the text of Amos. The answer was found in the editorial work of some person who added sections of the hymn as fillers for lost speeches of Amos. He concluded: "Sicherer als einem Abschluss bezeichnen diese Einschübe eine Lücke, die der Sammler nicht mit ursprünglichem Stoff auszufüllen wusste, so dass er, vielleicht nur vorläufig, Lückenbüsser dafür einfügte."[5] Budde failed to explain why an editor would see the need for such fillers, even if provisional, and how one hymn was torn apart and used in such a disorderly manner.[6] For the latter reason, Budde's reconstruction of the original hymn on the basis of logical sequence alone must be rejected.

At the other extreme is B. N. Wambacq, who has included passages outside the book of Amos in the original hymn to Yahweh the Creator God.[7] These passages consist of Jer. 10:12-16; (Jer. 51: 15-19); 31:35; Isa. 51:15. After a lengthy discussion of these passages and the doxologies, Wambacq concluded: "Amos a probablement emprunté ces trois passages à l'hymne en honneur de Jahvé créateur et les a inséré dans son oeuvre dans l'intention d'accentuer davantage l'ingratitude des Israélites."[8] The criteria for

---

[4]Budde, *JBL*, XLIV (1925), 106-07. 9:5ac is said to have been derived from 8:8 and does not belong to the original.

[5]*Ibid.*, 106.

[6]This is the basis for Maag's criticism of Budde's position, although he does not do Budde justice. See Maag, *Text, Wortschatz und Begriffswelt des Buches Amos*, 57-58.

[7]Wambacq, *op. cit.*, 208-20. He bases this on the work of A. Vaccari, "Hymnus propheticus in Deum Creatorem," *VerbDom*, IX (1929), 184-88.

[8]Wambacq, *op. cit.*, 218. A Weiser, *Das Buch der Propheten Jeremia* (Göttingen: Vandenhoeck & Reprecht, 1952), 132, 296-97, recognizes in Jer. 14:22 and 31:35 material from the temple cult. The first verse is said to be a complaint-liturgy having its setting in the Jerusalem temple where the community laments before the face of Yahweh (15:1). In 31:35 he finds the grounds for the promise in 31-34, and compares Ps. 8; 24:1f.; 33:6ff.; 65:7f.; 95:4ff.; 102:26; 135:6ff.; 136:5ff.; 146:6ff.

recognition of these passages as parts of a single hymn are two-
fold: first, theological content, and second, the phrase "Yahweh
of Hosts is his name" which concludes each. The weakness of his
argument stems from the inadequacy of the criteria by which parts
of the hymn are recognized, as well as failure to suggest any
satisfactory reason for such borrowing on the part of Amos, Isaiah and Jeremiah.[9]

Although Wambacq did not reconstruct the entire hymn in any
particular sequence, he did discuss meter in regard to the doxologies, which he recognized as hemistichs composed of 3 plus 3
rhythm. In fact, the short refrain ending the second and third
doxologies was lengthened to *YHWH 'ae lōhē ṣ e bhā'ôth sh e mô* on the
basis of textual variants, custom and rhythm.[10] Believing that
the doxologies were borrowed by Amos, Wambacq sought to remedy
the fact that the second interrupts its context by placing 5:7
before 5:10, where it is said to have belonged before a "careless
scribe" transposed the verses.[11] The author included 5:9 as a
part of the hymn, though following Hoffmann in his astral interpretation of the verse.[12] One other emendation is worth

---

[9]This view would presuppose familiarity with the hymn in
Israel and Judah, as is the assumption in the thesis advocated by
John Watts discussed above. Besides this difficulty, there is a
lack of theological unity in the other passages from Isaiah and
Jeremiah, especially that in Jer. 10:14-15. One wonders why Job
9:5-10 was not included, for it shows many more similarities to
the doxologies of Amos.

[10]Wambacq, *op. cit.*, 73-77.

[11]*Ibid.*, 199. He argued that such ideas as those expressed
in the doxologies are very ancient, appealing to van Honnacker's
view that *bārā'* and *śēḥô* are not late words. Highly questionable
is the denial that 4:13 refers to judgment: "L'idée du judgment
derniér est tout à fait absente du passage," (see 189, note 4).

[12]*Ibid.*, 190, note 6. Here he maintains this view despite
Mowinckel's objections in "Die Sternnamen im Alten Testament,"
NTT, XXIX (1928), 5-75. Mowinckel thinks of all star names in
the Old Testament as exilic or post-exilic, Jer. 18:14 being the
only exception (6). He recognizes nine star names (Venus as Morning Star, Corvus, Saturn, Pleiades, Orion, North Star, Antares,
Hyas, Mercury) and a word meaning zodiacal signs, possibly planets
(71). Against Hoffmann's view of star names in 5:9, he objects
that the verse is a gloss to 5:6 and that the refrain in 5:8 closes
the strophe so that a return to star references in the next verse
would be improbable. Finally, he observes that parallelism indicates that a line originally stood before 5:8a (66). Eric Burrows, *The Oracles of Jacob and Balaam* (London: Burns, Oates & Washbourne Ltd., 1938), *passim*, contends that the oracles of Jacob
allude to perhaps 28 constellations or stars in the space of 25

mentioning: he understood *ûmagîdh lᵉ'ādhām māh śēḥô* of 4:13 along lines laid down by A. Vaccari, translating "And pours the inundating waters upon the land."[13]

Between these two extremes--Budde, who thought of one strophe composed only of Am. 4:13, 5:8, and 9:5-6, and Wambacq, who wrote in terms of several strophes, remnants of which appear in Amos, Jeremiah and Isaiah--the other authors considering the problem have sought a solution. Friedrich Horst suggested two strophes of four lines of 3 plus 3 rhythm each; Hans Schmidt proposed three strophes of two 3 plus 3 lines with prologue and refrain for each; Theodore Gaster thought he discovered three strophes, each with a refrain, plus a fragment of a fourth in 5:9; Victor Maag contended for four strophes of two lines in 3 plus 3 beat; and John Watts argued for three strophes of four lines.[14]

Both Horst and Maag connected 5:8 with 4:13, excluding 5:9 from consideration, although the latter suspected a missing phrase that must have mentioned the movement of the stars.[15] Because of the interrelation of 4:13 and 5:8, a discussion of the doxologies cannot follow the easy procedure of taking up one at a time, but must overlap to some degree.

Horst considered 4:13 and 5:8 one strophe, originally connected but torn asunder by an accident. The following is his strophic arrangement:

יוֹצֵר הָרִים וּבֹרֵא רוּחַ וּמַגִּיד לְאָדָם מַה־שֵּׂחוֹ
עֹשֵׂה שַׁחַר וְעֵיפָה וְדֹרֵךְ עַל־בָּמֳתֵי אָרֶץ
וְהֹפֵךְ לַבֹּקֶר צַלְמָוֶת וְיוֹם לַיְלָה הֶחְשִׁיךְ

---

verses of the Masoretic text, and that their date is c. 1000 B.C. (44, 49). Burrows discovers allusions to Pleiades in Gen. 49:23 and to Orion in Gen. 49:24b, although the evidence for the latter is very questionable (36-37, 38-39, especially note 2). Even if Burrows' conclusions were accepted, his observation that *kesîl* is a late word would have to be taken into consideration (39, note 3). But the entire argument is highly questionable from the methodological point of view.

[13]Wambacq, *op. cit.*, 188, note 3. For *ûmagîdh* he read *ûmagîr*, *mē* for *māh*, and *'ādhamā* for *'ādhām*.

[14]Watts, *Vision and Prophecy in Amos*, 51, note 4, 52-59. Watts defended the following metrical system: 4-2-2-3,3-3-4; 3-2-2,4-3,3-3-3,3-3-2; 2-2-3,3-3-3,4-4,3-3-2.

[15]Maag, "Jahwäs Heerscharen," 46-47, note 4.

הַקּוֹרֵא לְמֵי-הַיָּם וַיִּשְׁפְּכֵם עַל-פְּנֵי הָאָרֶץ
יהוה שְׁמוֹ.[16]

Maag's reconstruction of these verses is quite similar:

יוֹצֵר הָרִים בֹּרֵא רוּחַ וּמַגִּיד לְאָדָם מַה-שֵּׂחוֹ
עֹשֵׂה שַׁחַר וְעֵיפָה וְדֹרֵךְ עַל-בָּמֳתֵי אָרֶץ
יהוה אֱלֹהֵי צְבָאוֹת שְׁמוֹ
עֹשֵׂה כִימָה וּכְסִיל
וְהֹפֵךְ לַבֹּקֶר צַלְמָוֶת וְיוֹם לַיְלָה הֶחְשִׁיךְ
הַקּוֹרֵא לְמֵי-הַיָּם וַיִּשְׁפְּכֵם עַל-פְּנֵי הָאָרֶץ
יהוה אֱלֹהֵי (צְבָאוֹת) שְׁמוֹ.[17]

In contrast, Gaster examined 4:13 as a separate strophe,
while Watts added 4:12b to the first strophe. Gaster's analysis
is as follows:

---

[16]Horst, "Die Doxologien im Amosbuch," 49. He writes that
māgadh does not occur as a verb in the Old Testament, but _megedh_
has the meaning of "costly" (Dt. 33:13,16). _ḥāshah_ is also lack-
ing, but in Aramaic (Dan. 3:16 _ḥashhâ_; Ezr. 6:9 _ḥashhû_, 7:20) it
does occur. Horst compares Accadian _ḥaśâḥu_ (desire or necessity),
and remarks that if the form _heshhô_ is a problem, then _ḥēsheq_ can
be read. He also calls attention to mythological allusions in
Am. 4:13, which remind him of Marduk's struggle with Tiamat.

[17]Maag, _Text, Wortschatz und Begriffswelt des Buches Amos_,
24-25, translates as follows:

Der die Berge bildet und den Wind erschafft,
    der dem Menschen kundet, was sein Sinnen ist,
Der die Morgenröte und das Dunkel macht
    und über die Höhen der Erde schreitet,
Jahwe, Gott der Heerscharen, ist sein Name.
Der Pleiaden und Orion macht,
Der das Dunkel zum Morgen wandelt
    und den Tag verfinstert zur Nacht,
Der den Wassern des Meeres ruft
    und die ausgiesst über der Erde Antlitz,
Jahwe, Gott der Heerscharen, ist sein Name.

This is a change from his earlier translation in "Jahwäs Heerscharen," 47, where he offers the following:

Der die Berge gebildet hat, der den Wind geschaff,
    der den Menschen kundtut, was sein Vorhaben ist,
Der Morgenröt und Dunkel macht,
    der einherschreitet auf den Höhen der Erde,
Jahwä, Gott der Heerscharen, ist sein Name.
                    ***
Der Siebengestirn und Orion machte,
....
Der das Dunkel zum Morgen wandelt
    und der Tag zur Nacht verfinstert,
Jahwä, Gott der Heerscharen, ist sein Name.

יוֹצֵר הָרִים וּבֹרֵא רוּחַ
וּמַגִּדיל לָאֲדָמָה שִׂיחָהּ
עֹשֵׂה שַׁחַר וְעֵיפָה
וְדֹרֵךְ עַל-בָּמֳתֵי אָרֶץ
יהוה צְבָאוֹת שְׁמוֹ.[18]

Finally, Watts' strophic arrangement proceeds in this manner:

הָכּוֹן לִקְרַאת אֱלֹהֶיךָ יִשְׂרָאֵל
יוֹצֵר הָרִים וּבֹרֵא רוּחַ וּמַגִּיד לְאָדָם מַה-שֵּׂחוֹ
עֹשֵׂה שַׁחַר עֵיפָה וְדֹרֵךְ עַל-בָּמֳתֵי אָרֶץ
יהוה אֱלֹהֵי צְבָאוֹת שְׁמוֹ.[19]

The second strophe was treated differently by the same authors; whereas Gaster limited himself to 5:8, Watts included 5:6-9. Gaster's suggestion is as follows:

עֹשֵׂה כִימָה וּכְסִיל
.....................(וּמוֹצִיא מַזָּרוֹת בְּעִתּוֹ)
הֹפֵךְ לַבֹּקֶר צַלְמָוֶת
וְיוֹם לְלַיְלָה הֶחְשִׁיךְ יהוה צְבָאוֹת שְׁמוֹ.[20]

---

[18]Gaster, *op. cit.*, 25, argued that in 4:13 the Yahweh or 'ae lōhē is a conflate, and that in 5:8 and 9:6 the original refrain has been redacted ("by the prophet himself?") to the simple "Yahweh." He translates:

He that formeth the mountains and createth the wind,
And maketh her foison [abundance] to grow unto the earth,
He that maketh the dawn and the gloaming,
And treadeth o'er the heights of the earth,
--the God of $ṣ^ebhā'ôth$ is His name.

[19]Watts, *Vision and Prophecy in Amos*, must argue for a single unit of four accents; for his defense see 52-53, note 8, where he cites references.

Prepare to meet your God, Israel.
Former of mountains
Creator of wind
    One revealing to man what His thought is
Making dawn of darkness
    And treading upon the heights of the earth
Is He whose name is Yahweh of Hosts.

[20]He that maketh the Pleiades and Orion,
....
He that turneth the gloom into dayspring,
And maketh the day dark with night,
--the God of $ṣ^ebhā'ôth$ is His name.

In 5:8 there is a mistake of vocalization, לְבֹקֵר appearing. Gaster, *op. cit.*, 24-25.

Watts argued for the following pattern:

דִּרְשׁוּ אֶת-יהוה וִחְיוּ פֶּן-יִצְלַח כָּאֵשׁ וְאָכְלָה וְאֵין-מְכַבֶּה
יהוה פָּֽהֶּ מִֽלְמַעְלָה מִשְׁפָּט וּצְדָקָה לָאָרֶץ הִגִּיחַ
עֹשֵׂה כִימָה וּכְסִיל וְהֹפֵךְ לַבֹּקֶר צַלְמָוֶת וְיוֹם לַיְלָה הֶחְשִׁיךְ
הַמַּבְלִיג שֹׁר עַל-עָז וְשֹׁר עַל-מִבְצָר יָבוֹא יהוה שְׁמוֹ.[21]

Textual emendation in 4:13a by Gaster is slight, and one
can easily understand how such a change could have taken place.[22]
But the complicated emendations suggested by Watts in 5:7 are not
in the least convincing, nor is his attempt to include 5:6 any
more satisfactory.[23] However, he has called attention to the fact
that the translator of the Septuagint understood 5:7 as part of
the doxology, and for that reminder one must be appreciative.

---

[21]Seek Yahweh and live.
Lest He break out like fire
Which consumes beyond quenching.
Yahweh (it is who) caused justice to trickle down from
above
And established righteousness for the earth,
Making Pleiades and Orion
Turning deep darkness to morning,
Who darkened day into night.
The One causing Taurus to vanquish Capella
And who will cause Taurus to set upon Vindemiatrix
Is He whose name is Yahweh.

[22]The l of $magdh\hat{\imath}l$ could have been omitted because of the l
in $l\bar{a}$'$^{a}dh\bar{a}m\bar{a}h$; from the latter phrase $m\bar{a}h$ could have become separated, and the suffix could have been changed after the other
alterations had rendered the phrase meaningless.

[23]First, the arbitrary omission of $b\bar{e}th$ $y\hat{o}s\bar{e}ph$ and $l^{e}b\bar{e}th$'$\bar{e}l$
in 5:6 cannot be accepted. In the second place, it is difficult
to understand how Yahweh could have been corrupted to hh, and
even more impossible to see how $milma^{aa}l\bar{a}h$ could have become
$l^{e}la^{aa}n\bar{a}h$. These criticisms gain force when one considers that
the verse makes perfectly good sense as it appears, being emended
only because of a desire to avoid the obvious break in the context posed by the doxology. Moreover, the versions do not present a unified witness in regard to 5:7; it may be true that Q
and L support the Septuagintal reading "κύριος ὁ ποιῶν εἰς ὕψος
κρίμα καὶ δικαιοσύνη εἰς γῆν ἔθηκεν," but B and C do not have
κύριος, and Swete merely notes its presence. In "Note on the
Text of Amos V:7," 215-16, Watts defended his emendations on the
basis of the following points: (1) the Septuagint, (2) the rare
Hebrew verb $p\bar{a}khah$, which was not known by the translator of the
Septuagint text of Amos, and (3) the mechanical preservation of
the Hebrew orthography despite its meaninglessness. In his opinion, this emendation was supported by the hymnic parallels which
contrast God's high dwelling with earth beneath, but this does
not follow at all.

Must the same verdict be reached regarding Watts' vocalization of the words in 5:9 so as to obtain names of stars, a tendency begun in 1883 by Georg Hoffmann and followed by Bernhard Duhm, G. R. Driver, B. N. Wambacq, Victor Maag and others?

Hoffmann's emendations were an attempt to clarify an admittedly difficult verse, one that seems out of place next to the second doxology. He changed $sh\bar{o}dh$ to $sh\bar{o}r$, $^c az$ to $^c\bar{e}z$, $mibhs\bar{a}r$ to $mabhs\hat{i}r$ and translated "Who makes the Bull (Taurus) to rise hard on (the rising of) the She-goat (Capella), and causes the Bull to set hard on (the rising of) the Vintager (Vindemiator)."[24]

Bernhard Duhm approved of Hoffmann's attempt and offered further emendation to confirm the conjecture.[25] Within the second $sh\bar{o}dh$, Duhm thought he found evidence for a reference to Gemma. He argued that the Septuagint's rendering of the two $sh\bar{o}dh$'s with different words indicates that something else was being translated. The second $sh\bar{o}dh$ is represented by ταλαιπωρίαν, sometimes a translation of $shebher$ (Isa. 51:19; 59:7; 60:18; Jer. 48:3). Duhm argued that the Septuagint translator read $shebher$, a corruption of $sh^e bh\hat{o}$ (Ex. 28:19).[26] In his opinion, this might stand for Gemma. Not satisfied with Hoffmann's translation of $^c al$ as "after," Duhm dropped it in favor of "with" (Am. 3:15, Job 38:32, I Kgs. 15:20, Gen. 32:12) and rendered "Who created Sirius and Orion (5:8a), who bids Taurus and Capella rise, who bids Gemma with Arcturus set" (5:9).[27]

---

[24]G. Hoffmann, op. cit., 110-11. Capella rose in April-May; Taurus, in May-June; Vindemiator rose in September; and the morning setting of Taurus was in October-November, probably corresponding to the time of the early rains. Cripps complains that Hoffmann forces the text here when maintaining that Taurus sets after the morning rising of Vindemiator in September; moreover, Cripps writes that the ancients usually referred to a setting (Cripps, op. cit., 297, note 1; and G. R. Driver, op. cit., 208, for the translation of Hoffmann's final rendition).

[25]B. Duhm, "Anmerkungen zu den zwölf Propheten," ZAW, XXXI (1911), 1-18 (especially page 10).

[26]Maag, Text, Wortschatz und Begriffswelt des Buches Amos, 26, suggests $sh^{ec}\bar{o}bh$ for Gemma.

[27]Duhm, "Anmerkungen zu den zwölf Propheten," 10, summed up his discussion of 5:9 as follows: "Von den Menschen, ihren Gedanken, ihren Festungen spricht der Dichter weder hier noch 4: 13." Nowack, op. cit., 144-45, accepted Duhm's suggestions. The understanding of $kh\hat{\imath}m\bar{a}h$ as Sirius raises the question of the meaning of the word usually translated Pleiades. In Job 9:9,10 and

The next major attempt to defend this understanding of the
verse was that of G. R. Driver.[28] To him the presence of references to the wicked in passages dealing with the heavenly bodies
was too much; thus he sought to get rid of such an interpretation.[29] Believing that Hoffmann's view made good sense, Driver
asserted that the refrain in Am. 5:8 "whose name is the Lord" is
out of place as a result of the work of a copyist who misunder-
stood the last two lines; Driver then sought to buttress this
understanding by a similar interpretation of Job 38:12-15.[30] In
this passage the phrase "wicked and high arm" was understood to
refer to heavenly bodies. Driver was so convinced of the merit
of his suggestion that he asserted that stars are intended whether
the text is kept or emended. Behind $r^e sha^c \hat{i} m$, he thought he saw
a reference to Sirius, the star of ill omen, the Dog-Stars (Canis)
Major and Minor). Or if the word has replaced $\acute{s}^{ec} \hat{i} r \hat{i} m$, "hairy
ones," Driver saw further evidence for Sirius in the Arabic word
for Canis Major, which means "hairy ones" and has a dual ending
for Canis Major and Minor. Furthermore, the Arabic word that is
the equivalent of "high arm" means the "Arm of Leo, A and B
Geminorum, the extended arm, and A and B Canis Minoris, the con-
tracted arm." Observing that these coincide almost entirely with

---

38:31-32, it appears along with the Bear and the Orion, the latter of which occurs with the meaning of "constellations" in Isa.
13:10. S. R. Driver, *op. cit.*, 182, calls attention to the myth
of a "heaven-daring rebel chained to the sky for his impiety" be-
hind this word $kh^e s \hat{i} l$. As for $kh \hat{i} m \bar{a} h$, it is uncertain which is
more nearly accurate. Hoffmann and Th. Robinson argue for Sirius,
while most other commentators prefer Pleiades, the case for which
has been presented most cogently by Mowinckel (see Hoffmann, *op.
cit.*, 110, 279; Th. Robinson, *op. cit.*, 88, and Mowinckel, "Die
Sternnamen im Alten Testament," 45-51).

[28] G. R. Driver, "Two Astronomical Passages in the Old Testament," *JTS*, IV (1953), 208-12.

[29] He interprets the context as a reference to the starry
firmament, the alternation of day and night, the distribution of
the seas over the earth, thus fixing the bounds of human habita-
tion. However, it is not certain that this is the correct interpretation; Th. Robinson, *op. cit.*, 89-90, and Harper, *op. cit.*,
116, think that the phrase "who calls for the waters of the sea
and pours them out upon the surface of the earth" is an allusion
to the Deluge, and even S. R. Driver, *op. cit.*, 182, thought this
possible. Other references to heavenly bodies mention the wicked
(Job 9).

[30] Compare Harper, *op. cit.*, who introduced 5:8 with the refrain.

the Navigator's Line: Sirius (A Canis Majoris), Procyon (A Canis
Minoris), Castor and Pollux (A and B Geminorum), Driver rendered
the verses in question as follows: "That it may grip the ends of
the earth, and the Dog-stars are shaken out of it...and the light
of the Dog-stars is withdrawn from it, and the Navigator's Line
is broken up."[31]

It must be admitted that such an interpretation of Am. 5:9
has one strong point: it gives to *hammabhlîg* a meaning more in
accord with its use elsewhere (Ps. 39:13; Jer. 8:18; Job 9:27;
10:20).[32] Furthermore, combined with 5:8, it gives a "dignified
and striking description" of Yahweh $s^e bh\bar{a}'\hat{o}th$: He made Pleiades
and Orion (5:8a); He is Lord of stars in their rising and setting
(5:9); He causes darkness and light (5:8b); wind and storm (5:8c);
Yahweh of Hosts is his name (5:8c).[33]

But the objections to such an understanding of 5:9 are very
strong. First, no suitable date for the reference to stars can
be suggested.[34] There is no indication that ancient Israel knew
them by such names, and if they emerged during the exile under
Babylonian influence, why are only two of them Babylonian?[35]
Moreover, if the passage is this late in origin, why did the
translator of the Septuagint misunderstand the references to
stars?[36] Again, it is difficult to escape the fact that star

---

[31]G. R. Driver, *op. cit.*, 209-12.

[32]Cripps, *op. cit.*, 298.

[33]*Ibid.*, 299. He also thinks that three other factors favor
this interpretation: (1) elsewhere the mention of Pleiades and
Orion always includes reference to at least one more star; (2)
the emendations are not drastic; and (3) one does not have to see
in this passage astrological or mythological significance. The
first and third arguments have no merit, and the second, though
true, does not demand acceptance of such an interpretation.

[34]Budde, *JBL*, XLIII (1924), 111; Cripps. *op. cit.*, 298.

[35]Taurus and Capella; see Cripps., *loc. cit.*

[36]Wellhausen, *Die Kleinen Propheten* (Berlin: Walter de
Gruyter & Co., 1898, 3rd edition, reprinted 1963), 81-82, recognized this difficulty, remarking that since the stars were so
well known a different reading would not have arisen. He also
thought the rising and setting of stars to be too ordinary a
matter for such a context, but this is less convincing.

imagery seems to be forgotten after 5:8a, while the refrain "whose name is the Lord" properly terminates the doxology.[37]

If the interpretation begun by Hoffmann is rejected, what better explanation of 5:9 can be given? Is it possible to interpret the verse as it stands or to emend it in another direction without creating too much objection? Theodore Gaster has made such an attempt:

$$\text{הַמַּבְלִיג שֶׁבֶר עַל־עוֹז}$$
$$\text{וְשֹׁד עַל־מִבְצָר יָבִיא.}^{38}$$

shebher was restored after the Septuagint, and *hammabhlîg* was explained from Judaeo-Arabic *balaja*, "reach, attain to." Moreover, $^c\hat{o}z$, parallel with *mibhṣār*, was connected with Arabic ^{c}*awadha*, "seek refuge," and with $m\bar{a}^c\hat{o}z$; Gaster denied any connection with the Hebrew root meaning "be strong" implied by $^c\bar{a}z$ of the Masoretic Text. The author ventured to translate: "He who maketh destruction to come upon men's stronghold, and bringeth ruin on their fortress."[39]

Friedrich Horst also offered a textual emendation having nothing to do with stars. In a footnote, Horst indicated his preference for *hammdallēg shûr* $ma^c\hat{o}z$, a restoration based on Ps. 18:30; II Sam. 22:30.[40] This emendation should probably be loosely translated as "He who leaps over the strong wall."[41]

Thus a satisfactory explanation can be given the verse by both approaches, although Gaster's interpretation has more to

---

[37]This is precisely Sellin's argument, which Weiser also used. Watts dismissed the argument solely on the basis of his hypothesis that 5:8b does not belong here but in 9:6b, so that star imagery is not interrupted (see Sellin, *op. cit.*, 228-29; Weiser, "Die Prophetie des Amos," 202-03; and Watts, *Vision and Prophecy in Amos*, 55, note 4).

[38]Gaster, *op. cit.*, 26.

[39]*Ibid.* Gaster suggested that 5:9 was out of place, and probably belonged after 9:6, the last two lines of the strophe having been lost.

[40]Horst, "Die Doxologien im Amosbuch," 46, note 5. He thought 5:9 was an addition placed here inadvertently by a copyist who quoted again the place from which 5:8 came.

[41]Mowinckel, "Die Sternnamen im Alten Testament," 67, makes sense of the text on the basis of the LXX. He sees a reference to Yahweh's power over fortresses and castles.

commend it. Does the content of 5:9, then, cause difficulty?
Is there no place for mention of destruction upon the evil in a
doxology praising Yahweh for his power over creation?[42] If it
could be shown that such a reference is not intrusive, then there
would be no necessity to take Hoffmann's way out. An answer to
this question can be found in a passage very similar to the one
in Amos, Job 9:9ff. Here the Bear, Orion and Pleiades are mentioned in a context of praise which recalls God's great and mar-
velous deeds; this allusion is immediately followed by an announcement of a theophany: "Lo, he passes by me and I see him
not....Behold, he snatches away; who can hinder him?" and specific mention of God's punishing wrath (9:13-19). Likewise in Isa.
13:9-16 a reference to the day of the Lord asserts that the stars
of the heavens and their constellations (Orions) will not give
any light on that terrible day of God's wrath.

Even within the doxologies there is confirmation of this
affirmative answer. The third refers to man's response to God's
touching of the earth: "All who dwell in it mourn." Horst has
rightly criticized Budde for eliminating this phrase from the
hymn. Moreover, 9:6b most probably contains an allusion to the
Deluge, so the third doxology has two references to God's punishment.[43]

If it is admitted that such praises of Yahweh's power over
creation can contain references to acts of punishment upon the
guilty, then one of the real causes for emending Am. 5:9 to names
of stars is removed. This means that, regardless of whether one
sees the phrase "who calls for the waters of the sea and pours
them out upon the surface of the earth" to be in its original
context at 5:8b or 9:6b, there is no real need to emend 5:9.

---

[42]Watts cannot adequately explain the reference to the
mourning of all the inhabitants in 9:5; in fact, he seems not to
have recognized the problem posed to his thesis by this verse.

[43]Harper, *op. cit.*, 116, points to four reasons for this
interpretation: (1) the word $q\bar{o}r\bar{e}$'; (2) the phrase "face of the
earth"; (3) the thought of the following verses; and (4) the
typical character of illustrations of Yahweh's power. A. Neher,
op. cit., 70, also recognizes the phrase in 5:8b and 9:6b as an
allusion to the Flood.

The third strophe does not present so much difficulty, Gaster being the only one who excludes 9:5 from consideration.[44] His reconstruction of the strophe is:

הַבּוֹנֶה בַמַּיִם עֲלִיָּתוֹ
וַאֲגֻדָּתוֹ עַל-אֶרֶץ יְסָדָהּ
הַקּוֹרֵא לְמֵי-הַיָּם
וַיִּשְׁפְּכֵם עַל-פְּנֵי הָאָרֶץ
יהוה צְבָאוֹת שְׁמוֹ.[45]

The other commentators include 9:5 in the hymn. Horst suggested the following arrangement:

הַנּוֹגֵעַ בָּאָרֶץ וַתָּמוֹג וְאָבְלוּ כָּל-יוֹשְׁבֵי בָהּ
וְעָלְתָה כַיְאֹר כֻּלָּהּ וְשָׁקְעָה כִיאֹר מִצְרָיִם
הַבּוֹנֶה בַשָּׁמַיִם עֲלִיָּתוֹ וַאֲגֻדָּתוֹ עַל-אֶרֶץ יְסָדָהּ
הַקּוֹרֵא לְמֵי-הַיָּם וַיִּשְׁפְּכֵם עַל-פְּנֵי הָאָרֶץ
יהוה שְׁמוֹ.[46]

Maag's reconstruction is exactly like that of Horst, except that the former included the introductory *wa'dhōnai YHWH haṣṣ^{e}bhā'ôth*.[47]

---

[44]Gaster, *op. cit.*, 25. Weiser's earlier work, "Die Prophetie des Amos," 31, recognized only 4:13, 5:8-9 and 9:6 as hymnic.

[45]He that buildeth in the seas His upper chamber,
And layeth His foundation on the earth,
He that calleth to the waters of the ocean,
And poureth them out upon the earth,
--the God of *ṣ^{e}bā'ôth* is His name.

[46]Horst ("Die Doxologien im Amosbuch," 54) interpreted the opening refrain as an oath particle used with the divine festal name, appealing to Johannes Pedersen's *Der Eid bei den Semiten* (Strassburg: Karl J. Trübner, 1914), 16.

[47]Maag, *Text, Wortschatz und Begriffswelt des Buches Amos*, 56-57. He translates:

(Mein) Herr Jahwe der Heerscharen,
Der die Erde anrührt, dass sie schwankt,
    und all ihre Bewohner in Trauer geraten,
Dass die ganze sich hebt wie der Nil,
    sich senkt wie der Nil in Ägypten,
Der im Himmel seinen Soller gebaut,
    sein Gewolb auf die Erde gegründet,
Der den Wassern des Meeres ruft
    und sie ausgiesst über der Erde Antlitz,
Jahwe ist sein Name.

His earlier view, "Jahwäs Heerscharen," 47, had included only 9:5.

Der die Erde anrührt, dass sie schwankt
und all ihre Bewohner in Trauer geraten,
dass ihr Gesamt sich hebt wie der Nil,
sich senkt wie der Strom Ägyptens
Jahwä, Gott der Heerscharen, ist sein Name.

On the other hand, Watts made several radical changes in the
text of 9:5-6. He reads:

וַאדֹנָי יהוה הַצָּבָא אוֹתוֹת הַנּוֹגֵעַ בָּאָרֶץ וְתָמוּג
וְאָבְלוּ כָל-יוֹשְׁבֵיהָ בָּהּ וְעָלְתָה כִיאֹר כֻּלָּהּ וְשָׁקְעָה כִיאֹר מִצְרָיִם
מִתְבּוֹנֵן בַּשָּׁמַיִם מַעֲלוֹתוֹ הוּא גִדְתוֹ עַל-אֶרֶץ יְסָדָהּ
הַקּוֹרֵא לְמֵי-הַיָּם וְיִשְׁפְּכֵם עַל-פְּנֵי הָאָרֶץ יהוה שְׁמוֹ.[48]

B. *Observations about the Vocabulary of the Doxologies*

1. *Terminology for Creation*

The various textual emendations have called attention to
several difficult words and phrases. Before venturing a translation of the doxologies, some consideration of the vocabulary
is in order. Since the doxologies extol Yahweh as Creator, primary attention should be given the words for his creative action.
These include *yāṣar*, *bārā'*, *ʿāsāh*, *bānāh* and *yāsadh*. The parallel
use of *yāṣar* and *bārā'* has already been pointed out. The former
is used in Am. 4:13 and 7:1 with the meaning "to form, to fashion." It is the normal word for forming something as with clay;

---

[48]Lord Yahweh
    The One summoning signs
        Is the One touching the earth so it will quiver,
    Though all its inhabitants mourn with it
        And its reservoirs rise like the Nile
            And irrigate like the Nile of Egypt.
    One determining his thoughts (works) in the heavens is He,
        His bounty which he will establish on the earth,
    The One calling to the sea's water
        That he might pour it over the earth's surface
            Is He whose name is Yahweh.

Watts' suggested emendations are unnecessary; besides they presuppose too many cases of single or double haplography to be
credible. Most dubious is the attempt to restore 9:6. The
change from *mithbônēn* to *habôneh* is a major one; so is that from
maʿalôthô hû' gᵉdhāthô to *ʿaliyāthô wa 'ᵃgûdhāthô*. It is difficult to see why so many mistakes would be made here, and less
convincing since *gᵉdhāthô* is not found elsewhere in the Old Testament. Finally, this emendation assumes that final *m* was written no differently (see Watts, *Vision and Prophecy in Amos*, 57-
59). In regard to the opening formula, Maag has suggested that
a mistake in dictation caused the change from *Yahweh 'elōhē
ṣᵉbā'ôth* to *'ᵃdōnai Yahweh ṣᵉbā'ôth* (Maag, "Jahwäs Heerscharen,"
47). On the other hand, J. Halévy thought of the *h* in *haṣṣᵉbā'ôth*
as dittography of the final *h* in Yahweh, while Wambacq believed
that *'elōhē* has dropped out, so that one should read with the
LXX *Yahweh 'elōhē haṣṣᵉbā'ôth* as in Am. 3:13 (see Wambacq, *op.
cit.*, 55, where Halévy's view is mentioned).

when referring to divine activity it has two basic meanings: (1)
to form, as the potter does, and (2) to frame, pre-ordain,
plan.[49]

Remarks in the preceding chapter about a pre-exilic use of
$b\bar{a}r\bar{a}$' need not be repeated; suffice it to say that Humbert's
thesis of a cultic cosmogonic use prior to Amos has little to
commend it. However, the same verdict must not be rendered regarding his analysis of the exilic and post-exilic uses of $b\bar{a}r\bar{a}$',
for here he has made a lasting contribution, and the influence
of his work upon the following discussion is strong.

Outside Second Isaiah there are three exilic uses of $b\bar{a}r\bar{a}$',
two within a prophetic lament that alludes to a cosmogonic myth
of creation (Ez. 28:13,15).[50] The first use of $b\bar{a}r\bar{a}$' within this
lament over the king of Tyre refers to the precious stones pre-
pared for him on the day he was created, while the second asserts
that the king was blameless in his ways from the day he was created, until iniquity was found in him. Humbert is certainly right
that this refers to an old myth, but his thesis that the "Qinah"
does not belong to the prophetic or narrative literary genre is
unconvincing, for the prophets certainly made use of it often.[51]
It is striking that Am. 4:13 is immediately followed by a lamentation over the fallen Virgin Israel. The third use of $b\bar{a}r\bar{a}$'
listed in Ezekiel appears within an announcement of judgment upon
the Ammonites (21:30), and accords completely with the other two
uses in this book. Consequently, there is no reason to consider
the text a use of $b\bar{a}r\bar{a}$', "to cut," as Humbert suggested.[52]

---

[49]The first meaning appears with many objects: Adam (Gen. 2:
7,8); beasts and birds (Gen. 2:19); Israel (Isa. 27:11); Servant
of Yahweh from the womb (Isa. 49:5); man (Isa. 43:7); Jeremiah
(1:5); eye of man (Ps. 94:9); locust (Am. 7:1); Leviathan (Ps.
104:26); dry land (Ps. 95:5); mountains (Am. 4:13); all things
(Jer. 10:16). Brown, Driver and Briggs think that the figure is
forgotten in the formation of light (Isa. 45:7); summer and winter
(Ps. 74:17); $r\hat{u}^a\underline{h}$ of man (Zech. 12:1); and $l\bar{e}bh$ of man (Ps. 33:15).
Another group of passages reflects the second meaning: Isa. 22:11;
37:26; 46:11; Jer. 18:11; 33:2; Isa. 43:10; 54:17; Ps. 139:16 (F.
Brown, S. R. Driver and C. A. Briggs, eds., *A Hebrew and English
Lexicon of the Old Testament* [Oxford: Clarendon Press, 1907], 427-
28).

[50]Humbert, *op. cit.*, 404-05, contrasts Gen. 2 and 3 where
the Yahwist never uses $b\bar{a}r\bar{a}$'.

[51]*Ibid.*

[52]*Ibid.*, 402.

Sixteen of the forty-eight uses of $b\bar{a}r\bar{a}$' listed in the con-
cordances are from Second Isaiah.[53] Humbert wrote, "Mais soudain
le verbe $b\bar{a}r\bar{a}$' brille comme un météore au ciel de l'exil, dans
les prophéties du Second Esaïe."[54] In characterizing this author's use of $b\bar{a}r\bar{a}$', Humbert suggested that to the classical
mythical cosmogonic meaning, Second Isaiah added a soteriological element far surpassing Jeremiah's fleeting glimpse, so that
even retrospective allusions to details of cosmogony have a soteriological mark.[55] For example, Humbert called attention to
the reference to the creation of stars (40:26) as the guarantee
of Yahweh's power over earth's mighty rulers, and to the assertion that Yahweh created the ends of the earth (40:28) as proof
that there are no limits to his power to deliver Israel.[56] It
must be noted, however, in view of the fact that no classical
cosmogonic use of $b\bar{a}r\bar{a}$' is suggested by a legitimate analysis of
the pre-exilic texts, that some correction of Humbert's views is
necessary. In actual fact, the earliest unquestionable use of
$b\bar{a}r\bar{a}$' may be soteriological (Jer. 31:22), while the other pre-
exilic use is embedded within a context that exalts God for his
mighty saving acts (Dt. 4:32).

Like his spiritual ancestor, Trito-Isaiah uses $b\bar{a}r\bar{a}$' exclusively in its soteriological sense, although 65:17 implies
the cosmogonic tradition.[57] The only other prophetic uses of
$b\bar{a}r\bar{a}$' are Mal. 2:10 and Isa. 4:5. In the former the prophet,
in order to castigate his hearers for having broken the covenant

---

[53]Humbert, *op. cit.*, 403. Humbert admits 44 (or 43) uses
of $b\bar{a}r\bar{a}$', "to create," in the Old Testament. They are: (1) historical pre-exilic, 0; (2) prophetic pre-exilic, Am. 4:13; Jer.
31:22; (3) legal pre-exilic, Dt. 4:32; (4) historical exilic, 0;
(5) prophetic exilic, Ez. 28:13,15; Isa. 40:26,28; 41:20; 42:5;
43:1,7,15; 45:7 (twice); 45:8,12,18 (twice); 48:7; 54:16 (twice);
(6) historical post-exilic, Gen. 1:1,21,27 (thrice); 2:3,4; 5:1
(twice); 6:7; Ex. 34:10; (7) prophetic post-exilic, Isa. 57:19;
65:17,18 (twice); Mal. 2:10; (8) Psalms, 51:12; 89:13,48; 102:19;
104:30; 148:5; (9) Wisdom, 0. See S. Mandelkern, *Veteris Testamenti Concordentiae Hebraicae Atque Chaldaicae*, F. Margolin and
M. Gottstein (eds.). (Tel-Aviv: Schocken), 1962.

[54]Humbert, *op. cit.*, 404-05.

[55]*Ibid.*, 405-06.

[56]*Ibid.*

[57]*Ibid.*, 406-07.

and committed idolatry, appeals to the fact that all have one
Father and one Creator. The passage from Isaiah 4:5, recognizably late, recalls the use in Ezekiel.[58] Once again, $b\bar{a}r\bar{a}$' appears within a context of judgment; it is promised that after God
has purged Jerusalem with a spirit of judgment and burning he will
create over the ruined site a cloud by day and smoke and flame by
night. One must ask whether this frequent association of $b\bar{a}r\bar{a}$'
with the Theophany of Judgment is accidental.

The texts leave no doubt about this matter, and it is a
serious weakness in Humbert's work that he did not recognize the
frequent connection of $b\bar{a}r\bar{a}$' with a Theophany of Judgment.[59] In
Jer. 31:22, the new thing created by the Lord (the situation where-
by a woman protects her husband) is the judgment upon Israel for
her faithlessness; while in Dt. 4:32, which alludes to the theophany at Sinai, a situation is depicted wherein Israel has broken
the covenant, bringing upon her head the judgment of God in the
form of curses spoken in ratification of a covenant. Similarly,
Ez. 21:30 is set within a threat that Yahweh will judge Ammon by
fire, and Ez. 28:13,15 is part of a lament over the fall of the
king of Tyre, a dirge that mentions God's punishment of him by
fire. Isaiah 4:5 is no different, except that here the theophanic
tradition is more pronounced. Even Mal. 2:10 follows a threat
that God will send a curse upon Israel (2:2) and make the priests
despised (2:9), and is concluded by a request that God destroy
every idolater (2:12). In view of all this, it is not at all
strange to find the use of $b\bar{a}r\bar{a}$' in Am. 4:13 within a context of
a Theophany for Judgment.

This connection is brought out even more clearly in Ex. 34:
10, which Humbert without justification considers a later gloss.[60]
Here the Priestly writer describes the theophany when God appeared
to Moses and proclaimed his name (33:17-34:9), after which he
makes a covenant with Moses, promising to do "terrible" things

---

[58]Compare Ex. 13:21-22, as well as the passages in Ezekiel
referred to above.

[59]In fact, he emends Isa. 4:5 almost solely on the basis of
his belief that there is no place for creation in a theophany
(Humbert, *op. cit.*, 402).

[60]*Ibid.*, 402-03. At first he did leave this matter open.

(awe-inspiring). It is a theophany of blessing, to be sure;
but one must recall that God had previously brought judgment by
fire, plague and sword upon those who worshiped the golden calf.
Other uses of $b\bar{a}r\bar{a}$' by the Priestly writer recall the cosmogonic
myth, so Humbert is correct that the soteriological reference is
missing in P (with the exception of Ex. 34:10).[61] The only other
passage where a soteriological element appears is Num. 16:30,
where Humbert has given strong arguments for considering this
another example of the root $b\bar{a}r\bar{a}$', "to split, to divide."[62]
But if one chooses to consider this another use of $b\bar{a}r\bar{a}$', "to
create," then it appears within a context of God's judgment upon
those who rebelled against Moses' leadership, and is in fact a
kind of ordeal. One other Priestly use of $b\bar{a}r\bar{a}$' is set within a
context of judgment, namely Gen. 6:7, where God vows to blot out
man whom he has created.

The Psalter contains six uses of $b\bar{a}r\bar{a}$' (51:10; 89:12,47;
102:18; 104:30; 148:5). The oldest of these (104:30) is immediately followed by a phrase from the theophanic tradition ("who
touches the mountains and they smoke"), while the other early
reference (89:47) follows mention of the prolongation of God's
burning wrath. This latter passage has certain affinities with
the *single* use of $b\bar{a}r\bar{a}$' in wisdom literature (Eccles. 12:1,
needlessly emended by Humbert).[63]

The third word dealing with Yahweh's creative action is
$^{c}\bar{a}s\bar{a}h$. It has already been observed that the Priestly writer
uses this word only as a parallel to $b\bar{a}r\bar{a}$'. In Amos it occurs
nine times: (1) make (4:13; 5:8,26); lay out (9:14); produce
(3:6,10); (2) do (3:7; 9:12); arrange (4:12).[64]

---

[61]Humbert, *op. cit.*, 407-08.

[62]His reasons are: (1) $b\bar{a}r\bar{a}$' never appears elsewhere in Yahwistic literature, not even in Gen. 2; (2) the context demands
$b\bar{a}r\bar{a}$' "to split." To the three elements of 16:30 (the ground
splits, the earth opens its mouth, the people and their posses-
sions are swallowed up) corresponds in perfect symmetry 16:31-
32, which depicts these three happenings. Finally, he appeals
to the Samaritan reading (*beriya* instead of *beri'a*) (*ibid.*,
401-02).

[63]*Ibid.*, 402. Humbert suggested the translation, "Remember
thy death," reading $b\bar{o}rek\bar{a}$ instead of $b\bar{o}r\bar{e}'ek\bar{a}$, referring to Isa.
38:18 and Ez. 26:20. He also called attention to the absence of
$b\bar{a}r\bar{a}$' in Job (415).

[64]Maag, *Text, Wortschatz und Begriffswelt des Buches Amos*,
93.

Finally, *bānāh* and *yāsadh* are used of Yahweh's creative activity. *bānāh*, meaning "build," occurs in 5:11, 9:6,11,14, while *yāsadh*, with *ᶜal*, means to erect something upon something (9:6), to found, to establish.

2. *Difficult Words and Phrases*

A passage that gives a great deal of difficulty is Amos 4: 13b; several explanations for the phrase *ûmaggîdh lᵉ'ādhām māh śēhô* have already been given. The earliest attempt to render the phrase meaningful is that of the Septuagint, which translates it by "he who announces to men his Anointed"; on the other hand, the Vulgate has "*suum eloquium*" (his musing, meditation), which is usually thought to be the meaning of *śēhô*, although *śîhô* is the normal form. A number of emendations for *śēhô* have been proposed, ranging from Budde and Ehrlich's *maᶜᵃśēhû* on the basis of the Targumim to Horst's *māh ḥeshhô* and Gaster's *māh śîhāh*. The latter two men must then change *ûmaggîdh* also in order to make sense of their emendation; Horst alters it to *ûmmaggēdh*, while Gaster changes the entire phrase to *ûmagdhîl lā'ādhᵃmāh śîhāh*. But these changes are not necessary, for the phrase makes good sense as it is.[65] *śiᵃḥ* is used in Ps. 104:34 with the meaning of "complaint, musing," while I Kgs. 18:27 speaks of Ba'al as musing.[66] In Ps. 147:19, *ûmagîdh* is used (within a context recalling God's power over nature) for God's declaration of his statutes to Israel.

A phrase that has received no special attention is *wᵉdhōrēkh ᶜal bhāmᵒthē 'areṣ* ("and treads upon the heights of the earth"). This idea, taken from the ancient theophanic tradition, has become an integral part of the prophetic lawsuit. Micah 1:2-4 is a classic example:

---

[65]Watts appears to be right here, especially when one interprets the phrase as Maag has done. Compare the Syriac "What is his glory" and Hirscht's view, who called attention to Gen. 3:11 and translated "to Adam." (For Hirscht's ideas, see Harper, *op. cit.*, 104; Watts, *Vision and Prophecy in Amos*, 53; and Maag, "Jahwäs Heerscharen," 47).

[66]The entire context is worthy of consideration, especially in view of Watts' thesis that the ancient hymn in Amos is a polemic against Ba'alism. In Elijah's contest with the prophets, one finds several themes parallel to those in Amos: the preparation to meet God, dark rain clouds, wind, Carmel. Compare Morgenstern, *op. cit.*, 12, note 7, who called attention to similarities between Amos and Elijah.

Hear, you peoples, all of you;
    hearken, O earth, and all that is in it;
and let the Lord God be a witness against you,
    the Lord from his holy temple.
For behold, the Lord is coming forth out of his place,
    and will come down and tread upon the high places of
                                                  the earth.
And the mountains will melt under him
    and the valleys will be cleft,
like wax before the fire,
    like waters poured down a steep place.

Likewise in the covenant lawsuit found in Dt. 32, the phrase
also occurs (32:19). Here Jacob is said to be made to ride vic-
toriously on the high places of the earth.[67] A similar use is
found in Dt. 33:29, where it is claimed that Israel's enemies
"will come fawning" to her, and she will "tread upon their high
places." This use of the phrase is also found in Hab. 3:15,19,
where one reads:

Thou didst trample the sea with thy horses,
    the surging of mighty waters.
. . . .
God, the Lord, is my strength;
    he makes my feet like hinds' feet,
    he makes me tread upon my high places.[68]

But in these three passages a shift can be observed from
the meaning in the lawsuit of Mic. 1:2-4, where Yahweh comes to
punish Israel. The ancient psalm preserved in II Sam. 22 (and
Ps. 18) also reflects this shift. In II Sam. 22:34 (Ps. 18:34),
it is said that "he made my feet like hinds' feet, and set me
secure on the heights." It may be observed that where Yahweh is
the subject the meaning is judgmental, but where his people are
subjects, the victory over enemies becomes central, along with

---

[67]G. E. Wright, "The Lawsuit of God: A Form-Critical Study
of Deuteronomy 32," *Israel's Prophetic Heritage*, B. W. Anderson
and Walter Harrelson, eds. (New York: Harper, 1962), 29, even
translates, following a suggestion of F. M. Cross, Jr., "He made
him ride on the back of Arṣ" (in his opinion, another name for
Môt). In Isa. 58:14, Israel is promised that she will ride upon
the heights of the earth provided that she turns back her foot
from the sabbath. This passage has in mind the blessing record-
ed in Dt. 32:13, as the mention of Jacob's heritage shows.

[68]Albright refers to Ugaritic texts which prove that *bmt*
meant "back" (see "The High Place in Ancient Palestine," *SVT*,
IV [1957], 256). He sees the same idea in Job 9:8, and argues
for literary dependence of Hab. 3:19 on Ps. 18:33 (see Albright,
"The Psalm of Habakkuk," 18).

an occasional substitute of $r\bar{a}kh\bar{e}bh$ for $dh\bar{a}rakh$.[69] Another way
of putting it is that judgment has shifted to the enemies of
Israel.

Another passage that has some connection with the doxologies
of Amos illustrates the condemnatory sense of the phrase (Job 9:
2-11). Here one notices terminology drawn from the prophetic
lawsuit, and at the same time praise of the Creator of the world.
In 9:8, God is extolled as he "who alone stretched out the heavens, and trampled the waves of the sea."[70] It would seem that
Job has taken up portions of a liturgy dealing with God's judgment of man, similar to the prophetic lawsuit in Mic. 1:2-4.

The above-mentioned connection of doxology and prophetic
lawsuit is very significant, for it adds weight to Horst's conclusions in regard to the Doxology of Judgment. Two of the most
recent discussions of the covenant lawsuit have alluded to the
close connection of special days of fasting with the $r\hat{\imath}b$.[71] In
view of this fact, an examination of recent literature dealing
with the prophetic lawsuit is in order.

In typical Hegelian fashion, scholarship has approached
the subject of the prophetic lawsuit. The thesis was proposed

---

[69]In II Sam. 1:19,25, David gives a lamentation over the
fallen Saul and Jonathan; he exclaims: "Thy glory, O Israel, is
slain upon thy high places." The comparison with Am. 4:13 is
striking, for this latter passage immediately precedes the lamentation over the fallen virgin daughter Israel. For a similar
idea using $d\bar{a}rakh$, compare Lam. 1:15, "The Lord has trodden as
in a wine press the virgin daughter of Judah." In Jer. 25:30-31,
Yahweh is said to tread upon the enemies because he has an indictment against the nations and is entering into judgment with
them (compare Ez. 36:2ff.).

[70]The RSV gives as an alternative translation, "and trampled
the back of the sea dragon." The similarities to the doxologies
in Amos are numerous and will be discussed more thoroughly at a
later time. One notices immediately the following: $r\hat{\imath}b$ (9:3);
removes mountains (9:5); shakes the earth...trembles (9:6);
trampled the waves of the sea (9:8); Bear, Orion, Pleiades (9:9);
passes by (9:11).

[71]Julien Harvéy, "Le 'rîb-pattern,' réquisitoire prophétique
sur la rupture de l'alliance," 172-96; and G. E. Wright, op. cit.,
40-41. Harvéy thinks of the prayers of a broken covenant (Neh.
1,9; Dan. 9; Ezr. 9) as confessions from special days of fasting,
which provide the occasion for the prophetic lawsuit (194-95).
Similarly, Wright argues that the "lawsuit was employed as a
means of public confession in a time of calamity..." (56) and
views Dt. 32 as a "broken" $r\hat{\imath}b$ adapted to serve a more general-
ized purpose in confession and praise (40-41).

by Gunkel and Begrich, who argued that the lawsuit had its origin in secular legal life, and viewed it as a *Scheltrede* clothed
with juridical terminology.[72] In recent works this view has
been advocated by Boecker and Westermann, but without considering the lawsuit a *Scheltrede*.[73] On the other hand, the antithesis was provided by Würthwein, who took seriously a suggestion by Weiser,[74] and sought to show that the real life setting
of the lawsuit was sacral law as promulgated by the cult.[75]
Hesse rightly criticized Würthwein's basic thesis and methodology, concluding that classical prophets are responsible for de-
riving from the lawsuit the idea of judgment against Israel.[76]
Nevertheless, Hesse still thinks of a cultic setting for the
lawsuit, the cultic prophets having used it for their messages
of judgment against Israel's enemies.[77] At this point, Gemser's
warning against taking metaphorical terminology too literally
must be heeded, for every mention of a judgment does not actually
imply a real event in the cult.[78]

The synthesis has been provided most astutely by Eberhard
von Waldow, who writes that the lawsuit's form derives from

---

[72]Gunkel-Begrich, *op. cit.*, 364-66; J. Begrich, "Studien zu
Deuterojesaja," *BWANT*, LXXVII (1938), 19-42.

[73]H. J. Boecker, *Redeformen des israelitischen Rechtslebens*,
Bonn Diss., 1959, *passim*; and C. Westermann, *Grundformen prophetischer Rede* (München: Chr. Kaiser Verlag, 1960), 143-44.

[74]Weiser, *Das Buch der zwölf Kleinen Propheten*, 278.

[75]Würthwein, "Der Ursprung der prophetischen Gerichtsrede,"
ZTK, XLIX (1952), 1-16. A hidden assumption of this work is
highly questionable, namely that since many authors use the same
form of lawsuit it must have an institutional origin (9).

[76]Hesse, "Wurzelt die prophetische Gerichtsrede im israelitischen Kult?" *ZAW*, LXV (1953), 45-53 (especially 46, 49).

[77]*Ibid.*, 49.

[78]B. Gemser, "The Rîb- or Controversy-Pattern in Hebrew
Mentality," *SVT*, III (1960), 120-37, particularly 128. Wright,
op. cit., 53, raises the same point, which has special force in
view of Würthwein's thesis that a real judgment was acted out
in the cult (see "Der Ursprung der prophetischen Gerichtsrede,"
11-12). Gemser's article is the most thorough treatment of the
vocabulary of the *rîb* yet written. For a good treatment of
legal procedure, see L. Köhler, *Hebrew Man* (Nashville: Abingdon,
1956), Appendix.

secular law but the content comes from Yahweh's covenant with Israel.[79] This author also proceeds to extract two literary types from the lawsuit, each with a different setting in life.[80] With emphasis upon the covenant as the origin of the lawsuit, Harvéy is in full agreement.[81] On the other hand, he seeks to discover the origin of the *rîb* in international sacral law.

> En d'autres termes, cette hypothèse de travail, c'est qu'il faut chercher l'origine de la Gattung dans le droit international, et plus précisément dans le même droit international qui a fourni le schéma de l'alliance. Dans ce contexte, le *rîb* à condamnation est le formulaire de la déclaration de guerre du suzerain au vassal infidèle, et le *rîb* à avertissement est celui d'un ultimatum au vassal qui a commencé à s'écarter des stipulations fondamentales de l'alliance.[82]

Regardless of the original life setting of the lawsuit, its value for an understanding of the doxologies is significant. In the prophetic lawsuit one finds the kind of background for a Doxology of Judgment that Horst sought in vain to provide, for the material was not available to him at the time. One final issue may be considered briefly--the date of the emergence of the prophetic lawsuit. Gemser has rightly discerned that Am. 1:3-2:3 almost amounts to a court officers' summoning accused and sentenced persons.[83] Nevertheless, Hosea is the first to

---

[79]"Der traditionsgeschichtliche Hintergrund der prophetischen Gerichtsreden," 20.

[80]*Ibid.*, 9. He distinguishes the "appeal for a trial" from the "speeches before a tribunal."

[81]Harvéy, *op. cit.*, 180.

[82]*Ibid.* Earlier, H. B. Huffmon, "The Covenant Lawsuit in the Prophets," *JBL*, LXXVIII (1959), 285-95, suggested that Hittite treaties provide the key to the interpretation of the covenant lawsuit (see especially 291-92). Huffmon also thought he distinguished two fairly distinct types of lawsuits, one connected with the divine council, the other associated with Yahweh's covenant with Israel (295). The former has been emphasized by Wright, *op. cit.*, 46; and F. M. Cross, Jr., "Yahweh and the God of the Patriarchs," *HTR*, LV (1962), 257, and "The Council of Yahweh in Second Isaiah," *JNES*, XII (1953), 275.

[83]Gemser, *op. cit.*, 129. Wright, *op. cit.*, 64, also thinks of Am. 3:1 as a *rîb*.

proclaim a lawsuit between Yahweh and Israel, and Jeremiah is the *'îsh rîbh* par excellence.[84]

Another word that has received no discussion by those who have examined the doxologies is *ṣalmāweth* in Am. 5:8. Outside this passage, the word meaning "deep darkness" occurs elsewhere seventeen times.[85] The earliest use is in Isa. 9:2, if this passage is authentic. The prophet declares that "the people who walked in darkness have seen a great light; those who dwelt in a land of deep darkness, on them has light shined." Albrecht Alt attempted to date this oracle between 732 and 722, thus arguing for its authenticity.[86] On the other hand, Sigmund Mowinckel does not think that the oracle comes from Isaiah, but sees its origin among his disciples.[87]

If Mowinckel is right, then the earliest use of the word outside Amos may be that of Jeremiah (2:6). The prophet refers to the wilderness experience, complaining that the fathers did not ask "who led us in the wilderness, in a land of desert and pits, in a land of drought and deep darkness, in a land that none passes through, where no man dwells?" This use of *ṣalmāweth* is followed by the declaration of a *rîb* between Yahweh and Israel: "therefore, I will contend with you, says the Lord, and with your children's children I will contend" (2:9). Here the word is used within the accusation that provides the basis for judicial procedure.

The other use by Jeremiah also deals with a judgment declared upon Israel (13:15-17). As is characteristic of the

---

[84]Gemser, *op. cit.*, 131. Wright, *op. cit.*, 60, writes that "the very theme of the Deuteronomic history is a *rîb*," while J. J. Stamm, "Die Theodizee in Babylon und Israel," *JEOL*, IX (1944), 104, maintains that the book of Job "ist kein Gespräch von Weisen, sondern eine 'Rede vor Gericht,' hebräisch ein *rîb*."

[85]Th. Nöldeke, "צַלְמָוֶת und צֵל," *ZAW*, XVII (1897), 183-87, defends the translation "deep darkness," "shadow of death." He concludes: "Es bleibt also bei der alten Aussprache צַלְמָוֶת und der Uebersetzung 'Todesschatten'" (187).

[86]In "Nonroyal Motifs in the Royal Eschatology," W. Harrelson accepts this view (see *Israel's Prophetic Heritage*, 150, for this and the reference to Alt's views).

[87]S. Mowinckel, *He That Cometh* (Oxford: Blackwell, 1959), 110.

lawsuit, the passage opens with an exhortation to listen; this
is followed by the appeal to "give glory to the Lord your God
before he brings darkness, before your feet stumble on the twi-
light mountains, and while you look for light he turns it into
gloom and makes it into deep darkness." Jeremiah concludes with
a warning that failure to listen will be Israel's downfall (13:
17).[88]

Ten uses of *ṣalmāweth* are in the book of Job (3:5; 10:21,22;
12:22; 16:16; 24:17 (bis); 28:3; 34:22; 38:17). Two of these passages are particularly interesting, the first because of its use of
bālag (compare Am. 5:9). In Job 10:21-22, one reads Job's plea:

> Let me alone that I may find a little comfort,
> Before I go to whence I shall not return,
> to the land of gloom and deep darkness....

The second is Job 34:22, which declares that there is no gloom
or deep darkness where evildoers may hide themselves from God's
sight. This same theme prevails in Am. 9:1-4, immediately before God's announcement that he will destroy the sinful kingdom.
Similarly in Job 34:23 the judgment of God is mentioned, although
the text is admittedly obscure.

The Psalter contains four uses of the word under discussion
(Ps. 23:4; 44:20; 107:10,14). The first is of indeterminable
date, while the second is exilic and the last two post-exilic.
In Ps. 44:20, the word seems to refer to the exile as "deep darkness," while this meaning is certainly applicable in Ps. 107:10,
14. Even Ps. 23:4 could have a foreign land in mind by the word.

This raises the question as to whether the word was used
exclusively in prophetic literature and Psalms with reference
to a foreign land. This is certainly the meaning in Jeremiah;
the only questionable use would be Isa. 9:2, which would refer
to those in exile if one accepts a late date for the oracle.[89]
At least it can be said that the word is used predominantly in

---

[88] Horst has called attention to this passage as confirmation of his view that such a cultic confession in which the
person on trial gave glory to Yahweh did exist ("Die Doxologien
im Amosbuch," 53).

[89] On the other hand, Isa. 9 may refer to Tiglath-Pilezer's
raid on Galilee during which time many could have been taken
into exile. For a discussion of this raid, see M. Noth, *The
History of Israel* (New York: Harper, 1958), 260.

prophetic literature and Psalms with reference to residence outside the Land of Promise. Moreover, the usage in Job would
merely be an extension of this idea to Sheol. Thus we are com-
pelled to ask how Am. 5:8 uses the word. Once again, an affinity to the book of Job is evident. Finally, one might ask whether infrequent usage of ṣalmāweth in prophetic literature indicates that the doxologies are a cultic text later than Amos.

Three other words need to be taken into consideration before
giving a translation; these are *hammabhlîg*, *ma^{ca}lôthāw* and
'^{a}gudhāthô. Reference to use of the root *bālag* in Job 10:21 has
been made. The meaning is unclear, although some light is thrown
upon it from Ps. 39:13, Job 9:27, 10:20, and Jer. 8:18. S. von
Grünberg connects it with Arabic *'aflaga* ("conquer, subdue"),
while Maag suggests the root *pālag-peleg*, ("a brook"). Gaster
connects *bālag* with the Judaeo-Arabic root *balaja* ("reach, attains
to"), and Horst emends to *hammdallēg*.[90]

The word *ma^{ca}lôthāw* is usually altered to *^{ca}lîyātho* (upper
chambers) on the basis of Ps. 104:3,13, although Watts has sought
to retain the form.[91] As for *'^{a}gudhāthô*, only Watts wishes to
change it; he emends to *hû' g^{e}dhāthô*.[92] Since the word makes
sense without emendation, there is no need to do so. It is used
in Isa. 58:6 with the meaning of "bands"; in Ex. 12:22 it means
"bunch," and in II Sam. 2:25 the word refers to a band of men.
The meaning in Am. 9:6 would be "vault" (of heavens fitted together).[93]

C. *A Strophic Reconstruction and Translation*

Any attempt to offer a strophic arrangement and translation
of the doxologies is to some extent subjective. Nevertheless, it
is hoped that the views offered here will be confirmed by exegesis of the passages. The analyses of Horst and Maag have been
most helpful, although all their suggestions have by no means

---

[90]Maag, *Text, Wortschatz und Begriffswelt des Buches Amos*,
69, 93; Gaster, *op. cit.*, 26, where mention of von Grünberg's
view is found; and Horst, "Die Doxologien im Amosbuch," 46.

[91]Watts, *Vision and Prophecy in Amos*, 59.

[92]*Ibid.*

[93]Gaster, *op. cit.*, 25, denies this meaning to it.

been followed. The real difficulty is 5:9, which seems to belong to the doxologies because of its form (the singular participle) and content. One might suppose that its original position
was before the strophe now found in 9:6, and that the refrain at
the beginning of 9:5 actually concluded 5:9. This view would be
strengthened if one followed Pedersen in interpreting the refrain as an oath particle plus the divine festal name, which is
especially appropriate after 5:9.[94] Furthermore, subject matter
and style are closely akin to 9:5 (note particularly the use of
an article with a participle, found only in the last two strophes
and 5:9, except for $haqq\bar{o}r\bar{e}$' of 5:8b, which also appears in 9:6b
where it probably belongs). Once 5:9 is seen as a sequel to 9:5a,
one can understand 9:5b as a gloss arising from 8:8.[95]

The question whether these four strophes make up a single
hymn must be left open, though content and meter would seem to
suggest it. The "hymn" contains a mixture of cosmogonic and
soteriological elements. Even the first strophe contains both a
mention of the creation of mountains and wind, and a reference
to the dispensing of oracles to man, together with a manifesta-
tion of God's victorious might. Only the second does not have
both elements, which might be an argument in favor of retaining
5:8b.

The doxologies can thus be reconstructed and translated as
follows:[96]

4:13aα	יוֹצֵר הָרִים וּבֹרֵא רוּחַ ׀ וּמַגִּיד לְאָדָם מַה-שֵּׂחוֹ
4:13aβ	עֹשֵׂה שַׁחַר עֵיפָה ׀ וְדֹרֵךְ עַל-בָּמֳתֵי אָרֶץ
4:13b	יהוה אֱלֹהֵי צְבָאוֹת שְׁמוֹ

***

---

[94]In 8:7, reference is made to the fact that Yahweh has
sworn by the pride of Jacob, and this is followed by an announcement that God will never forget any of their deeds. To this is
added a verse very similar to 9:5. Does this preserve the proper setting of 9:5 as Weiser argued? Weiser, "Die Prophetie des
Amos," 31-32.

[95]Robinson thinks of 9:5b as a gloss, while Fosbroke suggests that 9:5 was made part of the doxology in order to link
the latter to the book of Amos (Th. Robinson, *op. cit.*, 105; H.
E.W. Fosbroke, "Amos," *IB*, VI [Nashville: Abingdon, 1956], 847).

[96]The meter is 3:3, the only exception being 5:8a which
has lost half the verse, and the refrain, which seems to be made
up of three stresses. Even the refrain of 4:13 is probably to
be scanned in this way.

74

עֹשֵׂה כִימָה וּכְסִיל....	5:8aα
וְהֹפֵךְ לַבֹּקֶר צַלְמָוֶת ǀ וְיוֹם לַיְלָה הֶחְשִׁיךְ	5:8aβγ
יהוה אֱלֹהֵי צְבָאוֹת שְׁמוֹ	5:8bγ

***

הַנּוֹגֵעַ בָּאָרֶץ וַתָּמוֹג ǀ וְאָבְלוּ כָּל־יוֹשְׁבֵי בָהּ	9:5aβγ
הַמַּבְלִיג שֹׁד עַל־עָז ǀ וְשֹׁד עַל־מִבְצָר יָבוֹא	5:9
וַאדֹנָי יהוה אֱלֹהֵי צְבָאוֹת	9:5aα

***

הַבּוֹנֶה בַשָּׁמַיִם עֲלִיּתוֹ ǀ וַאֲגֻדָּתוֹ עַל־אֶרֶץ יְסָדָהּ	9:6a
הַקּוֹרֵא לְמֵי־הַיָּם ǀ וַיִּשְׁפְּכֵם עַל־פְּנֵי הָאָרֶץ	9:6aαβ = 5:8bαβ
יהוה אֱלֹהֵי צְבָאוֹת שְׁמוֹ.	9:6bγ

He who forms mountains and creates wind,
  Who declares to man what is *His* thought,[97]
Who makes of dawn darkness,
  and treads upon the heights of the earth,
Yahweh, God of Hosts, is his name.[98]
***
He who makes the Pleiades and the Orion
....
And turns deep-darkness into morning,
  Who darkens day to night,
Yahweh, God of Hosts, is his name.
***
He who touches the earth so that it melts,
  And all its inhabitants mourn,
He who makes destruction to flash against the strong
  So that ruin comes upon the fortress,
Is the Lord Yahweh, God of Hosts.
***
He who builds his chambers in the heavens
  And founds his vault upon the earth,
Who calls for the waters of the sea
  And pours them out upon the surface of the earth,[99]
Yahweh, God of Hosts, is his name.

---

[97]E. Kautzsch and A. E. Cowley, *Gesenius' Hebrew Grammar* (Oxford: Clarendon Press, 1910), 116gN.

[98]With the Septuagint, A and Q, although B points to the simple *Yahweh shemô*.

[99]Kautzsch and Cowley, *op. cit.*, 111u.

CHAPTER III

THE LIFE SETTING OF THE DOXOLOGIES

A. *The Refrain, "Yahweh (the God) of Hosts is his Name"*
    Each of the doxologies concludes with a refrain, "Yahweh
(the God of Hosts) is his name," which occurs elsewhere fourteen times, and provides the key for discovering the life setting of the doxologies. Two of these appear within the literature of the pre-exilic period: Am. 5:27 and Hos. 12:5 (Hebrew,
6). The authenticity of both is seriously questioned. Since
one's attitude to the genuineness of Am. 5:27 in particular, and
Hos. 12:5 to some extent, plays a major role in his view of the
doxologies, this matter must be given careful consideration.

1. *Use of the Refrain in Amos and Hosea*
    The use of the refrain in Am. 5:27 has been denied to Amos
by G. A. Smith, who wrote that the last clause was peculiar,
having been created by the combination of two clauses ("saith
Yahweh God of Hosts" and "God of Hosts is his name"), and considered the $sh^e m\hat{o}$ a later addition placed here to give the oracle the same conclusion as that in 4:13.[1] On the other hand,
S. R. Driver has responded that the refrain in 5:27 cannot be
dismissed so easily, especially in view of Hos. 12:5.[2] He further maintains that the phrase in the doxologies must not be
rejected too quickly, since the unusual form "Yahweh, God of
Hosts" (exactly as in Am. 5:14-16; 6:8, and with "God of *the*
Hosts" in Am. 3:13, 6:14, Hos. 12:5) is a "presumption in favor
of 'Yahweh of the Hosts' in 4:13, consequently of authenticity."[3]

    Such contrasting viewpoints are typical of all who have
ventured a verdict on the authenticity of the refrain in Am.
5:27. K. Cramer defends its genuineness on the basis of a

---

[1] G. A. Smith, *op. cit.*, 215, note 1.

[2] S. R. Driver, *op. cit.*, 121-22, note 1. B. N. Wambacq,
op. cit., 198, appeals to Ex. 15:3 ("Yahweh is his name") to
defend the refrain in Am. 5:27 and the passages in Isaiah and
Jeremiah where the same refrain occurs.

[3] S. R. Driver, *loc. cit.*

76

comparison with Hos. 12:5, about which he drew the opposite conclusion from that of Driver. Calling attention to the presence
of *zikhrô* in Hos. 12:5, Cramer asserted that this expression is
late, whereas *sh^{e}mô* in Am. 5:27 is early.[4] On the other hand,
both Maag and Weiser consider the refrain in Am. 5:27 "a hymnic
gloss,"[5] while Cripps suggests that this refrain might indicate
that 5:27 comes from the same late hand that inserted the doxologies.[6]

A final decision in regard to the genuineness of the refrain
in Am. 5:27 is complicated because Am. 5:26-27 is suspected of
being a gloss. A number of interpretations have been given to
these verses, no one of which has found general acceptance. Some
scholars understand Sakkut and Kewan as Assyrian deities (or one
deity, Saturn) and view 5:26 as the sequel to 5:25.[7] Others deny
the worship of Assyrian deities in the time of Amos and consequently label 5:26 a gloss.[8] On the other hand, Weiser reverses
5:24 and 5:25, viewing verses 24 and 26 as a prediction of judgment, and interpreting them in terms of North Israelite cultic
processions.[9] This differs greatly from Maag's view, who thinks

---

[4]K. Cramer, "Amos: Versuch einer theologischen Interpretation," 96.

[5]Maag, *Text, Wortschatz und Begriffswelt des Buches Amos*, 36,
note 1; Weiser, *Die zwölf Kleinen Propheten*, 172, note 5. Compare S. Jozaki, *op. cit.*, 78, who makes a similar observation
about the refrain in 5:27.

[6]Cripps, *op. cit.*, 301, note 1. R. E. Wolfe, "The Editing
of the Book of the Twelve," *ZAW*, LIII (1935), 109, writes that
the doxologist editor added 2:4-5; 5:26-27 and the doxologies with
the intention of combatting idolatry to clear the way for belief
in one supreme God.

[7]Karl Marti, *Das Dodekapropheton* (Tübingen: J.C.B. Mohr,
1904), 197; H. Junker, "Amos und die 'Opferlose Mosezeit': Ein
Beitrag zur Erklärung von Amos 5:25-26," *ThuGl*, XXVII (1935), 686-
695; Würthwein, "Amos-studien," 48; Th. Robinson, *op. cit.*, 93
(where references to Assyrian sources mentioning these deities are
given); R. H. Pfeiffer, "The Polemic against Idolatry in the Old
Testament," *JBL*, XLIII (1924), 232, 237; Hyatt, "Amos," 622; and
Fosbroke, *op. cit.*, 822.

[8]Wellhausen, *Die Kleinen Propheten*, 84, is the chief exponent
of this view. Cripps, *op. cit.*, 300-02, suspends judgment on the
authenticity of 5:26-27.

[9]Weiser, *Das Buch der zwölf Kleinen Propheten*, 172-74. He
writes that judgment will come like a flood, and the people will
take their cultic images erected by Jeroboam I on one last sadly
grotesque festival procession. If accepted, this gives still
another example of the use of the refrain in connection with judgment. However, against Weiser's rearrangement of the text is the
fact that it breaks up the natural unit in 5:21-24.

of 5:27 as a genuine word of Amos placed here by a redactor
since 5:26 seemed to suggest the East. Moreover, he understands
5:26 as a question.[10] In accord with Sellin's overall approach
to the attitude within Amos to the sanctuaries of the North, he
placed 5:13 before 5:27.[11] Finally, Julian Morgenstern sought
to connect 5:26 and 5:27 by interpreting *sikhûth malkekhem* and
khiyûn '*ae lōhēkhem* in terms of a nomadic pilgrimage with the
sacred ark.[12]

In view of these diverse views about Am. 5:26-27, what interpretation seems to have most to commend it? First, there can
be little doubt that Sakkut and Kewan refer to Assyrian deities
(or one deity). Nor does this constitute a serious historical
problem in view of Am. 8:14, which specifically mentions oaths
by Ashimah.[13] As for the relationship between 5:26 and 5:27,
the following can be noted. Cripps is certainly right in maintaining that 5:25 cannot be the end of the speech, and if the
end is 5:27, then something is needed between the two verses.[14]
Furthermore, there is no cogent reason for denying 5:27a to

---

[10]Maag, *Text, Wortschatz und Begriffswelt des Buches Amos*,
34-36. "And did you bear the tabernacle of your King, the ped-
estal of your gods, which you made, O Israel?" Compare the view
of Nathaniel Schmidt, "On the Text and Interpretation of Amos
V:25-27," *JBL*, XIII (1894), 1-15. This suggestion is attractive,
although based on a partial re-writing of the text.

[11]Sellin, *op. cit.*, 237-40.

[12]J. Morgenstern, *The Ark, the Ephod, and the 'Tent of
Meeting'* (Cincinnati: HUC Press, 1945), 109ff. Maag, *Text,
Wortschatz und Begriffswelt des Buches Amos*, 36, objects that
Am. 5:27 thinks of a settled situation in exile where the sacred
ark would serve no function. But did it not do so at Jerusalem
under David?

[13]It is not certain, however, that Ashimah is to be thought
of as an Assyrian deity. John Gray thinks of this and the similar use of the word in II Kgs. 17:30 as a deliberate misvocal-
ization of Ashera, the name of the Canaanite mother goddess.
On the other hand, he refers to the fact that Greek sources from
the Roman imperial period "attest a deity Simi or Seimios, who
may be named in the composite divine name Ashembethel in the
Elephantine papyri." Gray observes, however, that the first
element of Ashembethel may be a dialectic variation of *shēm* (see
J. Gray, "Ashima," *IDB*, I [1962], 252, and *I and II Kings* [Phila-
delphia: Westminster Press, 1963], 595-96).

[14]Cripps, *op. cit.*, 301. Likewise Harper, *op. cit.*, 138,
maintains that 25 is logically connected with 26.

Amos.[15] As for 5:26, it is difficult to make a decision in view of the corrupt text, which gives evidence of glosses and changes in vocalization.[16] In fact, the waw of 5:26 can be conjunctive, adversative or consecutive, and at least six interpretations of the verb *ûn^{e}sā'them* are possible.[17] Moreover, the refrain in 5:27 appears to be a gloss, or at least the final *sh^{e}mô*.[18] It may be noted that the use of *'āmar* with this refrain is unusual in Amos, which may indicate that only *sh^{e}mô* is secondary. In view of the obvious textual corruption of 5:26, Maag's reconstruction would seem to have most in its favor, although the question as to the original meaning must be left open.

Attention has been called to the use of *'āmar* with the refrain in 5:27. The oracular formula also occurs in Am. 6:8 with the phrase "Yahweh the God of Hosts," but here the word *n^e'um* appears.[19] If this phrase is original, it adds weight to the

---

[15]Hyatt, "Amos," 622; Th. Robinson, *op. cit.*, 93; Maag, *Text, Wortschatz und Begriffswelt des Buches Amos*, 35 (but out of place). However, Fosbroke and Jozaki argue against the authenticity of 5:26-27 (see Fosbroke, *op. cit.*, 822; and Jozaki, *op. cit.*, 65).

[16]"Star, your gods" is evidently a gloss, and perhaps "your king" (Procksch in *Biblia Hebraica*), while the vocalization of Sakkut and Kewan was altered to stress the worthlessness of the gods (*shiqqûṣ* being the paradigm), just as names including Baal were changed (see Pfeiffer, "The Polemic against Idolatry in the Old Testament," 232, 237).

[17]If conjunctive, it constitutes (1) a charge of idolatry in the wilderness period or (2) a question concerning that period; if adversative waw, (1) a charge of idolatry for the time from the wilderness wanderings to the present or (2) an accusation against Amos' contemporaries; and if consecutive, (1) a prediction of captivity or (2) a command (see Harper, *op. cit.*, 137).

[18]Besides the references listed above, one could mention Procksch in *Biblia Hebraica*, who considers *'ēlōhē* as "probably added" and *sh^{e}mô* as "added."

[19]Friedrich Baumgärtel, "Zu den Gottesnamen in den Büchern Jeremia und Ezechiel," 1-29, examines the phrases "Yahweh of Hosts" and "the Lord God," concluding that these are closely connected with the formulas *kōh 'āmar*, *n^e'um 'āmar*, *'āhāh*, *nishbā^c* and *kōh hir'ani*. Baumgärtel also thinks of *kōh 'āmar* as a liturgical oracular formula connected with the ark mediating the divine *d^{e}bhar* of Yahweh of Hosts (22-23). He further understands *n^e'um* as a prophetic formula emerging from divination and describing the divine word in less concrete terms than does *kōh 'āmar* (21); (see Baumgärtel, *ibid.*, *Verbannung und Heimkehr: Festschrift für W. Rudolph*, Arnulf Kuschke, ed. [Tübingen: J.C.B. Mohr, 1961], 1-29).

view that the refrain in 5:27 (except for $sh^e m\hat{o}$) is authentic. However, there is apparently no enthusiasm over considering the phrase in 6:8 a genuine word of Amos, especially since the Septuagint omits it.[20] Even those who defend the phrase seek to relocate it.[21]

It was observed above that S. R. Driver defended the refrain in 5:27 partly on the basis of Hos. 12:5, although Cramer came to a different conclusion from the same comparison. Here one reads "And Yahweh the God of Hosts, Yahweh is his name" ($zikhr\hat{o}$). This phrase is almost unanimously rejected, with many interpreters considering 3-6 as secondary.[22] It may be noted that the refrain is injected into a context that recalls the setting of the first doxology of Amos, especially the announcement of an indictment against Jacob, mention of a confrontation with God

---

[20]Th. Robinson, *op. cit.*, 93; Weiser, *Das Buch der zwölf Kleinen Propheten*, 178; and Fosbroke, *op. cit.*, 825, consider it a secondary formula. Maag, *Text, Wortschatz und Begriffswelt des Buches Amos*, 38, is an exception.

[21]Harper, *op. cit.*, 151, and Cripps, *op. cit.*, 210, argue that it must follow 6:7 if correct at all. Fosbroke, *op. cit.*, 825, suggests that it appears to be an editorial note referring to 6:1-7 or an attempt to solemnize 6:8.

[22]The following consider Hos. 12:5 a gloss: Procksch, *Biblia Hebraica*; Harper, *op. cit.*, 382; Th. Robinson, *op. cit.*, 47; Weiser, *Das Buch der zwölf Kleinen Propheten*, 89, note 3 (a liturgical hymnic formula introduced later for cultic reading); J. Mauchline, "The Book of Hosea," *IB*, VI (Nashville: Abingdon, 1956), 696-97 (who views 3-6 as "probably added," while 6 is said to be certainly parenthetical and to break the connection); Nowack, *op. cit.*, 95; H. W. Wolff, *Dodekapropheton I. Hosea* (Neukirchen Kreis Moers: Neukirchener Verlag, 1961), 276. Wolff's discussion deserves careful consideration. He observes that the use of $^{?a e}l\bar{o}h\hat{i}m$ (4,7), Yahweh (3), and $^{?}\bar{e}l$ (5) together is without parallel in Hosea, and argues against the entire section. Moreover, comparing Hos. 12:5 to the doxologies of Amos, Wolff accepts Horst's conclusions as to the literary type and place in life of these, while following Eissfeldt's interpretation of the phrase "Yahweh $\rlap{,}s^e bh\bar{a}\,^{?}\hat{o}th$." But Wolff does not think Hos. 12:5 comes from the same hand as the doxologies of Amos, for three reasons: (1) the difference in the title of God, "Yahweh the God of *the* Hosts" in Hosea, while Am. 4:13b has "Yahweh God of Hosts" and 9:5a has "Yahweh of the Hosts"; (2) the use of $zikhr\hat{o}$ in Hosea rather than $sh^e m\hat{o}$ as in Amos, and (3) the context into which the doxologies are inserted (in Amos after the announcement of judgment, but not so in Hosea). In regard to the second point, Wolff admits that $z\bar{e}kher$ occurs parallel to $sh\bar{e}m$ (Ps. 135:13; Ex. 3:15), but points out that the emphasis is always on the idea of "from generation to generation" (Pss. 102:13; 135:13), not found in Hosea. Finally, it may be observed that Marti, *op. cit.*, 71, defends Hos. 12:5, considering it the subject of $y^e dhab\bar{e}r$ in 12:4 (5).

(Bethel?), and the appeal to return to God. This is in no way accidental, as will become evident in the examination of the contexts into which the refrain is inserted elsewhere within the Old Testament.

Besides appearing in Amos and Hosea, the refrain, "Yahweh of Hosts is his name," occurs in Second Isaiah and Jeremiah. Uses in Jeremiah are almost universally acknowledged as later insertions, showing the influence of Second Isaiah or a common cultic language. An examination of these passages in Isaiah and Jeremiah is extremely helpful in establishing the life setting of Amos' doxologies.

2. *Deutero-Isaiah's Use of the Refrain*

The book of Isaiah deserves primary consideration; it contains four uses of the refrain (47:4; 48:2; 51:15; 54:5). The first passage occurs within a context of the description of Yahweh's judgment upon Babylon (47:1-15). Chapter 46 describes the fall of the gods, while the next chapter depicts the fall of the city itself, following closely in mood and content the preceding chapter.[23] Actually, the tone of the entire message dealing with Babylon is set by the oath of 45:22-23, "Turn to me and be saved, all the ends of the earth....To me every knee shall bow, every tongue shall swear." This emphasis on "turning" recalls Am. 4:6-11, 5:4,6 and Hos. 12:6. In Isa. 46:1-7, there is reference to the burden of carrying idols, while 8-13 continues the attack on idolatry by comparing man-made lifeless images to the living God, Yahweh (cf. Am. 5:25-27). Isaiah 47: 1-15 constitutes a "Mocking Song of the Virgin of Babylon,"[24] the fulfillment of the threat in 45:23. Verse two is very descriptive: "...Strip off your robe, uncover your legs, pass through the rivers" (of judgment),[25] while verse three asserts that no man will be spared (cf. Am. 9:1-4).[26] Verse five

---

[23]James Muilenburg, "Isaiah 40-66," *IB*, V (Nashville: Abingdon, 1956), 543.

[24]*Ibid.*

[25]D. R. Jones, "Isaiah- II and III," *Peake's Commentary on the Bible*, 523.

[26]For a picture of captives lifting their skirts, see A. Jeremias, *Das Alte Testament im Licht des alten Orients* (Leipzig: J. C. Hinrichs, 1930), 689.

recalls Am. 5:2,[27] and verse ten accuses the Babylonians of
self-confidence: "You felt secure in your wickedness, you said,
'No one sees me'" (cf. Am. 9:4). In 47:3 there is a minor textual difficulty, which is best solved by reading 'āmar with
three Greek uncials[28] instead of 'ādhām.[29] This would result
in the following translation: "Says our Redeemer--the Lord of
Hosts is his name--the holy one of Israel."

The second passage, 48:2, likewise places emphasis on the
taking of an oath, attacks idolatry, and announces judgment,
while adding the motif found in most of the passages using the
refrain: creation. In 48:1-2 one reads, "...Who swear by the
name of the Lord, and confess (yazkîrû, cf. Hos. 12:5) the God
of Israel, but not in truth or right. For they call themselves
after the holy city, and stay themselves on the God of Israel;
the Lord of Hosts is his name." "Swear by" and "confess" are
terms drawn from the cult (Isa. 65:16; Jer. 4:2; 12:16; Dt. 6:
13; 10:20; Ex. 23:13; Ps. 20:7).[30] Isaiah 48:4 refers to the
people's obstinacy, while verse five attacks idolatry and verse
eight asserts that Yahweh knew they would deal treacherously.
Finally, 48:10 refers to judgment by refinement, and 48:13 cli-
maxes the section, extolling Yahweh as Creator: "My hand laid
the foundation of the earth, and my right hand spread out the
heavens..."[31]

The next passage combines the emphases of exodus and creation, the former being understood as victory over the Chaos
Dragon. In Isa. 51:9-10, the question is asked, "Was it not
thou that didst cut Rahab in pieces, that didst pierce the dragon...?" (cf. Job 26:7-13). There follows a hymn in praise of

---

[27]Muilenburg, "Isaiah 40-66," 547.

[28]John Skinner, *The Book of the Prophet Isaiah* (Cambridge:
University Press, 1898), 82.

[29]Muilenburg, *loc. cit.*, translates: "I will take vengeance,
and will not spare, says...." The change is minor, and such a
corruption of two letters is easily possible.

[30]*Ibid.*, 554. Skinner, *op. cit.*, 89, writes that the reference is not specifically to false swearing, but to insincere
oaths, and observes that this is the first mention of swearing
by the holy city, Jerusalem, in the Old Testament, found elsewhere only in Isa. 52:1, Nehemiah and Daniel.

[31]Note the use of *qōrē'* here, as in Am. 9:6 and 5:8.

Yahweh the Creator (51:12-16); the hymn scolds the people for
fearing mere men, having forgotten their Maker, "who stretched
out the heavens and laid the foundations of the earth," (cf. Am.
9:6), and continues, "For I am the Lord your God, who stirs up
the sea so that its waves roar--the Lord of Hosts is his name"
(cf. Am. 9:5). Verse 16 is very significant, in view of Am.
4:13b ("and reveals to man what is his thought"); it reads: "And
I have put my words in your mouth and hid you in the shadow of
my hand, stretching out the heavens and laying the foundations
of the earth, saying to Zion, 'You are my people.'" As in the
other contexts, judgment occurs here, verse seventeen alluding
to the cup of his wrath.[32]

The last passage in Isaiah (54:5) also emphasizes Yahweh as
Creator and Judge, while recalling Yahweh's oath to Noah. The
section begins with a plea that Israel "Fear not, for you will
not be ashamed,"[33] and continues: "For your Maker is your husband, the Lord of Hosts is his name, and the Holy One of Israel
is your Redeemer, the God of the whole earth he is called."[34]
Once again God's overflowing wrath is alluded to, with the assurance that just as Yahweh swore to Noah that the waters would
no more cover the earth, so he has sworn again that he will not
be angry with Judah or rebuke her.[35]

3. *The Refrain in the Book of Jeremiah*

The contexts within Jeremiah in which the refrain occurs
are strikingly similar. The first of these is Jer. 10:16

---

[32]Many scholars consider this passage an addition, but Muilenburg, "Isaiah 40-66," 600, has cogently defended it on the
basis of (1) the emphasis on creation and its relation to Israel,
(2) the affinities with the Servant passages, and (3) the characteristic words and ideas of the prophet. Jer. 31:35 contains
part of Isa. 51:15, and it is difficult to decide to which passage the verse properly belongs, although the best argument can
be made out for Isa. 51:15 (see Muilenburg, *loc. cit.*). Skinner,
op. cit., 124, refuses to venture an opinion, while Wambacq, *op.
cit.*, 217-19, thinks Isaiah and Jeremiah borrowed the line from
an ancient hymn.

[33]The "shame of your youth" refers to the pre-exilic period
of infidelity (Hos. 2:17; Jer. 2:2; Am. 5:26; see Muilenburg,
"Isaiah 40-66," 635).

[34]This refrain is unique in that it has a complete sentence
after the reference to Yahweh as Lord of Hosts.

[35]Verse ten has its parallel in Jer. 31:35-36, where a similar promise occurs. For this entire passage, Isa. 40:19-22
should be consulted.

(51:19). The initial section of the chapter attacks astrology and idolatry (10:2-5), while a rhetorical question emphasizes Yahweh's uniqueness and awesomeness, which is followed by further attack upon idols as man-made (6-9), in view of the fact that the Lord is the living King, at whose "wrath the earth quakes" (10:10; cf. Am. 9:5). This is followed by a hymn in praise of the Creator (10:12-16).

> It is he who made the earth by his power,
> who established the world by his wisdom,
> and by his understanding stretched out the heavens.
> When he utters his voice there is a tumult of waters
>   in the heavens,
> and he makes the mist rise from the ends of the earth.
> He makes lightnings for the rain,
> and he brings forth the wind from his storehouses...
> Not like these is he who is the portion of Jacob,[36]
> for he is the one who formed all things,
> and Israel is the tribe of his inheritance,
> the Lord of Hosts is his name (12-13,16).

This hymn occurs within chapter 51 (15-19) in identical form, but has the striking introduction: "The Lord of Hosts has sworn by himself" that over Judah shall be raised the shout of victory. Once again the combined themes of judgment, attack on idolatry, oaths and creation occur. There seems to be no question about the spuriousness of this passage in both contexts.[37]

---

[36]For a discussion of two words for possession, see F. Horst, "Zwei Begriffe für Eigentum (Besitz): נַחֲלָה und אֲחֻזָּה," *Verbannung und Heimkehr*, 135-56.

[37]Hyatt, "Jeremiah," *IB*, V, 897, remarks that the verses reflect the tone of Second Isaiah (40:19-22; 41:7,29; 44:9-20; 46:5-7), Dt. 4:28 and certain Psalms (115:3-8; 135:15-18). He considers 10:11 an addition from the fifth century ("a formula for exorcism"). John Paterson, "Jeremiah," *Peake's Commentary on the Bible*, 546, writes that 10:1-16 intrudes, breaking the connection of 9:22 and 10:17. With the opinion of Hyatt and Paterson, W. Rudolph is in substantial agreement; *Jeremia* (Tübingen: J.C.B. Mohr [Paul Siebeck], 1958), 65. He observes that since Jer. 10:12-16 is repeated in 51:15-19, the entire section in chapter 10 (1-16) comes from the exilic period (see page 69). On the other hand, A. Weiser, *Das Buch des Propheten Jeremia* (Göttingen: Vandenhoeck & Ruprecht, 1952), 93-95, argues cogently for the authenticity of the core of the hymn. He admits that the mood is exilic (like that of Isa. 40:19-20; 41:6-7; 44:9ff.; 46:5ff.; Dt. 4:28; Pss. 115:4ff.; 135:15ff.), and that the present form is late (recognizing verse eleven as a liturgical formula of exorcism), but thinks that the policies of Manasseh and Joachim would have called forth in Jeremiah the denunciation of idolatry. Confirmation of this view he sees in the fact that the exilic author of 50-51 found this block of material in the Jeremianic tradition, and in the use of *hebhel* in verses 3 and

Another use of the refrain appears within the theologically revolutionary New Covenant section (31:35). In 31:38 the Lord promises to watch over his people to build and to plant, just as he had watched over Israel to break down (cf. Am. 9:8ff.). Verses 31-34 announce the coming of a New Covenant within the hearts of the people, while 35-37 gives the basis for the promise and assurance that it will never fail. In verse 35 one reads, "Thus says the Lord, who gives the sun for light by day, and the fixed order of the moon and the stars for light by night, who stirs up the sea so that its waves roar--the Lord of Hosts is his name." This is followed by the promise that if this fixed order departs, then shall Israel cease from being a nation, and "if the heavens above can be measured, and the foundations of the earth below can be explored, then I will cast off" Israel for her sin (36-37). The authenticity of the promise of the New Covenant has been vigorously challenged; most admit that Deuteronomistic elements appear in it.[38] The same must be said for the poetic verses following that promise (35-37), but like the former issue, this one is in no way settled today.[39]

The next use of the refrain in Jeremiah is that of 32:18. This prayer of Jeremiah (17-25) shows signs of interpolation,

---

15. As for the exact verses from Jeremiah, Weiser thinks 10:1-5,8,9 (paraenetic section) may have been spoken by Jeremiah in the festival of covenant renewal. More convincing, however, is Weiser's analysis of the hymn itself (95-96). Recognizing that the hymn is not limited to 12-16, he considers 6-7 a form of prayer, and 10,12-16 a form of confession, both making up a liturgy. Moreover, he recognizes that the mention of the *name* of Jahweh (6,16) suggests the revelation of the divine name in connection with the cultic theophany. Finally, Weiser writes that the cultic name "Yahweh of Hosts" is used in a hymnic confession ("Yahweh of Hosts is his name").

[38] Weiser, *Das Buch des Propheten Jeremia*, 296, prefers to think of common liturgical poetry, not a Deuteronomic system of ideas.

[39] Rudolph, *Jeremia*, 186, thinks of 35-37 as the completion of the entire promise of salvation about Ephraim. On the other hand, Hyatt, "Jeremiah," 1040, doubts that the verses come from Jeremiah, since they are too nationalistic and recall Isa. 40:12, 26; 42:5; 44:24; 45:7,18; 54:10. On the basis of a comparison of these verses with Jer. 33:20,25, Wambacq, *op. cit.*, 219, argues that Jeremiah's treatment of this subject matter is more prosaic, while the poetry of Jer. 31:35-37 is much superior. But the authenticity of Jer. 33:20,25 is certainly to be denied, and Wambacq's argument carries little weight. Like Rudolph, A. Weiser, *Das Buch des Propheten Jeremia*, 296, thinks of 35-37 as the conclusion of the great promise in 31-34.

the original being limited to 17a, 24-25 if at all genuine.[40]
Verses 17-20 praise Yahweh as Creator and Redeemer: "Ah Lord God.
It is thou who hast made the heavens and the earth by thy great
power and by thy outstretched arm!...O great and mighty God whose
name is the Lord of Hosts,[41] great in counsel and mighty in deed;
whose eyes are open to all the ways of men...." (cf. Am. 9:4),
and "who hast shown signs and wonders in the land of Egypt...and
hast made thee a name, as at this day." The Deuteronomistic style
and language are evident, and have been frequently pointed out.[42]
Verse 22 recalls the oath Yahweh swore in regard to the Promised
Land, while 33-35 mentions the reason for Judah's plight: "They
have turned to me their back and not their face..." and have committed idolatry, offering their sons and daughters to Molech and
serving Baal. Once again the themes of judgment, creation, idolatry and oath dominate the context in which the refrain is found,
and this is hardly accidental.

In Jer. 46:18 the refrain also appears, although here it is
generally conceded to be secondary.[43] Yet even if regarded as a
redactional gloss, the insertion of a refrain in this context
confirms the general impression gained above, for the immediate
subject matter constitutes an oath: "As I live, says the king,
whose name is the Lord of Hosts;" and the prediction of judgment: "...Prepare yourselves baggage for exile, O inhabitants
of Egypt" (cf. Am. 5:27). Moreover, this judgment is announced
in words that recall Am. 8:8; 9:5, namely "who is this, rising
like the Nile, like rivers whose waters surge?" (46:7). Finally,
verse ten asserts that Yahweh has a day of vengeance at the Eu-
phrates and that Egypt is doomed.

---

[40]Rudolph, *Jeremia*, 193; Paterson, *op. cit.*, 557; and Hyatt,
"Jeremiah," 1045. On the other hand, A. Weiser, *Das Buch des
Propheten Jeremia*, 304-05, defends the authenticity of 17-25
and feels that the cultic style (like Neh. 9) presents no problem.

[41]Notice the use of the "great and mighty God" ($h\bar{a}'\bar{e}l$) with
this refrain. The Septuagint omits $ṣ^ebh\bar{a}'\hat{o}th$ here.

[42]Hyatt, "Jeremiah," 1046, and Rudolph, *Jeremia*, 193, recognize the affinities with other cultic prayers, especially Neh. 9.
Paterson, *op. cit.*, 557, thinks the prayer in Jeremiah throws
light on synagogue liturgy.

[43]Hyatt, "Jeremiah," 1107. On the other hand, Rudolph,
Jeremia, 256, thinks the refrain in 48:15 comes from 46:18.

The next use of the refrain (48:15) is generally rejected on the basis of the Septuagint.[44] Once again the context is one of judgment and idolatry. Verse 13 sets the tone: "Then Moab shall be ashamed of Chemosh, as the house of Israel was ashamed of Bethel, their confidence,"[45] while verse 15 refers to the judgment falling upon Moab, concluding with "says the King, whose name is the Lord of Hosts."[46]

Jeremiah 50:34 has the refrain, although here it is set within the middle of a sentence. In verse 29 a favorite phrase of Isaiah ("the Holy One of Israel") occurs, the only use in the book of Jeremiah.[47] As in so many cases, the refrain is surrounded by references to judgment and attack upon idolatry (50: 27, 35-38—"For it is a land of images, and they are mad over idols").[48] The refrain is coupled with the assertion that "their Redeemer is strong," which points in the direction of cultic prayers (Ezr. 9; Neh. 9; Dan. 9; Jer. 32; Isa. 37) to be discussed later.

---

[44]Rudolph, *loc. cit.*

[45]Bethel is probably a deity (see Hyatt, "The Deity Bethel and the Old Testament," 81-98; O. Eissfeldt, "Der Gott Bethel," 1-30; K. Galling, "Bethel und Gilgal," *ZDPV* [1944], 26ff). Eissfeldt observes that *dārash* (Am. 5:4-5) is often used with a deity, but never with a place name, and that altar (3:14b) is frequently used with a genitive of deity, but not of place (16). He also finds a reference to Bethel as a deity in the passage cited above, as well as in Hos. 12:5 and 10:15, remarking that the doxologies of Am. 5:8-9 and Hos. 12:5 follow the mention of Bethel, their purpose being to deny that Bethel is the true God and to name Yahweh as He (17). Hyatt discusses additional evidence pointing to the worship of Bethel as a deity and suggests that the origin of this should be placed in Syria about 1500 B.C. (90). Like Eissfeldt, he prefers place-names for Gen. 31:13 and 35:7 (94-95; Eissfeldt, "Der Gott Bethel," 4-10).

[46]Verse 21 specifically names this destruction as the judgment of God. The use of n^e'um with the refrain is unique, although 'āmar occurs in Hos. 12:5 and Isa. 47:4.

[47]Hyatt, "Jeremiah," 1128, writes that Redeemer is the title of Yahweh in Second Isaiah; and Rudolph, *Jeremia*, 283, remarks that the reference to Sodom and Gomorrah is a reworking of Isa. 13:19-22. The affinity with Prov. 23:11 was pointed to by A. Weiser, *Das Buch des Propheten Jeremia*, 440. He also wrote that the refrain had its origin in the worship tradition.

[48]Verses 40 and 42 are striking. The first alludes to Sodom and Gomorrah (cf. Am. 4:11), while verse 42 mentions the sound like "the roaring of the sea" caused by the people. This theme occurs frequently in the previous passages discussed.

The last use of the refrain (51:57) is derived from 46:18 (48:15).[49] Like these latter two contexts that use the phrase, "says the King, whose name is the Lord of Hosts," this one announces judgment upon images (51:52) and heightens the horror by the promise that no one will escape though mounting to heaven (51:53; cf. Am. 9:1-4). Once again the judgment is described in terms of the roaring of many waters (51:55).

4. *"Yahweh is his Name"*

Before drawing any conclusions about use of the refrain and the contexts into which it is placed, attention should be given to the two uses of "Yahweh is his name" outside Amos (Ex. 15:3; Jer. 33:2), especially in view of the fact that Wambacq attributes great weight to the use in Exodus in establishing an early date for the longer refrain.[50] Too much importance should not be attributed to this use of *YHWH $sh^e m\hat{o}$*, especially in view of divergent views in regard to the date of the song.[51] Verse three

---

[49]Rudolph, *Jeremia*, 291.

[50]Wambacq, *op. cit.*, 198.

[51]Martin Noth, *Exodus*, J. S. Bowden, trans. (Philadelphia: Westminster Press, 1962), 123, considers this passage a relatively late piece. A. Bender, "Das Lied Exodus 15," *ZAW*, XXIII (1903), 47, and R. H. Pfeiffer, *Introduction to the Old Testament*, 281, thought in terms of 450-400 B.C., while Paul Haupt, "Moses' Song of Triumph," *AJSL*, XX (1904), 153-54, maintained that a date as late as 350 B.C. was possible. On the other hand, F. M. Cross, Jr. and D. N. Freedman, "The Song of Miriam," *JNES*, XIV (1955), 237-50, have argued cogently for a date "not earlier than the twelfth, and not later than the eleventh century B.C., *in its present form*" (see the anachronistic mention of Philistia, the significant omission of Ammon, the "orthographic data, linguistic characteristics, and metrical structure" (240). John Watts, "The Song of the Sea--Ex. 15," *VT*, VII (1957), 379-80, contends, however, that three factors indicate a period in the latter part of the United Kingdom: (1) the reference to Philistines among the defeated nations (14b); (2) the pointed reference to the establishment of a sanctuary for Yahweh's throne (17bc), which seems to indicate Jerusalem; and (3) the characterization of Yahweh in royal terms which seem to presuppose the elaborate ritual of the kingdom and the temple (6-7,11-12,17bc,18). But Watts believes that part of this hymn antedates the kingdom (380) and has been adapted for use in the royal temple and applied to Moses in the seventh-sixth centuries B.C. (379). J. Philip Hyatt, "Yahweh as 'the God of my father'," *VT*, V (1955), 134, also thinks that the first twelve verses "may well have been composed not long after the crossing of the Red Sea, and handed down orally for a period of time before being written down." See also Marc Rozelaar, "The Song of the Sea," *VT*, II (1952), 221-28, where structure is the main interest of the writer.

is crucial to this discussion: "The Lord is a man of war; the Lord is his name." This assertion is somewhat misleading; it does not claim that Yahweh is a God of war, but that Israel experienced him as one who fights for her.[52] Such language is reminiscent of theophany, where Yahweh is described as fighting for Israel (cf. Jdg. 5).

Jer. 33:2 is generally recognized to be spurious.[53] It reads, "Thus says the Lord who made the earth, the Lord who formed it to establish it--the Lord is his name." This is followed by a call to prayer: "Call to me and I will answer you, and will tell you great and hidden things which you have not known."[54] Weiser has rightly compared this passage (2-3) to the doxologies of Amos, for the similarity is strong.[55] With this passage the doctrine of creation has entered the dynamic of prophetic saving faith, Yahweh's power over creation serving as the guarantee that he will not let Jerusalem remain in chaos.[56] This promise occurs in verse 9, which reads: "And this city shall be to me a name of joy, a praise and a glory before all the nations of the earth who shall hear of all the good that I do for them; they shall fear and tremble because of all the good and all the prosperity I provide for it."

5. *Conclusion*

From this survey of the contexts in which the refrain "the Lord of Hosts is his name" appears, the following can be

---

[52]Noth, *Exodus*, 124.

[53]Hyatt, "Jeremiah," 1049; Rudolph, *Jeremia*, 199; Weiser, *Das Buch des Propheten Jeremia*, 311. Hyatt concludes that 1-2, 6-13 are late, and that 2-3 has ideas and phrases of Second Isaiah (45:18; 47:4; 48:6). Similarly, Rudolph accepts only 4-6a, 7b, 12, 13b as genuine, and suggests that the meaning of Yahweh is explained as "He who creates" (197).

[54]Hyatt, "Jeremiah," 1049, writes that a comparison with genuine prayers of Jeremiah (12:1-6; 15:15-21) reveals the artificiality of verse 3 in calling to prayer. In the same vein, Rudolph, *Jeremia*, 197, remarks that a prayer like this is foreign to Jeremiah and is an intellectual formulation.

[55]Weiser, *Das Buch des Propheten Jeremia*, 311.

[56]G. von Rad, "Das theologische Problem des alttestamentlichen Schöpfungsglaubens," *Gesammelte Studien zum Alten Testament*, 139, makes this observation about Isa. 43:1; 44:24ff.; 45:12-13, but it may also be appropriately applied to Jer. 33: 2-3, 9-11.

concluded. Four themes find frequent repetition, so that such
a juxtaposition of refrain and emphases on judgment, creation,
idolatry and swearing cannot be viewed as accidental. This can
be seen most clearly from the following analysis.

The praise of Yahweh the Lord of Hosts as Creator is found
in ten of the passages using the refrain, and those which do not
mention the creative act are precisely the questioned usages,
with two exceptions. The emphasis on Yahweh as Creator occurs
in Am. 4:13; 5:8-9; 9:5-6; Isa. 48:13; 51:12-16; 54:5; Jer. 10:
12-16; 31:35; 32:17-20; 51:15-19. Exceptions are Am. 5:27; Hos.
12:5; Jer. 46:18; 48:15; 50:34; 51:57; and Isa. 47:4. Of these
Am. 5:27; Hos. 12:5; Jer. 46:18; 48:15 and 51:57 are generally
thought to be glosses, the last three containing the unusual
"says (n^e'um) the King, Yahweh of Hosts is his name." This
leaves only two contexts that do not mention Yahweh's creative
act: Jer. 50:34 and Isa. 47:4. However, Jer. 50:34 is unusual
in that the refrain does not conclude the sentence, and while
the immediate context of Isa. 47:4 lacks any reference to creation, its *larger* context does allude to creation (46:4).

The theme dominating every use of the refrain (except perhaps Jer. 31:35) is judgment. This depiction of Yahweh's judgment is usually composed of three elements: (1) the threat, (2)
the basis for the judgment, and (3) an appeal to return to Yahweh. The third element is naturally absent from those passages
announcing Yahweh's judgment upon foreign peoples. The threat
of judgment may be made up of many vivid pictures, but the most
descriptive is the roaring waters or rivers of judgment (Am. 5:
8-9; 9:6; 5:24, if Weiser's interpretation is accepted; Isa.
47:2; 48:8). The motif of judgment occurs in Am. 4:13; 9:1-4;
Isa. 48:10; 51:9-10,17; 54:7; Jer. 10:10; 32:33-35; 46:10; 48:
21; 50:27; 51:52. The most frequent basis for the judgment is
the fact that the eyes of the Lord have seen the people's sins
(Am. 9:4; Isa. 47:10; 48:8; Jer. 31:28 which reverses the theme;
32:20). In Jer. 44:26-27 one discerns the significance of the
phrase "Behold, I am watching over them for evil and not for
good"; it is no accident that this motif occurs within a context
denouncing the Israelites for swearing, "As the Lord God lives,"
when their worship of the queen of heaven has polluted their
hearts. The third element, the appeal to return, can be found
in Am. 4:6-11; 5:6; Isa. 45:22; 48:4; Jer. 32:33-35 (though

implicitly), and in two other contexts that are very similar to these under discussion: Job 5:8 and 9:15.

The third theme that characterizes the contexts in which the refrain occurs is an attack on the idolatry of the people. Such an attack appears in Am. 5:5; 5:25-27; 8:14; Isa. 46:1-7; 48:5; Jer. 10:3-5,11,14-15; 32:35; 48:13; 50:35-38; 51:52. The connection of idolatry and swearing, the fourth theme, can be discerned most clearly in Jer. 51:14-19. But the oath is referred to in a number of contexts (Isa. 45:22-23; 48:1; Jer. 31: 36-37; 32:22; and 46:18). Moreover, it is tempting to understand Am. 4:12b as an oath.[57]

B. *Different Forms of the Refrain*

The preceding analysis of contexts in which the refrain is found has not paid particular attention to the style of the refrain itself. The following will seek to examine this aspect to see if there is any correlation between the different words of the refrains and the contents of their contexts. In short, it will seek to determine whether a particular refrain is always used with a fixed subject matter.

The most common refrain is "Yahweh is his name," "Yahweh of Hosts is his name," or "Yahweh God of Hosts is his name." The first occurs in Am. 5:8 and 9:6, while the second appears in Isa. 48:2; 51:15; Jer. 10:16; 31:35 and 51:19; the third is used only in Am. 4:13. In all of these creation is the central theme, and judgment is missing only in Jer. 31:35. Moreover, the attack on idolatry occurs in Isa. 48:5; Jer. 10:3-5,8-9,11; and the oath is an issue in Am. 4:12; Isa. 48:1; Jer. 51:14; 31:36-37 (implicitly).

The second type of refrain is the combination of an oracular formula (either n^e'*um* or '*āmar*) and refrain. It is found in Am. 5:27; Isa. 47:4; Jer. 48:15; and 51:57. The striking

---

[57]Sheldon Blank, "The Curse, Blasphemy, the Spell and the Oath," *HUCA*, XXIII (1950-1951), 89-90, points out that frequently the oath-taker gives no hint as to the ominous content of the "thus" and "the same" (in the phrase, "Thus shall God do to me and more too"). Blank thinks the potency of the word led to this hesitancy to specify the "thus." It may also be noted that Cripps, *op. cit.*, 175, and Harper, *op. cit.*, 103, recognized this use of *kōh* in Am. 4:12b. This understanding gives the best explanation of the *kōh* yet offered. Could it be that the "it" in Amos' oracles against the nations (*lō' 'ashibhēnû*) has the same background?

feature of this group is the absence of any reference to Yahweh as Creator, but the singular dominant note is an attack against idolatry. The refrain in Isa. 47:4 is unusual in that it has the short "Yahweh of Hosts is his name" in the midst of other adjectives ("Our Redeemer--the Lord of Hosts is his name--is the Holy One of Israel").

Another type of refrain is represented by Jer. 32:18 and Hos. 12:5. In the former the simple form is expanded to read, "The great (and) mighty God ('ēl), Yahweh of Hosts is his name," while Hos. 12:5 forms the transition between this and the fourth type which uses the refrain within the middle of a lengthy sentence. The refrain in Hosea reads, "And Yahweh the God of the Hosts, Yahweh is his name" (zikhrô). Because of the use of zikhrô instead of shemô, this passage probably should be excluded from consideration.[58] That being the case, the only remaining example of this third type emphasizes creation, judgment and idolatry, while mentioning Yahweh's oath to the fathers.

The final type has stylistic precursors in Hos. 12:5 and Isa. 47:4, but comes to full expression in Isa. 54:5; Jer. 46:18; and 50:34. In Isa. 54:5 one reads, "For your Maker is your husband, the Lord of Hosts is his name, and the Holy One of Israel is your Redeemer." Similarly, the refrain in Jer. 46:28 is followed by a long sentence: "As I live, says the King, whose name is the Lord of Hosts, like Tabor among the mountains, and like Carmel by the sea, shall one come." Jeremiah 50:34 is similar: "Their Redeemer is strong; the Lord of Hosts is his name. He will surely plead their cause, that he may give rest to the earth, but unrest to the inhabitants of Babylon." Creation finds only the faintest allusion here (Isa. 54:5 has "your Maker"), and judgment dominates. On the other hand, idolatry is only attacked in passing (50:35-38), while an oath occurs in the refrain itself (Jer. 46:18) and elsewhere (Isa. 54:8).

This leads to the following conclusions. Two types of refrain are used in contexts where creation is the basic issue, while another type is placed within an attack on idolatry, and still another appears where the announcement of judgment is central but swearing prominent. Second, by far the most

---

[58]This observation assumes that Wolff, *Dodekapropheton I. Hosea*, 276, is right that there is a difference between the two words. On the other hand, they may simply be synonyms.

references occur within a context emphasizing creation, although
the soteriological implications of the creative act are all important. This explains why judgment is the fundamental mood behind every use of the refrain (except Jer. 31:35, where the ex-
alted description implies that Yahweh will judge the enemies of
Israel); the God who creates is able to save, and in delivering
Israel judgment upon those who oppressed her is necessary.[59]
But even Israel is not immune from punishment at the hands of
her Creator, and the primary basis for such treatment is her
guilt in making idols and worshiping them, while a subsidiary
cause for the judgment is her practice of swearing but not in
truth or by Yahweh.

C. *The Refrain's Function: Combatting False Oaths*
These are the salient facts. What can be made of them?
In the writer's opinion, the following hypothesis best explains
the data at hand. After the confrontation between Israelite and
Assyro-Babylonian religion, Israel succumbed to the temptation
to swear by foreign deities (Am. 8:14; Jer. 12:16; and 44:26).
The prophetic response is seen in the taking up of the ancient
cultic refrain, "Yahweh of Hosts is his name," which almost always stands in direct connection with the asseveration that Yahweh is Creator. The emphasis is clear: "Yahweh is the *name* of
the only God, the Creator of heaven and earth, in whose name all
oaths must be taken." This creation is soteriological, recalling the ancient myth of the splitting of the seas (Ex. 15:3).
Consequently, creation and redemption are linked, and in the
name of the mighty Creator threats are leveled against enemies
who would thwart Yahweh's deliverance. Within this theme of

---

[59]The fundamental contribution made by G. von Rad, "Das
theologische Problem des alttestamentlichen Schöpfungsglaubens,"
136-47, must not be ignored. Creation faith plays a serving role
and is never the main theme even in Second Isaiah (139), except
in the Psalms influenced by Egyptian wisdom, namely 19, 104, and
9 (143-46). Von Rad finds classic illustration of the supple-
mentary, supporting character of creation faith in the doxologies
of Amos, where no new message independent of the rest of the prophetic words is said to be found (139). In a word, the supporting role of Old Testament creation faith must be recognized, even
if one does not go to the extent that von Rad does, especially in
regard to the teachings contained in the doxologies of Amos. It
would be more nearly accurate to observe that the distinctive
character of Old Testament creation faith is the association of
it with a first "historical" act of God.

creation, deliverance and judgment stand three motifs: (1) rivers
of judgment, the threat of punishment and its object; (2) the
assertion that the eyes of the Lord are watching over humanity
for judgment, and (3) the appeal to return to Yahweh. The prophets demand that oaths be taken in the name of Yahweh the Creator,
and that they be made in truth (Dt. 6:13; 10:20; Jer. 5:1-2; 12:
16; Isa. 65:16-17; 43:18; 48:2). Moreover, cultic prayers represent the attempt to educate people in this direction (Dan. 9:11,
where curse and oath as well as the "name" made at the Reed Sea
are recalled; Jer. 32; Neh. 9).

What is the life setting of this movement? An answer may
be derived from the following facts. Genesis 14 indicates that
about 1000 B.C. swearing was permissible in the name of 'ēl
'elyôn of Jerusalem, Maker of heaven and earth. After this one
can observe a growing tendency to swear by the God who delivered
Israel from Egypt, and at the stimulus of Second Isaiah the sub-
stitution of references to creation for allusions to the Exodus
began to take place. Like his contemporary, the Deuteronomistic
historian was emphasizing the same thing, as can be seen from
the prayer of Jer. 32 and those inserted into other texts. However, by 450 B.C., the end product of this emphasis on the Isrealite God as Creator was given its final form, namely Gen. 1.
By then the battle had been won and the refrain was no longer
needed. This leaves one question to be discussed: what place do
the doxologies have in this scheme? The answer seems to be that
they should be placed somewhere between 550 and 450 B.C.

The preceding hypothesis does not assume that creation faith
originated in the struggle with Assyro-Babylonian religion, but
that emphasis came to be placed on an idea that existed from the
earliest days of Israelite history.[60] *A priori*, there are six
reasons that almost demand an early belief in creation: (1) a
recognition that Israel's neighbors worshiped creator gods and

---

[60]W. Eichrodt, *Theologie des Alten Testaments*, II (Stuttgart: Ehrenfried Klotz Verlag, 1961), 59, thinks of the belief
in creation as "*uralt*"; and J. Philip Hyatt, *The Heritage of
Biblical Faith* (Saint Louis: Bethany Press, 1964), 94, calls it
early. Even G. von Rad, *Old Testament Theology*, I, 136, recognizes the antiquity of a belief in creation (Ps. 19:2ff.; Gen.
14:19,22; 24:3; I Kgs. 8:12, text emended).

gave this belief a place of major importance;[61] (2) the absence of a theogony in the Old Testament;[62] (3) the awareness that Gen. 1 is the final product of a long period of development;[63] (4) the desacralization of sex in the Old Testament;[64] (5) Israel's conception of God;[65] and (6) the original meaning of the name Yahweh, if Albright, Freedman and Cross are right.[66]

But acceptance of these arguments does not justify an uncritical analysis of texts dealing with creation, as can be seen in the work of B. N. Wambacq.[67] In his discussion of the material there are four methodological errors that have vast implications. In the first place, he uses recognizably late materials, although considering them early (Ex. 20:11; 31:17; Isa. 37:16;

---

[61]Th. C. Vriezen, *An Outline of Old Testament Theology* (Oxford: Blackwell, 1960), 184. The most obvious borrowing from Canaanitic religion can be seen in the ancient myth of the Chaos Dragon and the fertility motifs that imply an idea of creation (Hos. 2; Jdg. 5).

[62]*Ibid.*

[63]B. W. Anderson, "Creation," *IDB*, I, 726; G. von Rad, *Genesis*, John H. Marks, trans. (London: SCM Press, 1961), 62 (it had its beginning in the oldest Yahweh community and was nourished in ancient sanctuaries); Vriezen, *An Outline of Old Testament Theology*, 344. Von Rad observes that P preserves the older way of thinking (completely material) than J (62). See also G. Lambert, "La creation dans la Bible," *NRT*, (1953), 252ff.; and Johannes Baptist Bauer, "Der priesterliche Schöpfungshymnus in Gen. 1," *ThZ*, XX (1964), 1-9.

[64]G. von Rad, *Old Testament Theology*, I, 28, writes that the real motivation behind the desacralization of sex was Israel's doctrine of creation.

[65]Vriezen, *An Outline of Old Testament Theology*, 25, rightly emphasizes that Israel's conception of God contains implicitly "and probably not only potentially" the doctrine of creation.

[66]W. F. Albright, "Review of B. N. Wambacq, L'epithete divine Jahve ṣebā'ôt," *passim*; D. N. Freedman, "The Name of the God of Moses," *JBL*, LXXIX (1960), 151-56; and F. M. Cross, Jr., "Yahweh and the God of the Patriarchs," *HTR*, XV (1962), 225-59. Yahweh is understood as a causative ("He causes to be"), as are also various other divine names ('ēl qānnā', Yahweh ṣᵉbhā'ôth, Yahweh yir'eh). On the other hand, S. Mowinckel, "The Name of the God of Moses," *HUCA*, XXXII (1961), 121-33, has denied any causative element to the name Yahweh and has attempted to explain its origin in a cultic cry of ecstasy ("O He!").

[67]B. N. Wambacq, *op. cit.*, 197-98.

Mic. 4:13; Am. 4:13; 5:8-9; 9:5-6). Second, he mistakes references to Yahweh "the God of heaven and earth" for assertions that
the deity is Creator (Gen. 24:3,7; Josh. 3:11,18; I Kgs. 20:28).
Again Wambacq claims that since "Yahweh is his name" occurs in
Ex. 15:3, the longer refrain in Amos, Isaiah and Jeremiah is not
late, hence the doxologies are authentic to the text of Amos and,
together with verses from Isaiah and Jeremiah, constitute an ancient hymn antedating Amos but employed by him. Finally, he excludes any reference to historical events in the hymns in Job and
Psalms celebrating Yahweh's victory over Rahab, Leviathan or Tannim (Pss. 74; 89; Job 9:5-13; 26:7-13), and assumes that reference
to Yahweh's mastery over the forces of nature implies a doctrine
of creation (Am. 4:6-11; 8:8; Pss. 77:17-19; 105:17-18; Ex. 14:
26-28; Num. 16:31-33; Josh. 6:10; 10:11; Jdg. 5:20-21; I Sam.
14:15).

Despite the fact that belief in creation existed in Israel
from earliest times, most reflective thinking on the idea comes
from a comparatively late period in Israelite history. Von Rad
has recognized this fact and has given an explanation for it.
He notices that the early cultic summaries (Dt. 26:5-10; 6:20-25;
Josh. 24:2-13) did not refer to Yahweh as Creator, even if the
Israelite knew that his God controlled nature (Ex. 15:21; Jdg.
5:20-21).[68] Similarly, he observes that Lev. 25:23 does not have
in mind the doctrine of creation, but recalls Yahweh's gracious
act in giving the Land of Promise to Israel.[69] Von Rad's solution to the problem of the relative lateness of emphasis upon
creation faith is in the form of an assertion: Yahweh faith is
election faith, that is, primarily saving faith. In saying
this, von Rad poses the problem of combining a doctrine of creation with belief in a God who performs saving deeds in its stark-
est form. He writes that the means of combining these two views
of God was derived from Canaanite sources, namely the struggle
with the mythical Chaos Monster.[70] To the genius of Second

---

[68]G. von Rad, "Das theologische Problem des alttestamentlichen Schöpfungsglaubens," 137. This is all the more striking
when one compares the late summary in Neh. 9:6-31, which begins
with creation (see Anderson, "Creation," 726).

[69]Von Rad, *loc. cit.*

[70]*Ibid.*, 141.

Isaiah is credited the solution to the problem caused by creation faith and election faith: creation takes on a soteriological note, the Exodus being interpreted as a contemporary redemption.[71]

The need for a re-thinking of this solution to the problem
of the relative lateness of reflective thinking about creation
has recently been recognized by von Rad himself.[72] Walter Harrelson has suggested a new answer to this problem, one that
avoids the difficulty of attributing a temporal or logical pri-
ority to saving faith over creation faith.[73] Recognizing a two-
fold use of the motif of creation (the reconstituting of the
cosmos in cultic acts where mythological patterns and motifs of
ancient religions played a decisive part, and the point of departure for a more comprehensive understanding of God's saving
works in the world of men), he observes that the Yahwist por-
trays saving history in the form of creation-chaos.[74] Absence
of themes of creation and Sinai from the confessional statements
is explained by the fact that both are the presupposition and
the acts to be constituted at the New Year's Festival.[75]

---

[71]G. von Rad, "Das theologische Problem des alttestamentlichen Schöpfungsglaubens," 140, and *Old Testament Theology*, I, 28.

[72]"Aspekte alttestamentlichen Weltverständnisses," *EvTh*,
XXIV (1964), 57, 61-62. Von Rad writes: "Sehe ich recht, so sind
wir heute in der Gefahr, die theologischen Probleme des Alten
Testaments zu einseitig im Bereich des Geschichtstheologischen
zu sehen" (57). He points to the centrality of the prohibition
against idolatry in shaping the Israelite world view, discovering
in this prohibition the fact that "Jahwe war nicht eine der tra-
genden Weltkräfte, auch nicht ihre Summe, sondern ihr Schöpfer"
and recognizing that the question of the origin and antiquity of
creation faith assumes new dimensions because of this insight (61-
62).

[73]"Creation and Saving History in Genesis," 1-16, unpublished
paper read to Chicago Society for Biblical Research on April 18,
1964.

[74]*Ibid.*, 7-8. Harrelson thinks that the central theme of the
Pentateuch is the "Promise in process of fulfillment," which is
developed by the use of the creation-chaos motif of the ancient
Near East, although modified and transformed.

[75]*Ibid.*, 11-13. He writes that "Israelite religion, from
first to last, is also a religion of fertility" (10), and points
out that the New Year's Festival is a rite of fertility which
presupposes the "Lordship of Yahweh over the world, his calling
it into being and sustaining it in being" (11-12). Harrelson
believes that the purpose of the celebration was to reaffirm and
effect order--the order of creation and of Sinai (13).

Harrelson raises the question as to the manner in which Israel came to root the fertility dimension of creation in the story of creation at the beginning of historical time, and answers it from two perspectives: (1) the understanding of Yahweh as a kind of tutelary deity of a tribe, which includes the idea of historical involvement, and (2) Yahweh's claim to exclusive loyalty, together with the prohibition against worshiping other gods, which leads to a de-deification of the world.[76]

Regardless of whether von Rad or Harrelson is right in this matter, there can be no question about the fact that belief in creation played a more formative role in early Israelite thought than is generally recognized. This observation gains force when one considers early passages in the Old Testament that testify to such a faith: Gen. 2:4bff.; I Kgs. 8:12 (text emended); Pss. 19, 8, 33, 104, 24, 74, 89; Job 9, 26; Hos. 8:14.[77]

---

[76]"Creation and Saving History in Genesis," 14-15. Von Rad, "Aspekte alttestamentlichen Weltverständnisses," 61-73, wants to make the prohibition against idolatry the ground for reflection upon creation, but Harrelson thinks the second understanding of creation provides a more adequate ground for the prohibition against idols (15).

[77]G. von Rad, *Old Testament Theology*, I, 28, note 38, writes that the Yahwistic creation account may derive from pre-Palestinian traditions (arid earth and waterless steppe). The text of Gen. 14:18,19,22 is uncertain; the LXX and Syriac versions omit Yahweh in verse 22, the only place where it occurs in the Masoretic Text. The word *qōneh* occurs often in Ugaritic literature and must mean Creator in this context (see Paul Humbert, "'Qānā' en hébreu biblique," *Festschrift für A. Bertholet*, 259-66). The date of Gen. 14 is difficult to determine, although it would seem to come from about 1000 B.C. B. W. Anderson, "Creation," 726, considers it early but of "uncertain date." G. von Rad, *Genesis*, 175-76, and *Old Testament Theology*, I, 136, also considers it an old text, its purpose being to convince the country people to support the Davidic ruler and his religious organization. For a recent discussion of the relation between Yahweh and *'ēl ᶜelyôn*, see O. Eissfeldt, "Jahwes Verhältnis zu Elyon und Schadday nach Psalm 91," *Die Welt des Orients*, II, (1957), 343-48. Eissfeldt thinks that Ps. 91 does not use the two names as epithets of Yahweh but of separate deities, and comes from about 1000 B.C. (347). With this date, H. H. Rowley, "Melchizedek and Zadok," *Festschrift für A. Bertholet*, 461-72, agrees (see especially page 470).
B. W. Anderson, "Creation," 726, points out that some scholars think Pss. 24, 47, 93-100 were used in the annual fall New Year's Festival in celebration of Yahweh's creative work.
To these passages may be added Gen. 1:1-2:4a in its earliest form, and possibly Dt. 32:15,18, and Ez. 18:13,15.

The attempt must now be made to defend the interpretation
of the facts given above regarding the refrain "Yahweh of Hosts
is his name." What is demanded is nothing less than a historical
reconstruction. The one offered in the following includes three
major propositions: (1) the origin of swearing by false deities,
(2) the prophetic demand that oaths be taken in Yahweh's name,
and (3) the attempt to educate the people to recognize Yahweh
as Creator by means of cultic prayers.

1. *Swearing by Deities other than Yahweh*

First, oaths came to be taken by foreign gods. Two words
are used for oaths ($sh^ebh\hat{u}^{c}\bar{a}h$ and $^{c}\bar{a}l\bar{a}h$), the latter indicating
the close connection of oath and curse.[78] The actual content of
the curse is usually suppressed,[79] the formula being "May God
do so to me and more also if...." (Ruth 1:17; I Sam. 3:17; 14:44;
I Kgs. 2:23).[80] At least four types of oaths exist in the Old
Testament: (1) promissory, (2) an element of legal procedure,
(3) religious, and (4) divine.[81] The promissory oath plays a
major role in treaties (Gen. 25:31; Jdg. 21:1, etc.) and is
often connected with the throne of David and $\d{h}\acute{e}sedh$.[82] Four

---

[78]F. Horst, "Der Eid im Alten Testament," *Gottes Recht*, 301;
M. H. Pope, "Oaths," *IDB*, III, 576-77. J. Pedersen, *Der Eid bei
den Semiten*, 108, writes that the hypothetical curse is spoken
and the response of the people, '$\bar{a}m\bar{e}n$, given, "so wird klar, dass
die Grenze zwischen Fluch und Eid durchaus fliessend ist (Num.
5:22; Dt. 27:15ff.; Neh. 5:13)." He concludes: "Vor allen zwei
Erscheinungen liegen dem Eide zugrunde: Der Bund und der Fluch"
(128).

[79]S. H. Blank, *op. cit.*, 89-90; Horst, "Der Eid im Alten
Testament," 303 ("unausgesprochen bleibt eine Verwünschung");
and Pope, *op. cit.*, 577.

[80]Only a truncated formula remains in many oaths: "If" and
"If not" in the protasis, and the omission of the curse in the
apodosis (see Pope, *op. cit.*, 577; and Blank, *op. cit.*, 89-90,
where the reason for this is given as the fear that the spoken
oath might sometimes take place even though the person be inno-
cent). See also Josef Scharbert, *Solidarität in Segen und Fluch
im Alten Testament und in seiner Umwelt* (Bonn: Peter Hanstein
Verlag, 1958), *passim*.

[81]This is Horst's classification, although the distinction
between the third and fourth must be understood as a matter of
expediency, since legal procedure is a religious realm also (see
Horst, "Der Eid im Alten Testament," 292-314). In any case,
Horst's classification is more helpful than Pedersen's oath of
asseveration and promissory oath (Pedersen, *op. cit.*, 179ff.).

[82]See Horst, "Der Eid im Alten Testament," 292-94, and Pedersen, *op. cit.*, 179ff. for a discussion and references.

variations of the oath within legal procedure are evident: (1) purification oath (Lev. 5:21ff.; Ex. 22:7, 10; I Kgs. 18:10); (2) negative confession, or adjuration (Job 31); (3) oath of ordeal (Dt. 17:8-13; Num. 5:12-28; Jdg. 17:2; Zech. 5:3f.); and (4) the oath of obedience (Jer. 42:5).[83] Oaths in the specifically religious realm deal with offenses against the covenant (Josh. 24:2; II Chr. 15:4-5; Ezr. 10:2-6; Neh. 10:30), and may be called oaths of homage.[84] Finally, the divine oath must be examined. It is of two kinds, blessing and curse. The former topic is two-fold: Yahweh's gift of the Promised Land, and the oath in regard to the Davidic dynasty.[85] Outside these two areas one finds oaths of blessing only sporadically (Isa. 54:9; 45:23; 62:8; Dan. 12:7).[86] The oath of doom is frequently used with reference to the wilderness period (Num. 14:23; 32:10-11; Dt. 1:34-35; 2:14; Josh. 5:6) and to the later period of unfaithfulness (Dt. 4:21; Jdg. 2:15).[87] Friedrich Horst has noted the peculiarity of the fact that the divine threatening oath is limited to the beginning and end of the pre-exilic period,[88] although his examples are not quite convincing. Nevertheless, it is true that Deuteronomy and Ezekiel give to the threatening oath special prominence.

Ideas connected with the oath are manifold. The oath is tantamount to excommunication, so a connection with covenant on

---

[83]Horst, "Der Eid im Alten Testament," 295-97.

[84]*Ibid.*, 297-98. Horst rightly suggests that swearing by and in Yahweh's name is cultic, and indicates cultic festivals at sanctuaries in which the oath was an integral part (cf. Ps. 119:106). Pedersen, *op. cit.*, 144-45, maintains that the Israelite customarily swore in the sanctuary (Ex. 22:6; Hos. 4:15).

[85]Horst, "Der Eid im Alten Testament," 299, correctly writes that this has nothing to do with Deuteronomic theology, but is connected with the royal Zion festival (Pss. 132:11ff.; 89:4-5; 36; 50).

[86]*Ibid.*, 299.

[87]*Ibid.*, 299-300.

[88]*Ibid.*, 300. Horst writes: "Es ist eigenartig, dass der göttliche Strafandrohungseid nur am Anfang der vorexilischen Prophetie und dann wieder ganz an ihrem Ende sich vorfindet und dazwischen nicht zu belegen ist." He mentions Am. 4:2; 6:8; Jer. 22:5; Ez. 17:16,19, remarking that Deuteronomy and Ezekiel (16 times) give the threatening oath a special role (301).

the one hand and curse on the other is essential.[89]   In the ancient world the oath constituted an important means of holding
society together; consequently it was an integral aspect of cultic life, the legal procedure being associated with shrines and
priesthood.   Moreover, holy persons, places and objects were connected with the oath.[90]   The international context was also an
important arena of the oath, it being used in the formal ratification of treaties.[91]   Oaths were sealed by invocation of the
divine name, although this specific mention of the name may be
a secondary element.[92]   Certain gestures were connected with
oath-taking, the phrase "to raise the hand" later coming to mean
"to swear" (Gen. 14:22; Ex. 6:8; Num. 14:30; Dt. 32:4; Ez. 20:28;
Dan. 12:7; Ps. 106:26).   Sacrifices often accompanied an oath
(Gen. 15:10,17; 31:54; Jer. 34:18), and the oath-taker even laid
hold of sacred objects (Gen. 24:2; 47:29).[93]

But the oath was subject to misuse, primarily in one of two
directions.[94]   On the one hand, the oath could be used as a means
of assuring Yahweh's protection, in spite of continued disobed-
ience.   A number of texts denounce this use of swearing, the earliest of which are from Hosea.   In 4:15 the prophet declares,
"Though you play the harlot, O Israel, let not Judah become guilty.
Enter not into Gilgal, nor go to Beth-aven, and swear not, 'As the
Lord lives'."   Again in Hos. 10:46 there is a denunciation of
empty oaths made with covenants, and here the idolatrous nature
of these oaths is evident (cf. Am. 5:26-27).   This charge against
the people for false swearing is taken up by Jeremiah (5:2),
Second Isaiah (48:1-2), Zechariah (5:3), and Malachi (3:5); and

---

[89]*Ibid.*, 301-02; and Pedersen, *op. cit.*, "Der Bund und der
Bundeseid," 21-51, and "Der Eid als Fluch," 108-18.

[90]Pope, *op. cit.*, 575-76.

[91]Horst, "Der Eid im Alten Testament," 293-94.

[92]*Ibid.*, 305.   See Pope, *op. cit.*, 576, for a discussion on
the invocation of the divine name.   Pedersen, *op. cit.*, 151, observes that Gen. 31:53 preserves a remnant of the ancient form
of oath ("by the *paḥad* of his father Isaac").

[93]Pope, *op. cit.*, 576; Horst, "Der Eid im Alten Testament,"
308-09; Pedersen, *op. cit.*, 150-51.

[94]Pedersen, *op. cit.*, "Der Verfall des Eides," 190-93.

Lev. 19:12 demands that oaths not be taken in Yahweh's name
falsely. The other direction that the misuse of the oath took
is vastly more important, that is, swearing by gods other than
Yahweh.

The earliest witness to this problem is found in the book
of Amos (8:7-8,14).

> The Lord has sworn by the pride of Jacob
> "Surely I will never forget any of their deeds.
> Shall not the land tremble on this account,
>   and every one mourn who dwells in it,
> and all of it rise like the Nile,
>   and be tossed about and sink again, like the Nile of
>   Egypt?"....
> ....
> Those who swear by Ashimah of Samaria,
>   and say, "As thy god lives, O Dan,"
> and, "As the way of Beer-sheba lives,"
>   they shall fall, and never rise again.

Similarly, Hos. 10:4-6 leaves no doubt as to the idolatrous element in swearing. Such oaths are condemned in Dt. 6:12-13; 10:
20, etc.; Josh. 23:7; Ps. 16:4; Jer. 5:7; 7:9; 12:16-17; and
Zeph. 1:5-6. The last two passages are extremely important in
this regard. Jeremiah 12:14-17, most probably an addition to
the text,[95] deals with evil neighbors of Judah and promises that
if they learn "the ways of my people, to swear by my name, 'As
the Lord Lives,' even as they taught my people to swear by Baal,
then they shall be built up in the midst of my people." Zephan-
iah 1:4-6 reads as follows:

> I will stretch out my hand against Judah,
>   and against all the inhabitants of Jerusalem;
> and I will cut off from this place the remnant of Baal
>   and the name of the idolatrous priests;
> those who bow down on the roofs to the host of the heavens;
>   those who bow down and swear to the Lord
>   and yet swear by Milcom;
> those who have turned back from following the Lord,
>   who do not seek the Lord or inquire of him.

In view of all this, the skepticism of Ecclesiastes in regard
to taking an oath is understandable (9:2).

---

[95]Hyatt, "Jeremiah," 920.

With this background in view, it is possible now to examine the special materials in which the oath by the Creator is mentioned. In Gen. 14:18-23 there appears a blessing "by God Most High, maker of heaven and earth"[96] and the report of an oath by the "Lord God Most High, maker of heaven and earth." The prefixing of *YHWH* in the last phrase is suspicious in view of its omission in the Septuagint and Syriac versions. It is interesting to note that in Gen. 24:3 Abraham has his servant swear "by the Lord, the God of heaven and earth"; the absence of *qōneh* or its equivalent is especially noticeable. When compared with the ancient account in Gen. 31:43-54, this reference to "Creator of heaven and earth" in 14:18-23 is all the more striking. The old covenant between Laban and Jacob is sealed with Jacob's oath by the "Fear of his father Isaac," and Laban's appeal is that "the God of Abraham, and the God of Nahor, the God of their father, judge between us" (31:53). Likewise, in Josh. 9:19-20, in an undoubtedly early account of the deception of Joshua's men by the Gibeonites, the oath is said to have been by "the Lord, the God of Israel," and no reference to "Creator" appears.

On the contrary, in Jer. 38:16 King Zedekiah is said to have sworn secretly to Jeremiah, "As the Lord lives, who made our souls, I will not put you to death or deliver you into the hands of these men who seek your life." Here the emphasis is placed on the creation of man, as in the Yahwistic account.[97] Another passage from the book of Jeremiah is of utmost significance for this discussion, namely 44:24-30.[98] Here one reads:

> Thus says the Lord of Hosts, the God of Israel: You and your wives have declared with your mouths, and have fulfilled it with your hands, saying, "We will surely perform our vows that we have made, to burn incense to the queen of heaven and to pour out libations to her." Then confirm your vows and perform your vows! Therefore hear the word of the Lord, all you of Judah who dwell in the land of Egypt: Behold, I have sworn by my great name, says the Lord,

---

[96]The translation of *qōneh* as Creator is substantiated in the LXX, Vulgate, Targum Onkelos and Syriac.

[97]Could it be that the textual difficulty is caused by the omission of the first two consonants of *šebhā'ôth*? This verse is probably genuine (see Hyatt, "Jeremiah," 1076).

[98]The Deuteronomic character of this passage is clear; consult Hyatt, *ibid.*, 1100.

that my name shall no more be invoked by the mouth of
any man of Judah in all the land of Egypt, saying, "As
the Lord God lives." Behold, I am watching over them
for evil and not for good; all the men of Judah who
are in the land of Egypt shall be consumed by the sword
and by famine, until there is an end of them (25-27).

The connection of oaths with strange deities is extremely significant, for this linking of oath and idolatry is a noticeable
aspect of several passages. Isaiah 48:1-2 refers to swearing by
the name of the Lord, and confessing the God of Israel, but not
in truth or right. It goes on to make the specific charge that
the people "call themselves after the holy city, and stay themselves on the God of Israel." The connection with idolatry is
made in verse 5. The mention of an oath by Yahweh occurs twice
in contexts praising him as Creator (Jer. 32:16-25, especially
22; Isa. 54:4-10, especially 9).[99] Finally, in Jer. 51:14 an
oath introduces a hymn in praise of Yahweh as Creator, in the
midst of which appears an attack on idolatry (51:15-19).

The same picture can be discerned from an examination of
usage of the common formula for an oath: "As the Lord lives."
The clear association of oath with idolatry is seen in Dt. 32:
39-40, which represents God as saying: "See now that I, even I,
am he, and there is no God beside me; I kill and I make alive;
I wound and I heal; and there is none that can deliver out of
my hand. For I lift up my hand to heaven, and swear, 'As I live
forever'...." The threat of judgment follows. Likewise in Jdg.
8:10; Num. 14:28; I Sam. 28:10; 29:6; II Kgs. 5:16-20 the connection between idolatry and an oath must be recognized. The
prophets Jeremiah and Ezekiel were fond of the expression "As
the Lord lives," and their use provides a clue to interpreting
the oath in their day. Jeremiah 4:1-2 is crucial:

If you return, O Israel, says the Lord,
    to me you should return.
If you remove your abominations from my presence
    and do not waver,
and if you swear, "As the Lord lives,"
    in truth, in justice, and in uprightness,
then nations shall bless themselves in him,
    and in him shall they glory.

---

[99]Compare Jer. 31:35-37 to Isa. 54:10. The appeal to "fear
not" with the promise that "you will not be ashamed" occurs in
more than one context dealing with our topic, and deserves careful consideration (Isa. 51:12-16; Jer. 5:18-24).

Likewise Jer. 5:1-3 emphasizes the necessity for Israel to return to Yahweh, do justice and seek truth, in spite of the fact that they swear "As the Lord lives" (cf. 12:16, which has previously been discussed). But the most important passages for this discussion are Jer. 16:14-18 and 23:7-8.[100]

The former passage proclaims that the time will come when the oath will be changed from "As the Lord lives who brought up the people of Israel out of the land of Egypt," to "As the Lord lives who brought up the people of Israel out of the north country and out of all the countries where he had driven them" (14-15). Verse 17 assures the people that Yahweh's eyes are upon all their ways, so that no iniquity is hidden; and verse 18 gives as the reason for Yahweh's punishment of his people the fact that the land has been polluted by idols and abominations. The same idea is expressed in Jer. 23:7-8 in regard to the change in oath formula. Now the feature that strikes one upon reading these passages is the movement within the oath formula toward the mention of Yahweh as Creator. This final step can be taken when Second Isaiah perceives that the deliverance at the Reed Sea can be understood as a creative act. In fact, from an examination of the contexts in which the refrain "As the Lord lives" is used, one notices a growing tendency to expand it from the brief form to a longer one (II Sam. 4:9, "As the Lord lives, who has redeemed my life out of every adversity"; 15:21; I Kgs. 18:15, "As the Lord lives, before whom I stand"; Jer. 38:16, "As the Lord lives, who made our souls"; and 46:18, "As I live, says the King, whose name is the Lord of Hosts," to the last of which may be compared Gen. 24:3 and Rev. 10:5-6).

From the book of Ezekiel one notices the same association of idolatry and the oath formula, seen most clearly in 5:11; 20:31,33; 35:11. In 33:11 one finds the frequent appeal to Israel to return:

> Say to them, As I live, says the Lord God,
> I have no pleasure in the death of the wicked,
> but that the wicked turn from his way and live;
> turn back, turn back from your evil ways;
> for why will you die, O house of Israel?

---

[100]The crucial verses (16:14-15; 23:7-8) are exilic or post-exilic (see Hyatt, "Jeremiah," 947, 988).

As has been indicated above, this link between oath and idolatry
is also alluded to in Hos. 4:15; moreover, it is quite clear in
Zeph. 1:5.

The preceding has shown that there was a strong tendency
within Israel to misuse the oath, either by false swearing in
Yahweh's name or through swearing by foreign deities. Only in
Gen. 14:19, 22 is this deity called Creator, but there can be
no question that the gods of the ancient Near East were understood as creators of the world. In such a context the prophetic
response is clear. At first the simple demand to swear by Yahweh alone was made,[101] but this soon was changed into an emphasis upon Yahweh as Creator, hence able to save and destroy.
Finally, one can discern a development from appeal to Yahweh the
God of Israel, through reference to Yahweh as the one who gave
deliverance at the Reed Sea, to the claim that Yahweh created
heaven and earth--a claim made possible by Deutero-Isaiah's understanding of the Exodus as a creative act.

2.   *The Prophetic Response*

The second point of the historical reconstruction is the
suggestion that the prophets responded to this situation with
the demand that swearing be done in Yahweh's name. This is a
dominant motif in Deuteronomy and can be seen vividly in 6:13
and 10:17-22. The former demands that Israel fear Yahweh and
serve him, swearing by his name. The following verse warns
against worshiping other gods and reminds the people that Yahweh is a jealous God. Deuteronomy 10:17-22 has overtones of
late cultic prayers:

> For the Lord your God is God of gods and Lord of lords,
> the great, the mighty, and the terrible God, who is
> not partial and takes no bribe. He executes justice
> for the fatherless and the widow, and loves the so-
> journer, giving him food and clothing. Love the so-
> journer therefore; for you were sojourners in the land
> of Egypt. You shall fear the Lord your God; you shall
> serve him and cleave to him, and by his name you shall
> swear. He is your praise; he is your God, who has
> done for you these great and terrible things which
> your eyes have seen. Your fathers went down to Egypt
> seventy persons; and now the Lord your God has made
> you as the stars of heaven for multitude.

---

[101]At this point appeal could be made to the Third Command-
ment which forbade the taking of Yahweh's name in vain.

The same emphasis on praising Yahweh for his great name is discernible in Ps. 96:4-9 (I Chr. 16:25-30).

Again in I Kgs. 8:31-32 (Solomon's speech at the dedication of the Temple) the request is made that Yahweh hear oaths taken at the altar in the Temple at Zion. Similarly, Jer. 4:1-2 promises that if the people return to Yahweh and swear "As the Lord lives" in truth, justice and uprightness, then nations will bless themselves in him. The same emphasis occurs in 12:16 where the neighbors of Israel are rebuked for having taught Israel to swear by Baal, but are promised weal if they learn to swear by Yahweh's name, "As the Lord lives." But this emphasis is not only Deuteronomistic (and Jeremianic?); it also finds a promoter in Second and Third Isaiah (48:1, 65:16-17). The first allusion is implicit; in form it is an attack on false swearing by Yahweh's name. Isaiah 65:16-17 is important in that it combines this emphasis upon swearing by Yahweh's name with the idea of a new creation:

> So that he who blesses himself in the land
>   shall bless himself by the God of truth,
> and he who takes an oath in the land
>   shall swear by the God of truth;
> because the former troubles are forgotten
>   and are hid from my eyes.
> For behold, I create new heavens and a new earth....[102]

From these passages it becomes increasingly clear that the later prophets demanded that oaths be taken in the name of the Lord. Corresponding to this prophetic demand was the cultic attempt to educate the people to recognize Yahweh as Creator; examples of such an effort are preserved in Jer. 32; Dan. 9; Neh. 9; Ezr. 9; and Isa. 37.[103] An analysis of these passages will be valuable in providing background for the proposed historical reconstruction.

---

[102]The parallelism between blessing oneself and swearing must not be overlooked. This also appears in Jer. 4:1-2. Does this give an indication of the content and purpose of at least one kind of oath? This use of swearing to secure Yahweh's protection and blessing is confirmed by the frequent allusions to "As the Lord lives" in a context denouncing Israel for staying themselves on Jerusalem.

[103]A. Weiser, *The Psalms*, 43, writes that cultic prayers were marked by a desire to pass on the tradition.

3. *Cultic Prayers*

The four basic themes extracted from the contexts in which
the refrain "Yahweh of Hosts is his name" appears--judgment,
creation, idolatry and oaths--run like a scarlet thread through
cultic prayers. This does not seem accidental. Moreover, a
development can be traced in these prayers from simple allusion
to elaborate discussion of certain themes.

The emphasis on creation is of foremost importance. The
Deuteronomistic passage that has overtones of later cultic pray-
ers (Dt. 10:12-22) does not contain a reference to Yahweh as
Creator, although it is but a step from the claim that to the
Lord belong "heaven and the heaven of heavens, the earth with
all that is in it" to the explicit mention of Yahweh as Creator.
Likewise in Solomon's prayer at the dedication of the Temple (I
Kgs. 8:12-53) the Masoretic Text lacks any reference to Yahweh
as Creator, but the Septuagintal reading, "The Lord has set the
sun in the heavens," may be original. In any case, this is quite
different from the usual reference to Yahweh as he who made all
things. Such an assertion can be found in Neh. 9:6, "Thou art
the Lord, thou alone; thou hast made heaven, the heaven of heavens, with all their host, the earth and all that is on it, the
seas and all that is in them; and thou preservest all of them;
and the host of heaven worships thee."[104] Somewhat more elaborate

---

[104]The verdict of K. Galling in regard to Neh. 9 is repre-
sentative: "Das Gebet als solches zeigt keinen Bezug auf die Zeit
Nehemias...." (see Galling, *Die Bücher der Chronik, Esra, Nehemia*
[Göttingen: Vandenhoeck & Ruprecht, 1954], 240). However, it is
not agreed as to what period the prayer does reflect. A. C.
Welch, "The Source of Nehemiah IX," *ZAW*, XLVII (1929), 130-37,
thought of it as a litany written for the worship of Northern
Israel on a day of fasting, confession and prayer soon after 722
B.C. On the other hand, L. E. Browne, "Ezra and Nehemiah,"
Peake's Commentary on the Bible, 376, thinks that the mention of
Assyrians as oppressors suggests Samaritan authorship; Browne believes that the prayer was probably written in the fourth century
and used by the Chronicler. The Greek period is suggested as the
date of the prayer by L. W. Batten, *The Books of Ezra and Nehemiah* (Edinburgh: T. & T. Clark, 1913), 365. A late date is also
accepted by C. C. Torrey, *Ezra Studies* (Giessen: J. Ricker'sche
Buchhandlung, 1896), 246, who calls the psalm a "tissue of quotation" characteristic of the Chronicler's work elsewhere; by Rudolph, *Esra und Nehemia* (Tübingen: J.C.B. Mohr, 1949), 156-57,
who thinks the Chronicler used an available prayer; and by R. A.
Bowman, "The Book of Ezra and the Book of Nehemiah," *IB*, III, 746,
who thinks of it as an independent composition used by the Chronicler or a later editor (see also G. von Rad, "Das formgeschichtliche Problem des Hexateuchs," *Gesammelte Studien zum Alten Testament*, 19-20).

is this than the simple claim of Jer. 32:17, "Ah Lord God! It
is thou who hast made the heavens and the earth by thy great
power and by thy outstretched arm!" The simple statement also
appears in Isa. 37:16, where Hezekiah is said to have prayed:
"O Lord of hosts, God of Israel, who art enthroned above the
cherubim, thou art the God, thou alone, of all the kingdoms of
the earth; thou hast made heaven and earth."[105]

Judgment, a central theme in each of the passages mentioned
above, plays a prominent role in the prayers of Ezra 9:6-15 and
Dan. 9:3-19. The former refers to Yahweh's punishment of Israel
at the hands of enemies (9:7) and laments that "none can stand
before thee because of this" (9:15);[106] on the other hand, Dan.
9:11 connects the judgment therein mentioned with the curse and
oath written in the law of Moses, and identifies the nature of
the punishment in terms of the calamity of Jerusalem (9:12).[107]

---

[105]The secondary character of this prayer is evident; the
language recalls Second Isaiah and exilic psalms (see R.B.Y.
Scott, "The Book of Isaiah," *IB*, V, 1366).

[106]Compare Job 9:2-12. There seems to be no reason to reject the prayer of Ezra, in spite of C. C. Torrey and A. S. Kapelrud; Torrey, *op. cit.*, 270, note n; and Kapelrud, *The Question of Authorship in the Ezra-Narrative* (Oslo: I Kommisjon Hos
Jacob Dybwad, 1944), 70. The prayer is defended by Rudolph,
Esra und Nehemia, 90, who writes that "Dieses ist im Zusammenhang
unentbehrlich"; Batten, *op. cit.*, 336-37 (substantially genuine);
and Bowman, *op. cit.*, 647.

[107]There are indications that this prayer is an insertion:
(1) redactional touches in 3-4a, 20-21; (2) use of the tetra-
grammaton; (3) Palestinian orientation; (4) theme that does not
correspond to the context; (5) prayer for immediate deliverance
while future assistance is spoken of elsewhere; (6) extensive
borrowings from Neh. 1,9; I Kgs. 8; Jer. 32; Ezr. 9. However,
it is not clear whether the author of Daniel placed it here, as
A. Jeffery, "The Book of Daniel," *IB*, VI, 484, thinks probable,
or whether its presence is due to the work of a later redactor,
as A. Bentzen, *Daniel* (Tübingen: J.C.B. Mohr, 1951), 75, suggests. Perhaps the hesitancy to make a final decision on the
part of J. A. Montgomery, *The Book of Daniel* (Edinburgh: T. & T.
Clark, 1927), 361, is wise. The most exhaustive treatment of
the prayer is that of Edmund Bayer, "Danielstudien," *Alttestamentliche Abhandlungen*, III, 5 (1912), 1-188. Bayer viewed the
prayer as a work of art, the totality of strophes as well as
single strophes showing parallelism of antithesis and synthesis
(17-18). He observed further: "Wir sehen also, das ganze Gebet
ist nach Inhalt und Form ausgezeichnet abgerundet und geradezu
also Juwel der prophetischen Poesie zu bezeichnen" (21). Bayer
also recognized the close relationship between Dan. 9 and the
prayers preserved by the Chronicler (II Chr. 6; Neh. 1,9; Ezr.
9); after a careful analysis of the literary relationship of

The threat posed to Jerusalem is also the content of the judgment in Jer. 32:24 and Isa. 37:17-20.

The polemic against idolatry appears in I Kgs. 8:22; Ezr. 9:11 (implicitly); Neh. 9:6,19; Isa. 37:19; and Dan. 9:18. Moreover, this is mentioned in connection with curse and/or oath in Dt. 10:20; I Kgs. 8:31; Ezr. 10:5; Neh. 10:29; Dan. 9:11; and Jer. 32:22. The emphasis upon Yahweh's name and elements of the theophanic tradition must not be overlooked. These appear in Dt. 10:17-20; I Kgs. 8:29; Neh. 9:10-13,17-19; Jer. 32:18; and Dan. 9:15. In three of these passages Yahweh is said to have gotten a name at the Reed Sea (Neh. 9:10-11; Jer. 32:20; Dan. 9:15), hence the association of creation and "name" theology.[108] Very striking is the description of God in terms of Ex. 34:6-7, the theophany at Sinai. Equally noticeable is repeated emphasis upon Yahweh's justice despite his wrath (Ezr. 9:13,15; Neh. 9:33; Dan. 9:7,14)[109] and the appeal that Yahweh look with favor upon his people (I Kgs. 8:29; Jer. 32:19; Isa. 37:17; Dan. 9:17-18).[110] In view of the emphasis upon the name of Yahweh in the refrains treated earlier, the promise in I Kgs. 8:29 is most expressive: "My name shall be there" [in the Temple at Jerusalem]. The meaning of this promise becomes clear when compared with Ezekiel 48: 35, "And the name of the city [Jerusalem] henceforth shall be, 'The Lord is there'" (YHWH shāmmāh).

Several observations about these findings are in order. First, there is a recognizable development in the treatment of

---

these prayers (26-33), Bayer concluded that the author of Daniel used the prayers of the Chronicler (33-37). Moreover, the relationship of Dan. 9 and Bar. 1:15-3:8 came into consideration; the prayer in Baruch was said to have been borrowed from Dan. 9 (44). Finally, Bayer offered cogent defense of the genuineness of the prayer in Daniel (48-53), concluding that "Das Buch Daniel ist ein einheitliches Werk eines und desselben Verfassers" (109). Bayer's conclusion in regard to Bar. 1:15-3:8 was also reached by B. N. Wambacq, "Les prieres de Baruch (1,15-2,19) et de Daniel (9,5-19)," *Bib*, XL (1959), 463-75. Wambacq wrote: "Il s'agit d'un travail redactionnel: l'auteur a reuni plusieurs textes de l'Ecriture et les a ajoutes à la priere telle qu'elle se lisait dans le livre de Daniel" (469).

[108]Compare Gen. 11:4; Isa. 63:12,14; II Sam. 7:23.

[109]See Am. 5:8; 9:6; Jer. 7:20; 42:18; 44:6; II Chr. 12:7; 34:25.

[110]Compare Jer. 1:12; 31:28; 44:27,11; Am. 9:4.

Yahweh as Creator, older texts being less elaborate. Lack of
any reference to Yahweh as Creator in Dan. 9 may be explained
by the fact that by this late date the battle against those who
denied that the Lord created all things had been won; a similar
explanation for the absence of the phrase "thou alone" in Dan. 9
could be given. Ezra 9 poses a special problem, since it contains no reference to creation; however, this prayer seems authentic, which may explain the absence of the usual cultic emphasis on creation, this being a spontaneous prayer not shaped
by cultic models. Second, the emphasis on Yahweh as Creator
comes from passages that must be dated somewhere between 550 and
400 B.C. In the third place, the intimate association of this
emphasis with the "name" theology in connection with the theophany must be taken into consideration. Finally, Jerusalem's place
in this complex of ideas is significant.

This leads to the question of the life setting of the refrain, "Yahweh of Hosts is his name" and emphases connected with
it. The phrase "Yahweh of Hosts is his name" is an ancient hymnic liturgical formula from the time of the ark at Shiloh.[111]
However, since the ark was moved to Jerusalem by David and sub-
sequently placed in the Solomonic temple, the city of Zion came
to play an important role in the contexts using the refrain.
This forces one to conclude that the life setting of the refrain
as it appears in the Old Testament is not that of its origin but
of its resurgence in Israelite thought in connection with Jerusalem. Moreover, the refrain appears to have been used after
the destruction of the temple in 587 B.C., becoming in a sense
a confession of faith in the God who sits enthroned on the cherubim in the temple at Jerusalem, despite the fact that this God
appears to be impotent.[112] Finally, the central position given

---

[111]In his analysis of the special names of God in Jeremiah
and Ezekiel ("Yahweh of Hosts" and "The Lord God" respectively),
F. Baumgärtel, *op. cit.*, 13, reached this same conclusion.

[112]Baumgärtel, *op. cit.*, 27-29, makes a similar point in
regard to Ezekiel's use of "the Lord God," which Baumgärtel considers an ancient cultic name like "Yahweh of Hosts," but which
is more appropriate after 587 B.C. For a discussion of the
emergence of Zion as an eschatological symbol, see Norman Porteous, "Jerusalem-Zion: The Growth of a Symbol," *Verbannung und
Heimkehr*, 235-52. Porteous writes that Ps. 132 calls Jerusalem
the city of Yahweh's choice, so that after 587 B.C. it could
only be concluded that Yahweh had been proved impotent or that
he had changed his mind (237).

Zion in the phrase would seem to indicate a feeling of those away from Jerusalem,[113] whose longing to return to the city of God's choice is expressed in their phraseology. If this is granted, the exilic period provides the setting for the refrain.

It must not be overlooked that the emphasis upon Yahweh's name is an early phenomenon, perhaps going back to a theophany in connection with the New Year Festival of epiphany and covenant renewal.[114] Artur Weiser has pointed out that the proclamation of God's name is an integral part of theophany (II Sam. 7: 5ff.; Ex. 20:24; 3:14; 6:2; 24:3ff.; 33:19; 34:5f.; Hos. 12:9; 13:4), along with a recapitulation of sacred history (Josh. 24: 2ff.; I Sam. 12:8ff.; Jdg. 5:11) and the proclamation of God's will in the form of the Decalogue.[115] Weiser has also indicated that the prophetic emphasis on judgment grew out of the idea of theophany[116] and that an attack on idolatry occupied a special position in the theophanic tradition.[117] Weiser also suggested that kingship and creation are secondary phases of the tradition.[118] If the last point is correct, no revision of the conclusion above is necessary; and if there really were such a ceremony, the original life setting of the phrase would be clarified.

Does the presence of an attack on idolatry within the contexts in which the refrain appears also point to the exile? An affirmative answer can be given, although the period of religious syncretism under Jehoiakim indicates such a problem in Jeremiah's time (44:17-18,26-27). Indeed, idolatry was a primary concern even from the earliest period (Josh. 24).[119] Nevertheless, the

---

[113]Compare Isa. 46:13; 48:2; 51:16; Jer. 31:35ff.; 50:5,28.

[114]Weiser, *The Psalms*, 29-43; S. Mowinckel, "The Name of the God of Moses," 126.

[115]Weiser, *ibid.*, 31-34. Mowinckel, *ibid.*, 126, also connects the Decalogue with this covenant renewal ceremony.

[116]*Ibid.*, 46; he points to Am. 1:2 and 9:1ff. and remarks that "Yahweh the God of hosts" reflects the idea of a celestial court of heavenly hosts which belong to the sphere of theophany.

[117]*Ibid.*, 51.

[118]*Ibid.*, 34.

[119]See Eduard Nielsen, "The Burial of the Foreign Gods," *StTh*, VIII (1955), 103-22; and Walter Harrelson, "Worship in Early Israel," *BR*, III (1958), 10.

association of idolatry with oaths and creation (Jer. 12:14-17; 10:3-5,11,14-15; 32:35; Isa. 48:5) and the intensification of the idolatry problem most probably should be understood as an exilic or early post-exilic phenomenon. The presence of caustic attacks on idolatry in Second Isaiah and in additions to Jeremiah points to such a conclusion.

One other factor must be mentioned: the emphasis upon creation in connection with the refrain, idolatry and oaths. Once again the exilic or post-exilic situation is indicated. This is seen most clearly in the oath formula. The earliest occurrence simply mentions Yahweh as God of Israel (Gen. 31:53; Josh. 9:19-20), but there can be discerned a growing tendency to swear by and pray to Yahweh who delivered Israel from Egypt (Jer. 16:14-18; 23:7-8), and finally, by Yahweh who created heaven and earth (Jer. 38:16, "who made our souls"; 32:22; Isa. 54:9; 65:16-17). This means that all three considerations (the life setting of the refrain, the polemic against idolatry in the context of oath-taking, and the emphasis upon creation) point to the exile when idolatry was a basic issue, Zion an emerging eschatological symbol, creation a working soteriological concept, and an ancient refrain a confession of faith in Yahweh the God of Hosts.

What is the place of the doxologies of Amos in this context? The four emphases discovered in contexts surrounding the refrain find striking use here. This can be seen most clearly in the combination of creation and judgment, as well as in the elements making up the description of the latter. All three themes discussed above occur in direct connection with (or within) the doxologies. First, use of the metaphor of the "waters of judgment" is discernible in Am. 5:8b and 9:6b. Second, the basis for judgment is given in 9:4, which appears in the strikingly similar form of "I will set my eyes upon them for evil and not for good." Third, 4:6-11 and 5:6 recall the appeal to return to Yahweh, although in the former the complaint appears several times, "Yet you did not return to me." Moreover, judgment is the theme of 5:9.

The emphasis upon creation gives indications of being subsequent to Second Isaiah, for there is a linking of creation, revelation and judgment. This can be seen in 4:13, the first part of which refers to the creation of mountains and wind and to the giving of oracles to the human spokesman of God, while the second part of the verse refers to Yahweh's appearance in victory, implying judgment upon enemies and sinners within the people of God. This same combination of creation and judgment appears in 5:8-9 and 9:5-6. Moreover, the ancient theophanic tradition can be discerned in 4:12b ("Prepare to meet your God"), 4:13b ("who treads upon the heights of the earth"), and 9:5 ("he who touches the earth and it melts, and all who dwell in it mourn"), as well as in the refrains of 4:13; 5:8; and 9:6. However, as has been suggested above, this should be understood as an archaizing tendency within exilic or post-exilic Israel.

The connection with idolatry and oaths is less clear, although there are several things indicating such an association. It has been suggested above that 4:12a should be viewed as a curse in connection with an oath. There can be little question that such an interpretation of kōh provides the best explanation for the vagueness of the threat in 4:12. In addition, it has been shown that 9:5a contains an oath particle with the divine festal name. Moreover, it has also been pointed out that 5:5a may contain an allusion to worship of the god Bethel; if this is true, the association of the doxologies with polemic against idolatry can also be made.[120] One further point can be given in defense of this connection of doxology and oath. It has long been recognized that 8:8 and 9:5 are closely related in thought. Now it may be noted that 8:7 contains an oath by Yahweh, and 8:8 relates Israel's response to that threat. Thus it can be argued that the oath was in mind when someone placed the doxologies into the book of Amos. Whether one can go further and conclude that 9:5 once stood at 8:8 is difficult to say, but in view of the nature of 8:9-9:4, this is possible.[121] On the other hand, 8:14 may have stood next to the doxology in 9:5-6, for there is good reason to think 9:1-4 does not belong in its present place. However, there is no need to make such claims, since 8:14 is closely connected with the doxology as it now stands. Here the association of oath and idolatry is particularly vivid: "Those who swear by Ashimah of Samaria, and say, 'As thy god lives,

---

[120]O. Eissfeldt, "Der Gott Bethel," 17, made this association for Am. 5:8-9 and Hos. 12:5.

[121]Weiser, "Die Prophetie des Amos," 202-03, reached this conclusion on other grounds (see above, page 25).

O Dan,' and 'As the way of Beer-sheba lives,' they shall fall, and never rise again." Finally, the association of doxology and idolatry may find additional support in 5:26-27 or 3:14b, if one chooses to view either as the threat originally mentioned in 4:12 ("*Thus* will I do to you, O Israel"). However, the close association of doxology and idolatry does not depend upon this suggestion.[122]

In view of these considerations, it appears that the doxologies of Amos belong to the life setting described above--the exilic or early post-exilic period--and must be viewed as confessions of faith in the God who created all things, who demands complete allegiance, and who appears to judge his people. They express the profound belief that Yahweh, far from being impotent now that the temple lies partly in ruins, is both Creator and Judge of all mankind; furthermore, the doxologies indicate that even a judged people can be grateful to its God. Therefore, these doxologies in Amos are in the fullest sense of the term "Doxologies of Judgment." Finally, the doxologies are to be understood in close connection with the prayers of the post-exilic period which serve the same function in the worship of the people.[123]

---

[122]One notices that the second doxology does not present as clear-cut a case of relationship with the four emphases as do the other two, although it does have enough to convince one of the validity of the comparison even without resort to Horst's view that 5:8 originally stood with 4:13. It would appear that the catch-word principle was more influential in bringing about the insertion of 5:8-9 than was the complex of forces discerned above for the other uses of the refrain, "Yahweh of Hosts is his name." That is, unless Bethel in 5:4 has reference to a deity!

[123]Kraus, *op. cit.*, 265, points to the important role of prayers in the exilic community.

CHAPTER IV

EXPOSITION OF THE DOXOLOGIES IN THEIR CONTEXTS

A. *Amos 4:13*

The first doxology of Amos is preceded by a series of divine chastisements marked off as a unit both by form and content. Formally, the refrain: "Yet you did not return to me, says the Lord," may indicate that "the prophets sometimes composed oracles in series of strophes."[1] A comparison with Isa. 5:25; 9:12,17,21; 10:4 is instructive both in form and content. The presence of the oracular formula ("says the Lord") dividing the larger unit into five strophes in no way nullifies the argument that the series of chastisements belong together, as can be seen from a similar phenomenon in Am. 1:3ff.[2] To the formal connection by means of a refrain corresponds one of thought sequence.[3]

It may be asked whether the thought sequence does not extend to 4:4-5 as Sellin has maintained.[4] On the face of it, these verses seem to deal with a different subject matter--the sanctuaries at Bethel and Gilgal and the misdirected zeal on the part of the worshipers at these holy places. However, the presence of $w^e gam$ '$^a n\hat{\imath}$ in 4:6 calls into question this conclusion, since its implied contrast appears to be $kh\bar{e}n$ '$^a habhtem$ of 4:5.[5] Furthermore, the recognition that 4:12b probably contained a reference

_____

[1]Hyatt, "Amos," 621. On the other hand, Th. Robinson, *op. cit.*, 87, thinks that a redactor put this passage together, as he may also have done in 1:3-2:5. Robinson is not convincing at this point. Weiser, *Das Buch der zwölf Kleinen Propheten*, 154, writes that "auf diesem Kehrvers liegt das Hauptgewicht der prophetischen Kritik." Cripps, *op. cit.*, 172, compares the refrain to Isa. 9:13; Jer. 15:19; and Hos. 7:10.

[2]Maag, *Text, Wortschatz und Begriffswelt des Buches Amos*, 23.

[3]Weiser, *Das Buch der zwölf Kleinen Propheten*, 154.

[4]Sellin, *op. cit.*, 221.

[5]*Ibid.*; Cripps, *op. cit.*, 171; Marti, *op. cit.*, 180. Nowack, *op. cit.*, 138, while recognizing this contrast, attributes $w^e gam$ '$^a n\hat{\imath}$ to a redactor. Likewise Guthe, *op. cit.*, 37, thinks of this phrase as the addition of a redactor who wrongly thought of the divine chastisements as future.

115

to the destruction of sanctuaries[6] implies that the strophe thus
returns to its point of departure--the sanctuaries.[7] On the
other hand, the connecting of these verses may be the work of a
collector, so the question must be left open.

The irony of Amos' invitation to the people is clearly seen
in the phrase, "For so you love to do, O people of Israel," as
well as implicitly in the admonition to *proclaim* their freewill
offerings (4:5). Although the text is somewhat obscure, Amos
apparently urges the people to bring their sacrifices in the
morning and their tithes on the third day of the feast.[8] According to the Deuteronomic law (Dt. 14:22-29), tithes were to be
paid every year, and on the third year given over to the Levites,
sojourners, widows and fatherless. Leaven was not supposed to
be mixed with sacrifices (Lev. 2:11; 6:17; Ex. 23:18), but it is
not certain that these laws were in existence at this time. By
no means is one to assume that Amos was castigating the Israelites for an offense against accepted ritual procedure.[9] Rather,
this is an attack on a people for whom religion is defined as
cult, moral demands being completely ignored. As alternatives,
Amos poses Yahweh or the sanctuaries, for in his sight the two
have become mutually exclusive.

The series of divine chastisements emphasizes Israel's obstinacy and dullness in face of instruction.[10] These punishments
are to be placed in the past, as the refrain indicates, but must
not be denied to Amos simply because they do not fit into the
prosperous era of Jeroboam II,[11] for Amos does not otherwise
limit himself to recent history (2:12; 5:25f.). Nor are the

---

[6]See below.

[7]Sellin, *op. cit.*, 221-22.

[8]Hyatt, "Amos," 621; Wellhausen, *Die Kleinen Propheten*,
79.

[9]Hyatt, "Amos," 621.

[10]Maag's argument that, since Amos usually emphasizes pride
and unrighteousness, not obstinacy and dullness to instruction,
this unit may not come from the prophet, is unconvincing (see
Maag, *Text, Wortschatz und Begriffswelt des Buches Amos*, 24).

[11]Sellin, *op. cit.*, 220-21, rightly perceives this, refusing also to use the analogy with Isa. 9:7ff. or the vagueness
of the language to support such a view.

plagues to be viewed as chronological, for the sequence is dra-
matic, beginning with the mildest and concluding with the harsh-
est.[12]

Seven chastisements are recalled: famine, drought, blight
and mildew, locust, pestilence, battle, and earthquake.[13] Each
failed to bring Israel to repentance (the real meaning of *shûbh*),
so a final judgment is threatened. The phrase for famine is
particularly striking, cleanness of teeth implying that nothing
passed between them. This is a real famine in contrast to that
of 8:11-12, which from the theological perspective is even more
horrible. Despite the hunger pangs, Israel did not return
c̄adhai ("all the way to me").[14] Drought, which chronologically
precedes famine, is treated at length; hence many commentators
think of 7b as a gloss.[15] However, the phrase "when there were
yet three months to the harvest" belongs to the original oracle,
for it adds particular force to the statement--the drought oc-
curred when rain was most needed to insure a bountiful harvest.[16]
Verse eight indicates that the drought was not only disastrous
to the farmer but also to the city dweller, whose deepest cis-
terns were dry.[17] The change in tense to the imperfect should
be noted, for the emphasis is upon repeated action.[18]

---

[12]*Ibid.*, 221.

[13]Some interpreters consider locusts and battle as glosses,
thus only five chastisements are viewed as authentic (see S. R.
Driver, *op. cit.*, 171).

[14]Fosbroke, *op. cit.*, 806; Sellin, *op. cit.*, 223.

[15]Marti's reconstruction, accepted by Fosbroke and Weiser,
is as follows: "And I also withheld the rain from you, so two or
three cities wandered to one city to drink water and were not
satisfied; yet you...me" (see Marti, *op. cit.*, 182; Fosbroke,
op. cit., 807; Weiser, *Das Buch der zwölf Kleinen Propheten*,
153).

[16]Sellin, *op. cit.*, 223.

[17]*Ibid.* Marti, *op. cit.*, 182, calls attention to Amos'
use of numerical climax in 1:3 also. Samuel Terrien, "Amos and
Wisdom," *Israel's Prophetic Heritage*, 109, points out that Amos'
use of consecutive numerals in pairs is a device typical of the
wisdom style.

[18]Hyatt, "Amos," 621. But Cripps, *op. cit.*, 172, prefers
to see the imperfect as descriptive of the process of development.

The third and fourth chastisements were directed against
Israel's means of sustenance. The blight and mildew laid waste
her gardens and vineyards, while the locust devoured her fig and
olive trees (cf. Hag. 2:17). The terrible devastation brought
about by locusts can be discerned from Joel's use of eschatological imagery drawn from an invasion by a swarm of locusts. The
fifth plague, pestilence, is said to be "$b^e dherek\ mi\d{s}r\bar{a}y\hat{\imath}m$," the
b^e probably having taken the place of k^e, which in this context
means "like."[19] The allusion is not to the slaughter of the
firstborn but to a "thorough-going Egyptian" plague.[20] The next
punishment took the form of war, in which young men were slain,
horses taken away, and camps burned.[21]

The last punishment was an "overthrow" as when God overthrew
Sodom and Gomorrah, most probably by means of an earthquake. Israel is described as a "brand plucked out of the burning."[22] The
absolute use of $'^{ae}l\bar{o}h\hat{\imath}m$ is unique in Amos and may indicate that
he knew another form of the tradition (than that of Gen. 19),
according to which an earthquake was sent by $'^{ae}l\bar{o}h\hat{\imath}m$ upon the
cities.[23] For Amos, the earthquake is the apex of divine chastisement (1:1; 2:13ff.; 3:15; 9:1).

---

[19]Hyatt, "Amos," 621. Maag, *Text, Wortschatz und Begriffswelt des Buches Amos*, 21, emends the word to read "like," and
Sellin, *op. cit.*, 223, prefers $k^e derek$ as in Dt. 7:15 and 28:60.
There is no reason to view this as a gloss (against Marti, *op.
cit.*, 183; Nowack, *op. cit.*, 139; Guthe, *op. cit.*, 37), nor to
assume with Th. Robinson, *op. cit.*, 87, that this may refer to
a plague within the Israelite army at Sinai.

[20]Cripps, *op. cit.*, 174.

[21]$\d{s}^e bhi$ may be preferable to $sh^e bhi$, and $b\bar{a}'\bar{e}sh$ to $b\bar{o}sh$.
Fosbroke, *op. cit.*, 807, thinks of the reference to horses as
an addition. Marti, *op. cit.*, 183-84, considers the mention of
battle a gloss; on the other hand, Wellhausen, *Die Kleinen Propheten*, 80, writes that Amos has in mind the year-long Syrian
skirmish. Wellhausen also calls attention to the peculiar use
of $^c im$, which is said to be more Aramaic than Hebraic.

[22]Marti, *op. cit.*, 184, thinks that this refers to the
time of Jehoahaz (II Kgs. 13:7) when Israel was as a brand
plucked out of the burning, and denies that an earthquake is
meant. Fosbroke, *op. cit.*, 808, follows Marti.

[23]Maag, *Text, Wortschatz und Begriffswelt des Buches Amos*,
23-24, recognizes this problem, admitting that the use of
$'^{ae}l\bar{o}him$ could indicate that it does not come from Amos. However, Maag suggests that Amos may not have identified $'\bar{e}l\bar{o}him$

But all seven chastisements failed in their purpose. Yahweh thus has one final punishment to inflict upon the sinful
people. The threat is not specified; for this reason many think
that the original conclusion has been removed.[24] On the other
hand, the vagueness of the threat adds to its terror; this is
confirmed by the fact that an oath formula is employed, which by
its very nature is unspecified.[25] In view of this imminent
threat, Amos calls upon Israel to get ready to meet her God in
judgment.[26] The reversal of the purpose of the theophany is
striking, and finds echo also in 5:17; 7:8; 8:2; 9:1.[27]

---

who destroyed Sodom and Gomorrah with Yahweh. Sellin's observa-
tion that $^{\,ae}l\bar{o}h\hat{i}m$ is frequently used with Sodom and Gomorrah (Isa.
13:19; Jer. 50:40), so that it amounts to a fixed formula, is much
more to the point (Sellin, *op. cit.*, 224). On the other hand,
Marti, *op. cit.*, 184, and Nowack, *op. cit.*, 139, consider $^{ae}l\bar{o}h\hat{i}m$
a gloss, and Guthe, *op. cit.*, 37, thinks of Sodom and Gomorrah as
an addition. Wellhausen, *Die Kleinen Propheten*, 80, calls attention to the unusual use of "overthrow" and $^{ae}l\bar{o}h\hat{i}m$, which suggests that the material derives from an ancient non-Hebraic legend
(as also is the case with the basic form of Gen. 18-19).

[24]See above. Marti, *op. cit.*, 180, 185; Th. Robinson, *op.
cit.*, 87; Nowack, *op. cit.*, 140, who thinks the content can be
discerned from parallels in 2:13ff. and 3:11ff.; Harper, *op. cit.*,
102; Wellhausen, *Die Kleinen Propheten*, 80; K. J. Grimm, *Euphemistic Liturgical Appendixes in the Old Testament* (Leipzig: August
Pries, 1901), 77-78. Grimm thinks the aversion to completing a
passage of reading in the synagogue on a note of curse or evil import led to euphemistic additions to the text of the Old Testament,
especially in Psalms and the prophetic literature (1-2,8-22 for
Psalms, 22-96 for prophetic books). On the other hand, Sellin,
op. cit., 224-25, argues that one should read, "Because you did
this to me," i.e., failed to repent, and insert 3:14b as the
threat. E. Baumann, "Der Aufbau der Amos Reden," *BZAW*, VII
(1903), 15, thinks 5:21-27 is the conclusion of 4:12a.

[25]See above. Cripps, *op. cit.*, 175, and Harper, *op. cit.*,
103, call attention to this use of $k\bar{o}h$.

[26]Marti, *op. cit.*, 185, writes that 4:12b-13 has in mind the
last judgment, in which all nations participate, and that it calls
Israel to prepare for this meeting as she did at Sinai (Ex. 19:
15). He finds in the use of "your God" proof of the lateness of
this half-verse. On the other hand, Sellin, *op. cit.*, 224, thinks
the god to be met is that of Bethel, the bull image of 2:8 and 5:
26, and both worshiper and deity will be destroyed by Yahweh. In
rabbinic literature this verse was used to justify attention to
bodily functions, posture and clothing before prayer. See H. J.
Routtenberg, *Rabbinic Interpretations of Amos*, unpublished Ph.D.
Diss., Boston University, 1943, 97-98.

[27]Weiser, *Das Buch der zwölf Kleinen Propheten*, 156, writes:
"Die Begegnung mit dem Gott der Katastrophen ist radikal anders.
Als Gegner steht Gott jetzt dem Volk gegenüber, das achtlos an
ihm vorüberging."

It is tempting to surmise that Amos is here alluding to cultic emphasis upon a theophany for judgment against the enemies of Israel, perhaps on the occasion of the covenant renewal ceremony. At this point Watts has made a significant contribution to the understanding of Amos' message, even if one cannot accept that author's view of Amos' role in the cult. It is difficult to imagine Amos functioning in the cult and conforming to ritual necessity in the sense suggested by Watts.[28] Much nearer the truth is Morgenstern's view that Amos preaches within the sanctuary at a special festival, but that his message is radically different from that expected at the New Year's Festival.[29] The speech itself may have been patterned after the cultic procedure of reciting the saving deeds of Yahweh (Jdg. 5:11; Mic. 6:5), the reverse being recounted.[30]

This series of chastisements depicts Yahweh as Lord of nature; yet he is a loving God who uses natural calamities to lead his people to repentance. His patience has a limit, after which point Israel can expect to confront her God in all his awesomeness. The idea that Yahweh was Lord of nature is not new with Amos, nor is the recognition that calamity comes from Yahweh's hand (Am. 3:6); but it was felt that ritual zeal could speedily remove the effects of divine wrath (I Sam. 12:15; II Sam. 12:16ff.).[31] Amos puts an end to this illusion in no uncertain terms.

The threat of a final confrontation with God is followed by a doxology that combines creation faith and saving faith in wondrous fashion. In form and content the doxology differs from the rest of the book, excepting the other two doxologies. By means of several vivid images, Yahweh is described as Creator, Revealer and Judge.

References to creation deserve primary consideration. Yahweh is said to have formed the mountains and created the wind. The Septuagint has βροντήν, the equivalent of $h\bar{a}ra^{\mathbf{c}}am$ (thunder), which to many seems a better reading alongside the reference to

---

[28] Watts, *Vision and Prophecy in Amos*, 66.

[29] Morgenstern, *Amos Studies*, 36, 172-74.

[30] Weiser, *Das Buch der zwölf Kleinen Propheten*, 154.

[31] *Ibid.*

wind.[32] This interpretation understands the imagery in terms of Canaanite ideas about the storm god, Yahweh here being described as Creator of storm clouds and accompanying violent winds.

Another possibility is to attribute eschatological dimensions to the imagery, emphasis being placed on the mountain of God to be created in the future on Zion (Mic. 4:1-4; Isa. 2:2-4). Such an understanding of the symbolism would do justice to the later place of creation in eschatology, but several problems are raised. The two basic objections to such a view are use of the plural "mountains" and the presence of reference to the "wind," which seems to mean storm-wind. On the other hand, $r\hat{u}^a\dot{h}$ can be translated spirit, although an absolute use would be unique (cf. Zech. 12:1); and the motif of judgment in the doxology finds its closest parallel in the passage from Micah. One could argue that the doxology is an early form of the eschatological hope that finds a more elaborate statement in Mic. 4:1-4 and Isa. 2:2-4. Such an argument might be strengthened by the fact that the doxology mentions the revealing function of Yahweh, which finds its parallel in eschatological passages. Here the nations say: "Come, let us go up to the mountain of the Lord, to the house of the God of Jacob, that he may teach us his ways and we may walk in his paths."[33]

In spite of the attractiveness of this interpretation, it seems more advisable to pursue another path. It has been suggested above that the $r\hat{i}b$ provides the background for a correct understanding of the doxologies. This observation takes on particular force when one notices how much the first doxology recalls motifs found in the genuine lawsuits of prophetic literature (Hos. 12:2-6; 4:1-6; Mic. 1:2-6; 6:1-8; Isa. 1:2ff.). Furthermore, the threat in Am. 4:12b points to the correctness of such an interpretation.

In the prophetic lawsuit the mountains are called upon to hear the controversy of the Lord (Mic. 6:1-2), and Yahweh is described as he who treads upon the heights of the earth in victory (Mic. 1:3; cf. Dt. 32:13). But there is in the doxology a significant change from the normal emphasis of the lawsuit as

---

[32]Nowack, *op. cit.*, 141; and S. R. Driver, *op. cit.*, 177.

[33]See G. von Rad, "Die Stadt auf dem Berge," *Gesammelte Studien zum Alten Testament*, 214-24.

to the role played by the mountains. The idea of the spirit of the mountain which originally belonged to the concept of the lawsuit has completely given way to the affirmation that Yahweh is Lord of the mountains since he created them. But the polytheistic context is not completely removed, for the doxologies are placed within the text of Amos in connection with attacks on idolatrous worship at the sanctuaries of Bethel and Gilgal (cf. Hos. 12:5). Not only is there a change in the role played by the mountains, but there is also a transformed introductory formula. "Prepare to meet your God" has taken the place of the formula, "The Lord has a controversy with his people, Israel."

Once the lawsuit is accepted as the background of the doxology, the reference to Yahweh as the one who "declares to man what is his thought" takes on new meaning. In the prophetic lawsuit there must naturally be a verdict; such a decision on God's part may well stand behind this allusion.[34] Moreover, "he who darkens the morning" can be understood in terms of Jdg. 5:4-5, which conveys the idea that the judge employs natural elements in meting out punishment upon the guilty.[35]

Can the doxology thus understood be attributed to Amos? It is possible to argue that the difference between the doxology and lawsuit implies that the doxology is an early form rather than an adaptation to later emphases. And there is nothing within the doxology that Amos could not have taught. Finally, the doxology gives a magnificent description of the God to be confronted, and justifies the threat.

Nevertheless, it is more likely that the doxology comes from a much later time, so the following hypothesis seems justified. On the basis of the analysis in chapter three of the

---

[34]On the other hand, this phrase may provide the basis for the verdict, namely that God sees and knows every thought of man and declares it in the hour of judgment. S. R. Driver, *op. cit.*, 177, understands the reference in terms of man's thoughts. Similarly, in rabbinic literature this phrase was understood to imply that on the day of judgment Yahweh would remind a man of all superfluous conversation, even that during intercourse with his wife (see Routtenberg, *op. cit.*, 103-05).

[35]For a discussion of the meaning of *shaḥar*, see L. Köhler, "Die Morgenröte im Alten Testament," *ZAW*, NF III (1926), 56-59. Köhler examines the twenty-three uses of *shaḥar* in the Old Testament, seeking illumination from the versions, and concludes that *Morgenröte* is preferable as a translation to *Morgengrauen* (59).

refrain, "Yahweh of Hosts is his name," one may suggest that the same phenomenon detected there was at work in the text of Amos. The emphases on idolatry, oath, creation and judgment are unmistakable; and combination of these motifs is not accidental. Thus it is necessary to conclude that the text of Amos has been adapted to meet the needs of the worshiping community, just as was also the case in Jeremiah and Hosea.

In view of the analysis of passages where the refrain "Yahweh of Hosts is his name" was used, it was possible to make certain observations about the form and function of the material under consideration. However, the major emphasis was placed upon form; this must now give way to a discussion of function. The doxology is not only description; on the contrary, it also contains affirmation (and implicitly denial). The affirmatory character of the refrain in the doxology provides a clue to its function. In the liturgical formula, "The Lord, the God of Hosts, is his name," there is an implicit attack on other gods. The significance of such an attack cannot be over-emphasized for Israel after 587 B.C., because her God had apparently been proved impotent.

Against such a view the doxology is directed. This can be seen in the fact that it immediately follows passages claiming that Yahweh sent calamity upon Israel and even threatened extinction. Thus the doxology asserts that Yahweh, far from being impotent, is Creator of both the foundations of the earth and powerful wind, and is actually responsible for Judah's downfall. Moreover, it claims that this same Lord reveals his will to man, so resorting to astrology is useless. Finally, the doxology describes Yahweh as the Judge of mankind ("to judge" being thought of here as executing justice).

This leads to the following observation: the doxology is a confession of God's justice in spite of the bitter facts of history. It has been added to the text of Amos by those who at a later time affirmed the fundamental truth of his message and were convinced that even a fallen nation could still utter a doxology of judgment. In form, the doxology was patterned after the prophetic lawsuit, both because of the situation of judgment reflected, and perhaps because the lawsuit had given way to special penitential prayers, the doxology being an earlier form than those preserved in the Old Testament. If this is true, the fundamental insight of Friedrich Horst that the doxologies find their life setting in the sacred legal context of the post-exilic community is substantially correct for this one.

B. *Amos 5:8-9*

Unlike the first, the second doxology interrupts its context. Verses 4-6, 14-15 must be taken together, but it is difficult to discern the precise relationship of the intervening material.[36] It has been argued above that verse 7 belongs to 6, not 10 as is generally thought, and that 10-12 is a genuine word of Amos set off on each side by spurious material. Verses 16-17 probably were the original conclusion to 12, but this is not certain. In this block of material the prophet is depicted as having urged the people to seek Yahweh rather than the sanctuaries (or gods of these sanctuaries) and having held up before them the possibility of escape from the catastrophe facing the nation. Specific sins are mentioned, and a doxology in praise of the Creator and Judge is included.

The most recognizable division is 5:4-6 (7?), 14-15. Here the word of life is placed next to the dirge over the fallen Virgin Israel. "Seek Yahweh" is a fixed liturgical phrase connected with pilgrimages and possibly with the question of the priests, "Where is Yahweh?" (Jer. 2:8).[37] Amos places two types of religion side by side, sanctuary religion and obedience to Yahweh's demands; in the succeeding verses he clarifies what the

---

[36]Marti, *op. cit.*, 187, recognized the close relationship of 14-15 to 4-6. Against this Sellin, *op. cit.*, 227, has argued that 14-15 contains a different mood, one of hope and appeal, rather than grim resignation and irony. Marti thought that a copyist, confused by three verses beginning with *dārash*, omitted 14-15, but upon seeing his error, put the two verses in their present position.

[37]Weiser, *Das Buch der zwölf Kleinen Propheten*, 159. Fosbroke, *op. cit.*, 810-11, contends that *dir^{e}shû* has a dual meaning here: (1) the old idea of seeking answers from prophets, priests and seers (Ex. 18:15; I Sam. 9:9; II Kgs. 3:11), and (2) turning one's desire Godward (Dt. 4:29). To this passage should be compared Hos. 4:15; 5:6; 6:1-3; 10:12; 13:2-4. In Makkoth 24b Rabbi Simlai is said to have remarked: "The 613 commandments that were given to Moses were reduced by David to eleven (Ps. 15); Isaiah reduced them to six (33:15); Micah reduced them to three (6:8); Isaiah further reduced them to two (56:1); finally, Amos came and reduced them all to one, as it is said, 'For thus saith the Lord unto the house of Israel: Seek ye me, and live'" (see Routtenberg, *op. cit.*, 48).

latter entails, but no such illumination is thrown on the nature of the former.

As a matter of fact, there is good reason to believe that Bethel in verse 5 is a deity, so the attack is leveled against idolatry. This is certainly the most natural interpretation in view of the parallelism in the verse, and presents no particular historical problem in view of explicit proof in Jer. 48:13 that Israel revered a deity named Bethel. However, if one assumes that Bethel of 5:5a is a divine name, it may be necessary to consider 5:5bc later additions; but this is not mandatory. Actually, many interpreters think of these as glosses, even while considering Bethel a sanctuary.[38] The holy places of Bethel and Beersheba[39] could boast of patriarchal sanction (Gen. 12:8; 28: 10-22; 26:23-25; 21:33; 35:2), while Gilgal was able to appeal to the patronage of Joshua (Josh. 5:13-15). Nevertheless, Amos goes against hoary tradition and denies that Yahweh can be found in these sanctuaries. Then where could the God of Israel be sought and found? It might be thought that Amos intended to imply that Jerusalem was the locus of genuine worship (1:2), but such a conclusion is not likely.[40] If not to Jerusalem, where did Amos expect the people to go? Perhaps the question is asked wrongly.

In popular opinion Yahweh could only be sought at the sanctuaries, so Amos' message came as a total paradox to them.[41]

---

[38]Th. Robinson, *op. cit.*, 88; Marti, *op. cit.*, 189; Fosbroke, *op. cit.*, 811. But Maag, *Text, Wortschatz und Begriffswelt des Buches Amos*, 29, defends the authenticity of the entire verse on the basis of a distinction between Yahweh's word and Amos' exposition of it. According to these parts of the verse, Yahweh threatens both Gilgal and Bethel with punishment. There is a word play on both words. Wellhausen, *Die Kleinen Propheten*, 5, puts it vividly: "Denn Gilgal wird Galgen gehn und Bethel wird des Teufels werden."

[39]Pilgrimages to Beersheba are mentioned in Am. 7:9; 8:14; I Kgs. 19:3; Hos. 4:15. Terrien, *op. cit.*, 113-14, thinks the fact that only Amos among the prophets spoke of Beersheba (5:5; 8:14) may indicate the source of wisdom influence upon his message--the semi-nomads in the south and southeast of the Dead Sea. This argument is not convincing at all.

[40]Th. Robinson, *op. cit.*, 89.

[41]Weiser, *Das Buch der zwölf Kleinen Propheten*, 159-60, writes that the cleft between prophet and people must be located in these two attitudes to the holy places and their function.

Between the prophet and his hearers there was a fundamental difference: according to the people the purpose of the cult was to
insure their welfare, but Amos recognized that the promotion of
divine purpose was the only legitimate aim of the cult.[42] If
this is the correct approach to the passage, one must conclude
that Amos rejected the cult in favor of the ancient amphictyonic
tradition as represented by the laws of God.

On the other hand, if emphasis is placed upon Bethel as a
deity, then one may legitimately suggest that idolatrous worship
is the sin of the sanctuaries. Such an interpretation certainly
finds confirmation in 8:14 and 5:26.[43] There is no need to assume that these cults were anti-Yahwistic in practice; on the
contrary, Yahweh was probably worshiped at the sanctuaries, although the heart of the cult was Canaanitic.[44]

In explanation of the divine word of 5:4-5, Amos adds his
own words (5:6-7,14-15). Verse six is not to be viewed as secondary exegesis of 5:5, but (together with 14-15) it gives an
indication of deep concern for the people felt by the prophet.[45]

---

[42]*Ibid.*, 160. Weiser sums up the people's belief in a word:
"Sicherung des 'Heils' [ist] letztes Motiv und Ziel dieses Kultus,
in dem Gott und die Gemeinschaft des Menschen mit ihm letztlich
menschlichen Zwecken dienstbar gemacht wird."

[43]On the other hand, Wellhausen, *Die Kleinen Propheten*, 78-
79,93, points out that Amos shows no antipathy toward the calf
of Israel (cf. Hos. 10:5-6), and that the sin of the people is
"die Illusion, dass Jahve dadurch sich suchen und finden und an
Israel ketten lasse; von fremdem Dienst oder von ungesetzlichen
Brauchen sagt Amos nichts." But J. D. Smart, "Amos," *IDB*, I,
121, rightly perceives that silence as to the bull cult does not
indicate that Amos condoned such practice.

[44]Sellin, *op. cit.*, 222, observes that these are legitimate
Yahwistic cults.

[45]Maag, *Text, Wortschatz und Begriffswelt des Buches Amos*,
28-29, thinks that these verses show the humanity of Amos, the
'ûlay of hope. This is a conscious rejection of Weiser's view
that 5:6 does not go back to Amos. But Weiser recognizes the
uncertainty of this issue, although writing that it is not Amos'
custom to give an explanation of his words (see Weiser, *Das Buch
der zwölf Kleinen Propheten*, 161). Fosbroke, *op. cit.*, 812,
argues that these verses are probably late since Amos does not
otherwise leave open any chance of escape (7:8; 8:2), but this
assumption must be rejected.

In face of the divine threat against the sanctuaries, Amos urges
the people to seek Yahweh so they might escape the catastrophe.[46]

The grounds for the threat are delineated in verse 7; justice
is being changed into a bitter thing, and righteousness cast down
to the earth.[47] A similar charge occurs in Hos. 10:4, where the
sins of idolatry and false swearing are described as the cause of
justice's sad plight. The second doxology follows verse 7, and
there can be no question about its intrusive character. The most
cogent reason for its position seems to be suggested by the word
$h\bar{a}phak$ used in 5:7 and 5:8.[48] By means of this doxology, placed
as it is beside the threat of judgment by fire and the reasons
for it, the Lord is praised both as Creator and Judge. Weiser
has written:

> Die polare Spannung des Glaubens, der erschauerende
> Ehrfurcht vor dem richtenden Gott vereinigt mit
> jubelnder Begeisterung für die Grösse und Macht des
> Schöpfers, bindet die beiden Pole der Auffassung von
> Gott als dem Richter und dem Schöpfer zu einer lebend-
> igen Einheit zusammen, so dass aus der Schöpfermacht
> Gottes sein Recht und seine Macht zum Gericht abge-
> leitet wird.[49]

The doxology begins by praising Yahweh as Creator of the Pleiades
and Orion[50] and as the One who controls the alternation between

---

[46]Wellhausen, *Die Kleinen Propheten*, 81, calls attention to
the prevalence of fire as a divine punishment in Amos (1:4,7,10,
12; 2:2). "For Bethel" is generally conceded to be a gloss (see
Wellhausen, *ibid.*,; Maag, *Text, Wortschatz und Begriffswelt des
Buches Amos*, 26; and Th. Robinson, *op. cit.*, 88).

[47]Weiser, *Das Buch der zwölf Kleinen Propheten*, 163, suggests
that a large unit consisting of three sections beginning with "Woe"
--5:7,18; 6:1--once existed, although the arrangement should not
be attributed to Amos. Several scholars wish to add "Woe" to 5:7
which would be partial support of Weiser's position; this is true
of Sellin, *op. cit.*, 229; Maag, *ibid.*, 30; Fosbroke, *op. cit.*,
812 (or read "they that turn"). But against these Th. Robinson,
op. cit., 89, suggests that 5:7 is a remnant of a lost speech,
part of which appears in 5:6 ("for Bethel"); however, there is
little basis for this view.

[48]Weiser, *Das Buch der zwölf Kleinen Propheten*, 164. Against
this it may be observed that the catchword principle does not
otherwise play a significant role in the text of Amos.

[49]*Ibid.*

[50]It seems that the last half of verse 8 has dropped out;
its subject matter will have been similar to the first half (see
above, page 74).

day and night; it then proceeds to praise the Lord as the One who sends the Deluge as punishment upon sinners, and as the powerful avenger who crushes man's strongest defenses.

The point of the reference to Yahweh as Creator of the stars may be polemical, especially in view of Am. 5:26. The reference to deep-darkness is not at all strange in a context dealing with alternation of day and night, as a comparison with "The Hymn to the Aton" makes abundantly clear. Here one reads that when the sun sets in the western horizon "the land is in darkness, in the manner of death."[51] However, it is possible to understand the allusion to deep-darkness in terms of eschato-logical deliverance (cf. Isa. 9:2, Heb. 1).[52] Some difficulty is presented by the allusion to the pouring out of the waters of the sea, which some take to imply heavy rains, while others think in terms of a deluge. Against the former view is the use of the verb shāphak and the noun hayyām.[53] In view of these words and the reference to the "surface of the earth," it is probable that a flood is in mind, perhaps the Noachian Deluge.[54]

The presence of the refrain at the end of 5:8 makes it like-ly that 5:9 did not originally belong to the doxology, unless it followed 9:5a as has been argued above. This verse announces that exaltation of human power is ended for all time.[55] Sellin's

---

[51]See James B. Pritchard, ed. *Ancient Near Eastern Texts Relating to the Old Testament* (Princeton: Princeton University Press, 1955), 370.

[52]Wellhausen, *Die Kleinen Propheten*, 81, recognizes "deep-darkness" as a late word and suggests that it should be pointed $ṣ^e lāmôth$ (fem. pl.) on the analogy of Arabic *tzulamat*.

[53]*Shāphak* is most frequently used in contexts implying vio-lence and bloodshed, although later texts do use the verb in connection with spirit (Joel 2:29). Sellin, *op. cit.*, 228, per-ceives the difficulty posed by *hayyām* but suggests that it is a scribal error for "the heavens," or that "the sea" refers to the heavenly ocean (Isa. 55:10; Job 38:34-38).

[54]Th. Robinson, *op. cit.*, 89-90. This verse is frequently quoted in Midrashic literature, and the predominant opinion ap-pears to be that the prophet here has reference to the deluge during the generation of Enosh (see Routtenberg, *op. cit.*, 113).

[55]Weiser, *Das Buch der zwölf Kleinen Propheten*, 164. This interpretation, defended also by Wellhausen, *Die Kleinen Pro-pheten*, 81-82, and Sellin, *op. cit.*, 228-29, is certainly pref-erable to the attempt to see star names in the verse.

suggestion that 5:9 is a gloss to 5:6 has much to commend it.[56]
Besides explaining the presence of the unusual *hammabhlîg*, it
also provides a referent for the participle in verse 9 ("Seek
Yahweh" of verse 6).[57]

Verse 10 has been considered an independent speech, since
it differs in content from 5:7.[58] On the other hand, it has
been connected with 5:7 and 6:12.[59] One wonders why 16-17 has
not been suggested as the conclusion of the verse, for there is
just as much in favor of such an interpretation. This assumes
that 5:11 is not the sequel to the verse now standing immediately
before it.[60] On the contrary, 11-12 appears to be a brief, independent speech denouncing the people for social unrighteousness and announcing that the wealth gained in their perversion
of justice will benefit them in no way. The houses of hewn
stone are to be understood as having been constructed at the ex-
pense of the poor, and the reference to pleasant vineyards is
probably to be regarded as an allusion to the sad lot of tenant
farmers.[61] In verse 12 "For I know" has two objects: both the
multitude and the greatness of Israel's sins.[62] The aphorism
of verse 13 is not the conclusion of the oracle, but must be a

---

[56] Sellin, *op. cit.*, 229; he compares Hos. 8:14, which is
unique in that it contains the only reference to Yahweh as Creator in Hosea, and also threatens a fire upon the cities and
strongholds.

[57] Fosbroke, *op. cit.*, 813, thinks that 8-9 were linked with
"Seek" of 5:6 by the interpolators.

[58] Th. Robinson, *op. cit.*, 90.

[59] Fosbroke, *op. cit.*, 814, and Marti, *op. cit.*, 191, think
of it as a continuation of verse 7; on the other hand, Weiser,
Das Buch der zwölf Kleinen Propheten, 165, argues that 6:12 is
its natural conclusion.

[60] Fosbroke, *op. cit.*, 815.

[61] Th. Robinson, *op. cit.*, 90-91; and R. Bach, *op. cit.*,
26. Weiser, *Das Buch der zwölf Kleinen Propheten*, 165-66,
thinks of 6:11 as the sequel to 5:11b and writes that the former recalls the earthquake.

[62] Maag, *Text, Wortschatz und Begriffswelt des Buches Amos*,
31.

later wisdom speech.[63] Weiser has rightly pointed out the difference between Amos' message despite personal danger and the
advice given here to be cleverly silent,[64] a difference that
Sellin's defense of 5:13 fails to remove.[65]

The next two verses belong to 4-6 (7?) and represent Amos'
explanation of what it means to seek Yahweh.[66] It is remarkable
that Amos speaks in terms of good and evil, assuming that the
people know the meaning of each. The conditional character of
God's grace could not be more clearly stated: "Seek good, and
not evil, that you may live; and so the Lord, the God of Hosts,
will be with you, as you have said" (5:14; cf. Hos. 8:3). Amos
asserts that the only way to survive the catastrophe is by obedience to the ancient amphictyonic laws (the good). But even
here the escape stands under the divine "perhaps," that is, God
is not bound to spare Israel even if she meets the demands.
"Gott ist nicht an das Volk gebunden, wohl aber ist das Volk an
Gott gebunden."[67] This means that "God with us" can be nothing
else than divine grace.[68] It leaves no place for self-confidence
because of Israel's election by Yahweh (cf. 9:10; 3:2; 5:18;
6:1,13).[69] Only as she hates the evil, loves the good, and

---

[63]*Ibid.*, and "Zur Übersetzung von Maskil in Amos 5:13, Ps.
47:8, und in den Überschriften einiger Psalmen," *STU*, XII (1943),
108ff. It is peculiar that Terrien, *op. cit.*, 108-15, does not
mention 5:13 as a passage influenced by the wisdom school. To
this verse Mic. 2:3 should be compared.

[64]Weiser, *Das Buch der zwölf Kleinen Propheten*, 168. Fosbroke, *op. cit.*, 815, also notices this contrast.

[65]Sellin, *op. cit.*, 231. He wishes to place 5:13 between
5:26 and 5:27. On the other hand, Amos' use of irony may well
explain this passage.

[66]Th. Robinson, *op. cit.*, 91, thinks that the absolute use
of *kēn* suggests that 5:14b may be secondary, but compare 4:5.
Weiser, *Das Buch der zwölf Kleinen Propheten*, 161, agrees that
14-15 must be taken with 5:14-5 but does not say that it comes
from Amos. In fact, the allusion to the self-confidence of the
people is thought to derive from later discussion. Sellin, *op.
cit.*, 229, thinks that 5:14 can be the conclusion of 5:6.

[67]Weiser, *ibid.*, 162.

[68]*Ibid.*, 162-63.

[69]Here Amos takes up a word of confidence circulating
among the people ("God with us"); to this may be compared Mic.
3:11 ("Is not the Lord in the midst of us? No evil shall come
upon us") and the symbolism of the name Immanuel (Isa. 7:14).

establishes justice in the gate will even the possibility of
escape arise (cf. Mic. 3:2; Joel 2:14); and even it is limited
to the remnant of Joseph.[70]

Verses 16-17 may be the conclusion of 5:10. The theophany
is no longer an occasion of hope, for Yahweh will appear to bring
judgment upon Israel. The terrible result of his coming is described in terms of wailing, lamenting and mourning.

The life setting of the second doxology, if it be different
from that of the first, is difficult to discern. Nevertheless,
two elements deserve special notice, one in the opening verse of
the context (5:4) and the other at the end (5:17). The probable
allusion to Bethel as a deity recalls one motif discovered in
several passages where the refrain "Yahweh of Hosts is his name"
occurs. But even if Bethel is viewed as a sanctuary, there seems
to be no doubt about the idolatrous character of worship at the
sanctuaries (5:26; 8:14). The second point is the reference to
a theophany ("For I will pass through the midst of you"); this
is particularly significant in view of the conclusions above regarding a theophanic tradition preserved in passages using the
refrain examined in chapter three. Once again one could suggest
that the exilic period provides the setting for the doxology,
perhaps in special confessions after the order of the covenant
renewal ceremony in which the theophany played the central role
(cf. Dt. 29:12).

C.   *Amos 9:5-6*

The fifth vision (9:1-4) opens the section into which the
third doxology has been placed. Yahweh is seen standing beside
the altar, and his command is heard to smite the capitals and
shatter them on the heads of the people, as well as his threat
that he will slay with the sword every person who escapes the
collapse of the sanctuary. Verses 2-4 name every possible place
of escape, denying that even one will provide refuge from Yahweh's avenging hand. The doxology follows, and is in turn suc-
ceeded by the divine denial that Israel is any different from
other nations. Finally, a distinction between "sinners" and the
"righteous" among the people is made, and only the former are
threatened.

------

[70]Unless "remnant" here means "descendants," that is, Israel, as was argued above.

Weiser has argued cogently that the fifth vision formed
the original conclusion of the other four and provided the high
point of the oral proclamation.[71] Nevertheless, the difference
in introductory formula and subject matter casts serious doubt
on this conclusion,[72] and Weiser's attempt to justify this dif-
ference--on the basis that a vision of Yahweh himself and broader
diction occur--seems to have failed.[73] Nor is there any reason
to think of the temple in Jerusalem as the scene of this vision.[74]
On the other hand, Weiser is probably right that the vision suggests an earthquake.[75] The threat of death seems limited to
those worshiping in the sanctuary,[76] and the offenses described
in 8:14 appear responsible for the present position of the fifth
vision.

Whereas the vision depicts a natural calamity brought about
by Yahweh, it is forgotten in 1b-4; and punishment by additional
means is predicted. The second verse names the extremes within

---

[71]Weiser, *Das Buch der zwölf Kleinen Propheten*, 187.

[72]Maag, *Text, Wortschatz und Begriffswelt des Buches Amos*,
47; and Th. Robinson, *op. cit.*, 104. One would need to add,
"And behold," as well as the question about what is seen. But
there is no reason to assume that Amos would always use the same
formula, so that this argument may carry little weight. On the
other hand, Maag is certainly right that the first four visions
speak of the certainty of an imminent destruction, while the
fifth emphasizes its inescapability.

[73]Weiser, *Das Buch der zwölf Kleinen Propheten*, 187.

[74]Against Weiser, *ibid.*, 188. Bethel is almost certainly
the sanctuary intended; Sellin, *op. cit.*, 263; Fosbroke, *op.
cit.*, 845; and Cripps, *op. cit.*, 100. K. Galling, "Der Gott
Karmel und die Ächtung der fremden Götter," *Geschichte und Altes
Testament* (Tübingen: J.C.B. Mohr [P. Siebeck], 1953), 119, thinks
of a sanctuary on Mount Carmel.

[75]Weiser, *ibid.*; Th. Robinson, *op. cit.*, 104; Fosbroke,
ibid.; Maag, *Text, Wortschatz und Begriffswelt des Buches Amos*.
45. There is much to be said for the emendation to "And he
slew...and he said, 'I will break by means of an earthquake'"
(see Maag, *ibid.*). If this is not accepted, then one might argue that Yahweh addresses an angel in the vision, the heavenly
court providing the background and prototype for the earthly
temple where Yahweh is enthroned (cf. Isa. 6:4 and I Kgs. 22:19-
23). S. R. Driver, *op. cit.*, 202, suggests that an angel is
addressed, but Sellin, *op. cit.*, 264, writes that Amos never mentions an angel anywhere else--a questionable argument, since
there is always a first time.

[76]Sellin, *op. cit.*, 263.

and above the earth to which one might flee--Sheol and heaven. Terrien has pointed out that outside of Amos only the wisdom tradition (Prov. 15:11; Job 26:6; cf. 7:21?) and a hymnic meditation (Ps. 139:7) of the sapiential type dare to conceive poetically the imagery of a rapport between Yahweh and the sojourn of the dead.[77] Sheol was conceived to be deep, cavernous (Isa. 14: 4-20), below the earth (Dt. 32:22; Job 26:5; Ez. 32:18),[78] yet Yahweh's hand will extend even to the pit. Likewise he can reach the highest heaven (cf. Ob. 4; Jer. 51:53), so no escape is possible.

Verse 3 mentions two other places that might be thought to stand outside Yahweh's dominion. Mount Carmel is said to have had nearly 2,000 limestone caves in which robbers could hide (Strabo); besides this, the top of the mountain was thickly wooded, so one could easily hide from his pursuers. Moreover, Carmel's height was exceeded only by Tabor, so height, caves and forests should provide refuge from Yahweh. Nevertheless, such remote places are under his scrutiny (cf. Jer. 23:24). Carmel may also have been chosen for this warning because with its side projecting into the water, it is the last point before one comes to the sea. Again, even if one goes to the bottom of the sea to hide from Yahweh's sight, there is no safety; for the sea monster that dwells there stands ready to obey Yahweh's command (cf. Jonah 1:3,9).[79] These two verses have a counterpart in Ps. 139:7-9, but the mood there is one of awesome wonder rather than punishment.[80]

---

[77]Terrien, *op. cit.*, 110-11. In another vision (7:4) of Amos, Terrien thinks he discovers a possible affinity with the wisdom tradition (the creation of the deep; cf. Prov. 8:24,27-28).

[78]S. R. Driver, *op. cit.*, 221.

[79]This is an allusion to the mythological chaos dragon defeated by Yahweh, although elsewhere its body is said to have been used in creating the cosmos (*Enuma Elish*; see Th. Robinson, *op. cit.*, 105; S. R. Driver, *op. cit.*, 222; Weiser, *Das Buch der zwölf Kleinen Propheten*, 188; and Sellin, *op. cit.*, 266).

[80]Fosbroke, *op. cit.*, 846. In an Amarna Letter (264) the following appears: "If we go up into heaven, or if we descend into the earth, yet is our head in thine hands." For the literary relation of Am. 9:2, Ps. 139, and Tell el Amarna 264:15ff., see H. Hommel, "Das religionsgeschichtliche Problem des 139. Psalms," *ZAW*, XLVIII (1929), 110-24.

The fourth verse denies that an alien land could provide safety; even in captivity the mythological sword will find its mark (cf. Ez. 14:17; 21:8ff.; Jer. 47:6-7; Gen. 3:24). Fosbroke has observed that this reference to captivity has relevance at a time in the exile when many assumed they were finally outside Yahweh's domain.[81] But it is possible to view the verse as authentic, since Amos certainly believed in Yahweh's control over other nations. As a summary statement of the inescapability of destruction, verse 4b reads: "And I will set my eyes upon them for evil and not for good." This is in essence a threat that henceforth Yahweh's presence will be detrimental: "Der auf das Volk gerichtete Blick Gottes--seine Gegenwart--führt zum Unheil und nicht zum Heil."[82] Weiser calls this "eine Offenbarung, die für Amos zum Grundthema seiner gesamten Verkündigung wird."[83] Elsewhere the phrase "the eyes of the Lord" has been used benevolently (Jer. 24:6; 39:11; Gen. 44:21), but a reversal has taken place by the addition of "for evil" (Jer. 21:10; 39:16; 44:27).[84]

The third doxology glances back at 9:1 and praises the God who causes the earthquake;[85] at the same time it confesses the presence of the one under whose word of judgment Israel has been humbled (9:4).[86] Yahweh is described in terms taken from the theophanic tradition: "He who touches the earth and it melts, and all who dwell in it mourn" (cf. Nah. 1:5; Hos. 4:3; Ps. 104: 32; 97:4-5). This is obviously an allusion to an earthquake,

---

[81]Fosbroke, *op. cit.*, 846-47. Jonah 1:3 indicates the tenacity of the idea that Yahweh's presence could be escaped in an alien land.

[82]Weiser, *Das Buch der zwölf Kleinen Propheten*, 188.

[83]*Ibid.*, 189.

[84]See above.

[85]Sellin, *op. cit.*, 266. The Targum reads: "Shall not the land be destroyed for this and everyone who dwells therein be confounded, and a king will come upon it with his army which is as numerous as the waters of the river and will overrun it completely and drive out its inhabitants, and it shall sink like the river of Egypt?" (see Routtenberg, *op. cit.*, 150).

[86]Weiser, *Das Buch der zwölf Kleinen Propheten*, 189.

as the gloss in 9:5b based on 8:8 makes clear.[87] The imagery
could be derived from metallurgy, the earth melting and forming
the raw stuff from which the cosmos was created.[88] The doxology
moves on to praise Yahweh as one who builds his upper chambers
in the heavens and founds his vault[89] upon the earth, and closes
with an allusion to his use of the deluge as a means for punishing a guilty people. This doxology recalls a similar description of God in Job 26, where the shades below and the pillars
of heaven are said to tremble (5,11), the waters are spoken of
as bound up in thick clouds (8), and God is said to have described a circle on the face of the waters (10; cf. also Job 22:
4,11,12-14).

But the similarity of the doxologies and Job does not stop
here; on the contrary, two hymnic passages are strikingly like
the doxologies (5:8-18; 9:2-12). This can be seen most clearly
by means of the following chart:

Amos		Job	
5:6	"Seek the Lord"	5:8	"I would seek God"
4:13; 5:8	"Who makes" ($^c\bar{o}seh$)	5:9	"Who does" ($^c\bar{o}seh$)
5:8b; 9:6b	"Who calls for the waters"	5:10	"He gives rain upon the earth, and sends waters upon the fields"
5:8	"He turns darkness to morning, and darkens day to night"	5:14	"They meet with dark-ness in the daytime, and grope at noonday as in the night"
		9:7	"Who commands the sun and it does not rise, who seals up the stars"
5:10	"They hate him who re-proves in the gate"	5:17	"Behold, happy is the man whom God reproves"
4:13	"He who forms moun-tains"	9:5	"He who removes moun-tains"
9:5	"He touches the earth and it melts"	9:6	"Who shakes the earth out of its place, and its pillars tremble"
4:13	"Who treads upon the heights of the earth"	9:8	"Who trampled the waves of the sea"
5:8	"He who makes Pleiades and Orion"	9:9	"Who made the Bear and Orion, the Pleiades..."

[87]Th. Robinson, *op. cit.*, 104. In commenting on the phrase
in 8:8, Wellhausen, *Die Kleinen Propheten*, 93, observes that the
analogy is poor, since the Nile rises and sets over a period of
two months, whereas the earth quakes several times in a few min-
utes.

[88]Th. Robinson, *op. cit.*, 104.

[89]S. R. Driver, *op. cit.*, 223, and Sellin, *op. cit.*, 267,
write that vault here refers to $r\bar{a}qi^{a c}$.

The third doxology is followed by two rhetorical questions denying to Israel any place of privilege before Yahweh (cf. Jer. 7:1-15). Theodore Robinson writes that there is no doubt as to their genuineness, for the verse contains "eine Feststellung von ganz unerhörter Kühnheit und Neuheit."[90] This can be seen most clearly from a comparison with Jdg. 11:23-24, where Yahweh is said to have given Israel her land just as Chemosh gave Moab hers. But this "unheard-of idea" is not to be denied Amos on the basis of absence of any recognition concerning the special choice of Israel, or of its position at the end of the book next to spurious material.[91] On the contrary, this understanding arose from Amos' confrontation with God who "steht vor aller Geschichte und über ihr als der souveräne Herr."[92]

Maag asks whether the $h^a l\hat{o}$' of 7a is genuine, suggesting that it may have arisen from 7b;[93] if this is correct, one would translate: "Just like the Ethiopians you are to me, O Israelites. Have I not....?" But whether one accepts this emendation or not, the point is the same: Israel has no more claim on Yahweh than do the Ethiopians, Philistines and Syrians. However, the meaning of the rhetorical questions also contains a positive truth-- Yahweh is God of all peoples.[94]

Just why the Ethiopians were chosen for this comparison is not clear. At least three possibilities present themselves: their distance from Israel, the blackness of their skin, and the fact that they were frequently sold as slaves. The last two would seem more likely, especially in view of Jer. 13:23 and Isa. 20:4.[95] The Philistines and Syrians are mentioned

---

[90]Th. Robinson, *op. cit.*, 106.

[91]Against Fosbroke, *op. cit.*, 849, who suggests this possibility.

[92]Weiser, *Das Buch der zwölf Kleinen Propheten*, 200.

[93]Maag, *Text, Wortschatz und Begriffswelt des Buches Amos*, 58-59.

[94]Fosbroke, *op. cit.*, 848.

[95]Sellin, *op. cit.*, 268; and Wellhausen, *Die Kleinen Propheten*, 94. Against this, see Fosbroke, *op. cit.*, 848, and Norman H. Snaith, *Amos, Hosea and Micah* (London: Epworth Press, 1956), 49, who challenge the view that Ethiopians are despised because of their black skin, and Cripps, *op. cit.*, 262, who thinks remoteness is more probably the reason for the choice.

because of their proximity and the age-old rivalry between them
and Israel. Caphtor (Crete?) is not the original home of the
Philistines, who were perhaps from Illyricum, but could be the
last station on their migration to the south.[96] The exact loca-
tion of Kir is uncertain, although the general region is Mesopotamia.[97] These verses assert that Yahweh directed the migra-
tions of Israelites, Philistines and Syrians, so the deliverance
from Egypt cannot give Israel any assurance before Yahweh. On
the one hand, there is abundant evidence of Yahweh's concern for
Israel (2:10-11; 3:2; 7:15; 8:2 "my people"), but on the other,
Israel is no better than her hated rivals, for their history
serves the divine purpose just as hers does. Weiser has rightly
observed: "Aber gerade diese Paradoxie entspricht recht eigent-
lich dem Wesen Gottes."[98]

The first part of verse 8 recalls the threat of 9:4, but
this time the third person occurs ("Behold, the eyes of the Lord
God are upon the sinful kingdom"). On the basis of parallelism
with 8b, Maag and Robinson suggest a change to "Behold my eyes
...."[99] A different conclusion is drawn by Weiser, who recognizes that 9:8 knows 9:4 and depends on it, the purpose of the
addition being to correct an erroneous prophecy and to reaffirm
the validity of the threat in 9:4.[100] The gloss comes from a
period after the fall of Israel, and testifies to the preservation
of a remnant. According to the verse, the wrath of God will be
limited to "the sinful kingdom," that is, *every* sinful kingdom.[101]

---

[96]Weiser, *Das Buch der zwölf Kleinen Propheten*, 200. Th.
Robinson, *op. cit.*, 106, and Sellin, *op. cit.*, 268, understand
Caphtor as Crete. J. C. Greenfield, "Caphtor," *IDB*, I, 534,
thinks Caphtor was used by the thirteenth century "broadly for
the Aegean area from which the Philistines as one of the 'People
of the Sea' emerged."

[97]Th. Robinson, *ibid.*; and C. H. Gordon, "Kir," *IDB*, III,
36.

[98]Weiser, *Das Buch der zwölf Kleinen Propheten*, 199.

[99]Maag, *Text, Wortschatz und Begriffswelt des Buches Amos*,
59; and Th. Robinson, *op. cit.*, 106.

[100]Weiser, *Das Buch der zwölf Kleinen Propheten*, 201. He
claims that the style is different from that of Amos, specifically,
the joining of two sentences in different persons.

[101]Sellin, *op. cit.*, 268 (cf. Isa. 10:6); S. R. Driver, *op.
cit.*, 224; Th. Robinson, *op. cit.*, 107; and Cripps, *op. cit.*, 264.
This would mean that the article is generic. But against this,

There could be no more fitting conclusion to Amos' prophecy than the words that follow: "And I will destroy it [the sinful kingdom] from the surface of the ground." Robinson has perceived this fact most clearly; he writes that "Jahve würde sich selbst untreu, wenn er dies Israel weiter am Leben liesse."[102]

If this is correct, 9:8b must be considered an addition to the words of Amos. Wellhausen's comment on this clause and the following two verses is classic: "Hat Amos sich selbst hier völlig vergessen? Er hat noch so eben (9:1-4) gesagt, kein Einziger solle dem allgemeinen Verderben entgehn."[103] Driver has attempted to attribute these verses to Amos, but without success.[104] The difference in tone from this and the rest of the book is decisive and must be maintained despite the recent attempt of H. G. Reventlow to defend the authenticity of the end of the book.[105]

Verse 9 further limits the threat of 9:4,8a. The metaphor is not clear, although it seems that the good grain is expected to remain in the sieve.[106] It may be that the prophecy of an earthquake calls to mind this metaphor, but this is not certain.[107] In any case, 9:9 gives the purpose of the exile, that the survivors may form the basic stock of a new people,[108] and warns

---

see Harper, *op. cit.*, 193, and Wellhausen, *Die Kleinen Propheten*, 95. Wellhausen compares Ecclus. 47:21, where βασιλεία απειθής is used of Israel in distinction from Judah. Since Amos otherwise makes no distinction between Israel and Judah (3:1; 6:1,11), Wellhausen thinks of this verse as spurious.

[102] Th. Robinson, *op. cit.*, 107.

[103] Wellhausen, *Die Kleinen Propheten*, 95.

[104] S. R. Driver, *op. cit.*, 122-26, 224-26.

[105] Henning Graf Reventlow, *Das Amt des Propheten bei Amos*, (Göttingen: Vendenhoeck & Ruprecht, 1962), 90-110. The "prophetic office" cannot bear the heavy load Reventlow places upon it. One must object to this author's view of the essence of prophecy and its function.

[106] S. R. Driver, *op. cit.*, 268; Th. Robinson, *op. cit.*, 107. But see Sellin, *op. cit.*, 268, and the translation of the RSV.

[107] Weiser, *Das Buch der zwölf Kleinen Propheten*, 201-02. Weiser, Sellin, and Maag think of "among all the nations" as a gloss. See Weiser, *ibid.*, 201; Sellin, *op. cit.*, 268; and Maag, *Text, Wortschatz und Begriffswelt des Buches Amos*, 59.

[108] Th. Robinson, *op. cit.*, 107.

those in exile against lighthearted optimism.[109] In essence
the verse asserts that the exile was a refining action and that
judgment is not only a past event but comes even now upon all
the sinners who say, "Evil shall not overtake or meet us" (cf.
Mic. 2:6; 3:11; Jer. 23:17).[110]

If the observations concerning the life setting of the
other doxologies are in any way correct, this one strengthens
the conclusions significantly. One is struck by the presence
of every single motif outlined in the third chapter as characteristic of the passages using the refrain "Yahweh of Hosts is
his name." In 8:14 both the oath and idolatry are dominant,
while 9:5a contains the divine festal name with the oath particle. Preceding the latter is a vision of judgment, to which
is attached a threat that the Lord will set his eyes upon Israel
for evil and not for good, almost an exact quotation of the
phrase found elsewhere giving the basis for Yahweh's verdict.
Finally, the theme of creation appears, and its subservient role
is rather pronounced. In essence the creative act is appealed
to as proof that Yahweh has power to judge the world. It is
significant, therefore, that the judgment recalls the ancient
theophanic tradition (9:6a; cf. Nah. 1:5).

---

[109]Fosbroke, *op. cit.*, 850.

[110]Read with Maag, *Text, Wortschatz und Begriffswelt des
Buches Amos*, 59, *thiggash ûth^eqaddēm ^cādhēnû ra^cāh*.

CHAPTER V

CONCLUSION

The preceding chapters have drawn definite conclusions
about the form, function and life setting of the doxologies of
Amos. They have also indicated that the relevance of this thesis is not limited to the text of Amos but can be fruitfully
applied to other passages within the Old and New Testaments.
The discussion of numerous issues involved in an analysis of the
doxologies has also pointed to several areas of research which,
although not necessary to the completion of the task envisioned
in this dissertation, deserve careful consideration in the future. The purpose of this conclusion is to draw together the
results mentioned above, to indicate their relevance for other
biblical texts, and to suggest some areas for further study.

The first subject to be discussed is the form of the doxology. Friedrich Horst's fundamental insight into the literary
type (a Doxology of Judgment) has been accepted and additional
evidence provided for it.[1] The refrain, "Yahweh of Hosts is his
name," is taken as the key to the understanding of formal analysis of the doxologies. An examination of the contexts in which
this refrain and its variants are found yields four motifs: (1)
judgment, (2) creation, (3) idolatry, and (4) oath. The theme
that appears in every use of the refrain is that of judgment,
so the name of the literary type is appropriate. This takes a
three-fold form: (1) the threat, especially in terms of roaring
waters or fire; (2) the basis for the judgment, specifically the
fact that Yahweh's eyes are set upon the people wherever they
may be; and (3) an appeal to repent, although missing where for-
eigners are the object of Yahweh's judgment. The actual judgment is described in terms recalling a theophany, but one must
not assume that this fact demands a date for the refrain and its
contexts in the early days of Israelite occupation when theophany was an integral part of the covenant renewal ceremony. On
the contrary, close association of creation and theophany points

---

[1]Horst, "Die Doxologien im Amosbuch," 165-66.

141

to a later period when kingship and creation, both secondary features, have been added to this celebration.[2]

The motif of creation plays a major role in the contexts using the refrain. The ancient myth of the Sea Monster (Leviathan, Rahab, Tannim or Tannin) underlies the passages, but the influence of Second Isaiah can be discerned in the interpretation of the Exodus as a creative act.[3]

The third motif is idolatry, and the contexts contain vigorous attacks on the worship of gods other than Yahweh. Closely connected with this theme is an emphasis upon swearing in the name of Yahweh rather than by other deities. This association of oath and idolatry has prompted a historical reconstruction indicating the prevalence of oaths by alien deities and the prophetic and cultic responses to wipe out this practice. A clear development in oath-taking can be discerned, starting with the simple "As Yahweh the God of Israel lives" and expanding to "As Yahweh lives, who made our souls," and "As Yahweh lives who brought us from Egypt," to "As Yahweh lives who created heaven and earth." This latter emphasis becomes an integral element of the cultic prayers, which arose as a means of preserving traditions of the worshiping community (Jer. 32; Ezr. 9; Neh. 9; Dan. 9).

The refrain used with the doxologies appears here and in Isaiah and Jeremiah in four forms: (1) the simple "Yahweh (the God) of the Hosts is his name," and (2) the refrain followed by an appositional phrase, both of which are used with the motif of creation; (3) an oracular formula ($\bar{a}mar\ YHWH$ or $n^{e'}um\ YHWH$) followed by a refrain, used in contexts where idolatry is the central theme; and (4) the refrain plus a long sentence, employed in connection with judgment and oaths.

The second question to be discussed is the function of the doxologies. The background for an understanding of their function has been discovered in the prophetic lawsuit ($r\hat{i}b$), although in a late stage when one might correctly speak of the legal

---

[2]Weiser, *The Psalms*, 33-34.

[3]At this point, G. von Rad's observations in "Das theologische Problem des alttestamentlichen Schöpfungsglaubens," 136-47, seem to be justified. At any rate, the reflective thinking in regard to creation and saving faith found in these passages seems to be an exilic or early post-exilic phenomenon.

terminology as metaphor only. This means that Horst's view that the doxologies reflect an actual judgment in sacral law is correct to the extent that they must be connected with the oath required in sacral law.[4] Moreover, the doxologies seem to have been used on special days of penitence and confession which grew out of the prophetic lawsuits of earlier times.[5]

The theophanic elements (both in terminology and theological content) derive from the covenant renewal ceremony but possibly indicate a revival of the theophanic tradition in connection with special days of penitence when the subject of judgment would naturally recall an earlier judgment par excellence, namely Yahweh's epiphany for judgment. The doxologies were added to the prophetic text for use on special days of penitence and confession, and their function was later taken over by cultic prayers instead of prophetic word of judgment plus doxology. In a time when the destruction of the temple and the subsequent Babylonian exile seemed to indicate Yahweh's impotence, the doxologies were an expression of faith in Yahweh by a people smarting from wounds inflicted upon them by their God, but confident that he was able to deliver them if he so desired.

A discussion of the function of the doxologies cannot be separated from consideration of their life setting. The cumulative evidence with respect to the contexts of the refrain almost demands a date during the exilic or early post-exilic period. The following elements suggest this conclusion: (1) the life setting of the refrain; (2) the close association of idolatry and oaths; (3) the emphasis on creation, specifically the soteriological understanding of the Exodus; (4) the cultic prayers; and (5) the emerging eschatological symbol of Zion. In brief, the place of Jerusalem in the contexts using the refrain, the threat of idolatry, the view of creation as a working sacral concept, the emerging emphasis on prayer, and the use of an ancient refrain as a confession of faith in Yahweh the God of Hosts, all point to the exilic or early post-exilic period as the life setting of the doxologies.[6]

---

[4]Horst, "Die Doxologien im Amosbuch," 165-66.

[5]Julien Harvéy, *op. cit.*, 195.

[6]The evidence cannot be said to be decisive, however. It is possible to understand the doxologies as ancient material

This analysis of the refrain and doxologies has thrown light upon similar passages in Isaiah, Jeremiah, Hosea, Exodus and Job. But even parts of the New Testament have been illuminated by the study--Acts 12:23; Jn. 9:24; and Rev. 10:5-6. In addition, the discussion has indicated something of the exilic and post-exilic attitude to "scripture"; this "open stance" and desire to give contemporaneity to the ancient prophetic word closely resemble later levitical preaching discussed so ably by Gerhard von Rad.[7]

In the course of this discussion, several related problems, not germane to the present study, have come to light. First, the history-of-religions question as to the relation of the ancient covenant renewal ceremony to the later Tabernacles-New Year Festival appears to merit further study. Perhaps a key to this endeavor could be found in the place of theophany in both.[8] Second, a person trained in astronomy should seek to discover what was known about the subject in the ancient Near East and to

---

employed by Amos as Doxologies of Judgment. In such a view, the original life setting of the refrain at Shiloh would be stressed, together with the polemic against *Baalism* during the time of Elijah. Moreover, the theophanic elements of the doxologies would then be associated with an actual covenant renewal ceremony, and the fluctuating divine titles would point to a period before "Yahweh of Hosts" became a fixed phrase. The formula of the prophetic lawsuit would then be understood as a later variation of the demand in Amos: "Prepare to meet thy God, O Israel."

[7]"Die levitische Predigt in den Büchern der Chronik," 248-61.

[8]James Muilenburg, "The Speech of Theophany," *HDBul*, XXVIII (1964), 35-47, has made an impressive beginning in recognizing the importance of theophany for Israelite faith. He observes (38) that theophanic formulations contain a theology *in nuce*, possibly more representative of Israelite belief than the historical credo discovered by G. von Rad in "Das formgeschichtliche Problem des Hexateuchs," 9-86. Muilenburg extracts five elements from the theophanies in Genesis: (1) the divine self-predication ("I am Yahweh"); (2) exhortation not to fear ("Fear not"); (3) promise of presence ("Because I am with you"); (4) promise of help ("I will help you"); and (5) the *hieros logos*. The work of Muilenburg has been supplemented by that of Frank Schnutenhaus, "Das Kommen und Erscheinen Gottes im Alten Testament," *ZAW*, LXXVI (1964), 1-22, which examines the verbs used in the theophanic tradition ($y\bar{a}\d{s}a$', $y\bar{a}radh$, $q\hat{u}m$, $h\hat{o}ph\hat{\imath}a^c$, $z\bar{a}rah$, $n\bar{a}g\bar{a}h$, $r\bar{a}$'a and $b\hat{o}$').

evaluate the evidence in the Old Testament within that light.[9]
Third, the present study has indicated the need for a work dealing with the vocabulary and evolution of prayer in the Old Testament.[10] The proper stance for such a study has been suggested
by J.A.T. Robinson, although in a more general context.[11] Robinson observes that if he had the courage his teaching about prayer
would take its point of departure in καιρός, that is in "the mo-
ment that drives us to our knees."[12] The fruitfulness of such
an approach to the prayers of the Old Testament is immediately
clear. Again, there is need for an exhaustive study of contri-
butions made by the conflict between Yahwism and alien faiths.
This would seek to show how new concepts arose and old ones were
enriched because of the struggle between two apparently incom-
patible religious perspectives.[13] Lastly, and possibly the most

---

[9]O. Neugebauer, *Astronomical Cuneiform Texts*, I-III (London: Lund Humphries), 1955, has given the most recent treatment
of Chaldean documents. Mowinckel's great work, "Die Sternnamen
im Alten Testament," would form the basis for a comparison with
extra-biblical sources.

[10]This would be more philologically oriented than the com-
parable work of Norman B. Johnson, *Prayer in the Apocrypha and
Pseudepigrapha* (Philadelphia: Society of Biblical Literature and
Exegesis, 1948), 1-77, and would build upon the research of Adolf
Wendel, *Das freie Laiengebet im vorexilischen Israel* (Leipzig:
Eduard Pfeiffer), 1931.

[11]John A. T. Robinson, *Honest to God* (Philadelphia: Westminster Press, 1963), 103.

[12]*Ibid.*

[13]A recent article by Walter Harrelson, "Prophecy and Syncretism," *ANQ*, IV New Series (1964), 6-19, reveals the fruits of
such a study. Harrelson discusses the problem under the rubrics
of thought about Israel's past, present and future. He points
out that Amos' use of the concept of the Day of Yahweh combines
imagery from holy war and from non-Israelite and Israelite cultic practices (10). The prophetic descriptions of Israel's past
in terms of marriage to or adoption by Yahweh are said to have
been derived from old traditions about God's adoption of a people
as his son (Ex. 4:22-23) and from fertility cults of Canaan and
surrounding lands (11). Isa. 5:1-7 is described as a *love poem*
borrowed from the hated Canaanite religion and employed by the
prophet to serve the covenant faith of Israel (12-13). Harrelson writes that "the community historicized its borrowings; it
rooted the mythological elements in the record of God's saving
work here on this earth" (17). He concludes:
   But the anchor that prevents this syncretism from
   becoming just an amalgam of various religious

difficult, there is need for a work that will establish reliable
criteria for recognizing archaizing tendencies and dead symbols,
an especially acute problem in the hymnic literature of the Old
Testament.[14]

Finally, something may be said about the relevance of this
thesis for contemporary Christianity and Judaism. At three points
modern man is addressed with a message of particular force: (1)
the very name of the literary type, Doxology of Judgment, suggests
that the believer who finds himself the object of divine judgment
can nonetheless praise God; (2) the discussion of cultic prayers
likewise points to the situation of those who have been driven to
their knees as a starting point in genuine prayer; and (3) the
enrichment of old concepts and the emergence of new ones reveal
how creative a pluralistic society can be.[15]

> ideas and understandings is clearly recognizable:
> it is the history of God with his people, stretching
> from the creation to the consummation at the last
> day (18).

See also G. W. Ahlström, *Aspects of Syncretism in Israelite Religion*, (Lund: C.W.K. Gleerup, Horae Soederblomianae), 1964.

[14] W. F. Albright, "The Psalm of Habakkuk," *passim*, and Alfons Deissler, "Zur Datierung und Situierung der 'kosmischen Hymnen' Pss. 8,19,29," *Lex Tua Veritas: Festschrift für Hubert Junker* (Trier: Paulinus Verlag, 1961), 47-58, have implicitly indicated the importance of such a study.

[15] For a discussion of the exciting challenge presented by a pluralistic society, see Leander E. Keck, *Mandate to Witness: Studies in the Book of Acts* (Valley Forge: Judson Press, 1964), 18-22.

POSTSCRIPT

The editors of the Society of Biblical Literature's Dissertation Series have kindly consented to permit me a few observations about discussions of the doxologies of Amos since 1964, when this dissertation was presented to the faculty of Vanderbilt University. In these eleven years, major commentaries have appeared in the Old Testament Library,[1] Biblischer Kommentar,[2] and Kommentar zum Alten Testament[3] series, as well as individual commentaries.[4] In addition, two monographs have added significantly to our knowledge of hymnic literature[5] and theophany,[6] and an essay has examined anew our understanding of the judgment doxology.[7] None of these seriously alters the conclusions reached over a decade ago. I have, therefore, yielded to persistent requests by students and colleagues in the discipline to make my dissertation more readily available. My hope is that it will contribute in a small way to Old Testament scholarship, both in the thesis it argues and as a paradigm of form critical analysis.[8]

---

[1]James Luther Mays, *Amos* (Philadelphia: The Westminster Press), 1969.

[2]Hans Walter Wolff, *Dodekapropheton. Amos. BKAT* (Neukirchen-Vluyn: Neukirchener Verlag des Erziehungsvereins), 1967.

[3]Wilhelm Rudolph, *Joel-Amos-Obadja-Jona. KAT* (Gütersloh: Gütersloher Verlagshaus Gerd Mohn), 1971.

[4]Erling Hammershaimb, *The Book of Amos: A Commentary*, translated by John Sturdy (Oxford: Basil Blackwell), 1970. Unfortunately, Milos Bič's commentary on Amos is not available to me.

[5]Frank Crüsemann, *Studien zur Formgeschichte von Hymnus und Danklied in Israel. WMANT* (Neukirchen-Vluyn: Neukirchener Verlag des Erziehungsvereins), 1969.

[6]Jörg Jeremias, *Theophanie. Die Geschichte einer alttestamentlichen Gattung. WMANT* (Neukirchen-Vluyn: Neukirchener Verlag des Erziehungsvereins), 1965.

[7]Gerhard von Rad, "Gerichtsdoxologie," *Schalom (A. Jepsen zum 70. Geburtstag)*, ed. K. H. Bernhardt (Stuttgart: Calwer Verlag, 1971), 28-37.

[8]I want to take this opportunity to thank Gene Tucker and Robert Wilson for their kindness in reading the manuscript and making many helpful suggestions, and Anna Katheryn Pfisterer for valuable assistance.

147

A number of ideas contained within the dissertation have given birth to articles now familiar to students of the Old Testament. These have appeared in various journals, and move considerably beyond what is found in the dissertation itself. Two of them posit a theophanic tradition behind Amos,[9] and three essays examine refrains within the text of Amos.[10] Another essay grew out of dissatisfaction with von Rad's narrow definition of creation, which excluded powerful imagery of cosmogony and procreation. My attempt to discover the function of creation theology in wisdom literature will appear shortly in *Studies in Ancient Israelite Wisdom*.[11] I shall focus my remarks in this Postscript upon two topics: the doxologies of Amos and judgment doxologies.

A. *The Doxologies of Amos*

With one exception, discussions of the doxologies of Amos since 1964 have covered familiar territory. That exception is Frank Crüsemann, whose study of the hymn in Amos is part of a comprehensive analysis of Israelite hymnody. On the basis of style Crüsemann isolates an elementary form in Israel--the participial hymn.[12] The content of participial hymns is said to belong to international hymnody. Nothing specifically Yahwistic appears; on the contrary, constitutive elements of ancient Near Eastern religions characterize these hymns. They speak of the creation of wind, storm, stars, rain, earthquake, and so forth. Once this common material was put in the service of apologetics, specifically by means of the refrain, "Yahweh is his name," the result was a wholly new kind of hymn. Crüsemann writes that the refrain unifies this material and claims its affirmations for

---

[9]"The Influence of the Wise upon Amos: The 'Doxologies of Amos' and Job 5:9-16, 9:5-10," *ZAW*, 79 (1967), 42-52; "Amos and the Theophanic Tradition," *ZAW*, 80 (1968), 203-15.

[10]"YHWH s^ebā'ôt š^emô: A Form-Critical Analysis," *ZAW*, 81 (1969), 156-75; "A Liturgy of Wasted Opportunity (Am. 4:6-12; Isa. 9:7-10:4; 5:25-29)," *Semitics*, 1 (1970), 27-37; "w^edōrēk ^cal-bāmŏtê 'āreṣ," *CBQ*, 34 (1972), 39-53.

[11]Library of Biblical Studies (New York: Ktav), 1975.

[12]*Studien zur Formgeschichte von Hymnus und Danklied in Israel*, 95, 103-106.

the God of Israel.[13] It is Yahweh who creates the wind and sits
high above the earth in his own dwelling place.

The doxologies of Amos belong to the participial hymn. They
are not an integral part of the text of Amos, but owe their presence to the work of a redactor. Crüsemann searches for the decisive clue to the doxologies in the refrain, "Yahweh is his name,"
just as I have done. He views the doxologies as an independent
hymn, probably of northern provenance.[14] Isaiah 51:15 plays a
prominent role in dating the redactional activity resting behind
the doxologies of Amos. Believing this verse to be pre-exilic,
Crüsemann concludes that the doxologies of Amos are also from a
time prior to the exile. Confirmation of this early date is
sought along stylistic lines: the refrain occurs in post-exilic
literature *in association with* an oracle of salvation, the mes-
senger formula, and the self-predication formula.[15] The different use of the refrain in these texts prompts Crüsemann to date
the doxologies much earlier, presumably on the assumption that
simplicity of form indicates antiquity. My analysis of texts
using the refrain, which focuses upon content as well as form,
points to entirely different conclusions.

Perhaps we are closer in our views than the last statement
implies, for Crüsemann distinguishes *origin* from *use*.[16] Horst's
proposal about a judgment doxology carries sufficient weight to
compel Crüsemann to admit that the hymn in Amos may have func-
tioned as a doxology of judgment at some time in its history.
However, its origin is said to be something entirely unrelated
to sacred law. I am inclined to agree that the hymnic fragments
have been put to a use in Amos significantly different from that
of their inception.

Crüsemann's reconstruction of the participial hymn in Amos
depends largely upon his understanding of the genre itself, although he does appeal to Job 9:9 in restoring Amos 5:8. Of prime
importance in his rendering of the doxologies is the absence of

---

[13]*Studien zur Formgeschichte von Hymnus und Danklied in
Israel*, 104-105.

[14]*Ibid.*, 106.

[15]*Ibid.*, 97, 103.

[16]*Ibid.*, 106.

definite articles with the participles. Noteworthy, too, is
Crüsemann's deletion of introductory particles (כִּי הִנֵּה) as non-
hymnic, and his identification of Amos 5:9 as a hymn fragment.
Insisting that the refrain should be made consistent, he opts
for the simple form, יהוה שְׁמוֹ. Crüsemann renders the hymn as
follows:

4:13 Der die Berge bildet und den Wind schafft
        und der dem Menschen verkündet, was sein Sinnen,
     der Morgenröte 'und' Dunkel macht
        und der tritt auf die Höhen des Landes:
     Jahwe ist sein Name!

5:8 Der die Plejaden und den Orion macht,
        'den Löwen und die dunklen Kammern des Südens,'
     'der' zum Morgen das Dunkel 'wandelt'
        und den Tag zur Nacht verfinstert:
     Jahwe ist sein Name!

9:5 Derjenige, der die Erde anrührt, so dass sie wankt
        und alle ihre Bewohner trauern,
     dass sie sich hebt wie der Nil
        und sich senkt wie der Nil Ägyptens;
     derjenige, der im Himmel seinen 'Söller' baut
        und sein Gewölbe über der Erde gründet;
     derjenige, der die Wasser des Meeres ruft
        und sie ausschüttet auf die Oberfläche der Erde:
     Jahwe ist sein Name![17]

The other interpretations of the doxologies follow paths
traversed before. For the most part these address themselves
to questions of date, authenticity, scope, and meaning of individual words. Critics are evenly divided over the issue of authenticity. Hans Walter Wolff revives Sellin's theory of redactional activity at places where mention is made of Bethel's
downfall. Wolff goes a step further, insisting that the liturgy
in Amos 4:6-13 derives from the period of Josiah and reflects

---

[17]*Studien zur Formgeschichte von Hymnus und Danklied in
Israel*, 102-103.

the struggle against a syncretistic cult at Bethel.[18] In this way Wolff gives a credible explanation for כֹּה and זֹאת in Amos 4:12. During the liturgy appropriate gestures accompanied the unspecified threatening words. Such an interpretation also allows Wolff to take seriously affinities between Lev. 26 and I Kgs. 8:33f., on the one hand, and Amos 4:6-13, on the other.

Stylistic criteria also govern Wolff's assessment of the relative dates of the doxologies and similar passages in Isa. 5:25-29 and 9:7-20. In addition to matters of style, however, Wolff pays attention to explicit liturgical language and concrete allusions to political calamities. Comparison of these texts leads Wolff to attribute the doxologies to the early Deuteronomistic period. The comparable liturgy in Isaiah is said to derive from a considerably later time.[19] Wolff thinks a redactor of Amos saw in Josiah's reforms a fulfillment of the prophetic denunciation of the sanctuary at Bethel.

Accepting Horst's explanation for the combination of confession and doxology, Wolff emphasizes the formal characteristics of the doxologies of Amos: (1) participles at the beginning of a series; (2) the conclusion of such series with a refrain, "יהוה (אֱלֹהֵי צְבָאוֹת) שְׁמוֹ," and (3) the unusual regularity of the 3+3 rhythm. Although he recognizes the uncertainty of such reconstructions of ancient hymns, Wolff ventures the following restored text:

ומגיד לאדם מה שֹחו	יוצר הרים ובֹרא רוח
ודֹרך על במֹתי ארץ	עֹשֹה שֹחר עיפה
	יהוה שֹמו
ויום לילה החשֹיך	ההֹפך לבֹקר צלמות
וישֹפכֹ על-פני הארץ	הקֹורא למי-הים
	יהוה שֹמו
ואבלו כל-יושבי בה	הנֹוגע בארץ ותמוג
ואֹגדתו על-ארץ יֹסדה	הבֹונה בשֹמים מעלותו
	יהוה שֹמו[20]

---

[18]*Dodekapropheton. Amos*, 257.

[19]*Ibid.*, 258.

[20]*Ibid.*, 254-55.

The secondary character of the doxologies is defended in another way by James Luther Mays. Unlike Wolff, who thinks the hymn derives from a time later than Amos, Mays believes it ante-dates the prophet from Tekoa.[21] The presence of the old hymn in Amos' oracles arose from the fact that he quoted a line from the hymn in 8:8.[22] Mays describes the hymn as an announcement of theophany, as I have done above. Although devoting little space to the subject, he suggests in passing that the epithet "Yahweh of hosts" belongs to Israel's theophanic tradition.[23] The unusual form, "The Lord, Yahweh of hosts," is explained as the result of a redactor's attempt to identify אֲדֹנָי, the only title in the visions, with Yahweh of hosts from the theophanic tradition.[24] Like Crüsemann, Mays understands the refrain as an early polemical confession (cf. Ex. 15:3; Ps. 68:4).

Mays insists that the separate fragments of a hymn fit badly in their contexts and accord poorly with the subject matter, a conviction that needs some qualification. He objects to Walter Brueggemann's interpretation of 4:6-13 as a liturgy of covenant renewal.[25] Mays writes that Amos summons his people to judgment, or to covenant-keeping. Although Brueggemann makes an interesting case for a call to covenant renewal, I am convinced that Amos calls on Israel to prepare for a theophany of judgment.

Defense of the doxologies' authenticity has not been marked by any new arguments. Erling Hammershaimb objects to an *a priori* assumption that Amos cannot have written such verses since they interrupt his announcement of judgment or because they differ stylistically from the rest of the book.[26] Hammershaimb insists that the hymn functions to demonstrate Yahweh's ability to carry out the threat against his people.[27] I concur in this judgment without drawing Hammershaimb's further conclusion, for a redactor

---

[21]*Amos*, 83.

[22]*Ibid.*, 84.

[23]*Ibid.*, 155.

[24]*Ibid.*

[25]*Ibid.*, 82; W. Brueggemann, "Amos iv 4-13 and Israel's Covenant Worship," *VT*, 15 (1965), 1-15.

[26]*The Book of Amos. A Commentary*, 133.

[27]*Ibid.*, 74.

is certainly capable of using a hymn to justify a threat that he wishes to apply to a new historical situation.

Wilhelm Rudolph also emphasizes the appropriateness of the hymnic description of Yahweh who comes to punish a sinful people. The source of these hymnic fragments is said to be the cult, for such polemical emphasis is otherwise absent from the words of Amos.[28] The hymn's content, however, accords well with Amos' thought, Rudolph avers, and all talk of intrusion into the contexts of the first and third doxology carries little weight.[29] Rudolph's point is well taken. I have also exercised great caution in regard to both texts, and have insisted that Amos' thought leads to such views of God as are found in the hymn. We part company, however, over the force of the second doxology, which becomes decisive in my eyes.

Against Wolff's restoration of the hymn on the basis of consistency, Rudolph objects that Amos otherwise shows no preference for exact schematization.[30] Although he accuses Sellin of pure arbitrariness in placing 3:14b after 4:12, Rudolph does not hesitate to suggest that 5:9 may originally have rested beside 6:14.[31] In any event, Rudolph rejects the hypothesis that the doxologies occur whenever the fall of Bethel's sanctuary is mentioned. He writes that the connection between the fifth vision in Amos 9:1-4 and the third doxology has nothing to do with Bethel, which is not even mentioned, but rests entirely on an allusion to an earthquake.[32] On this particular issue I think the sanctuary at Bethel is indeed implied by the text in Amos 9:1-6, but certainty is not possible.

Rudolph underscores the difference between Amos 5:8 and the Priestly account in regard to the sending of rain. In the latter the heavenly ocean was suspended over the earth, and rain poured through special windows when God opened them. In Amos 5:8, from time to time Yahweh summons water from earth's streams in order to dispense it once again upon the earth below. Rudolph thinks

---

[28]*Joel-Amos-Obadja-Jona*, 182.

[29]*Ibid.*, 181, 183.

[30]*Ibid.*, 183.

[31]*Ibid.*, 201.

[32]*Ibid.*, 247.

the connection with 5:8a makes an interpretation of the rainfall as punitive highly unlikely.[33] Here Rudolph and I are in sharp disagreement, for I would contend that the language and context suggest that the verse alludes to the Deluge or to a particularly destructive flash flood.

Rudolph takes issue with my attempt to date the use of the refrain, "Yahweh...of hosts is his name," in post-exilic times.[34] However, he correctly notes my own recognition that "Yahweh of hosts" comes from the struggle with Canaanite religion. What Rudolph interprets as indecisiveness on my part arises from his failure to recognize the distinction I make between the *origin of the epithet* "Yahweh of hosts" and *use of the refrain*, "Yahweh of hosts is his name". In my view the former is an ancient title; the latter, a formula that came to its own in a much later historical situation.

Neither Rudolph nor Hammershaimb bring forward fresh philological evidence by which to adjudicate the date of the doxologies. Rudolph does appeal to Gunkel's admission that בָּרָא was already used in the pre-exilic cult.[35] No evidence is supplied in support of this claim. Of special interest is Hammershaimb's explanation of צַלְמָוֶת as an intensive plural of צלם (be dark), and his recognition of an oath in Amos 9:5 ("As surely as....."). The latter suggestion is qualified, and Hammershaimb offers an alternative translation: "But the Lord is Yahweh of Hosts, who ....."[36] My own inclination is to favor Hammershaimb's explanation for צַלְמָוֶת and to see this as further support for the association of exile and צַלְמָוֶת proposed in my dissertation.

This brief summary of research since 1964 hardly does justice to the works under survey. Hopefully it offers a foretaste of the riches awaiting the contemporary student of Amos. Perhaps, too, it dramatizes the problem of dating ancient literature. In a sense we find ourselves trapped in a vicious circle. We date texts on the basis of our understanding of the development of Israel's language, literature and thought, and we arrive at that

---

[33]*Joel-Amos-Obadja-Jona*, 200.

[34]*Ibid.*, 182.

[35]*Ibid.*

[36]Hammershaimb, *The Book of Amos*, 133.

understanding by means of the very texts we seek to date. Awareness of this fundamental problem led me to emphasize form and
content over date, and to exercise due caution in maintaining a
post-exilic date for the hymnic texts being studied. I do not
find it cause for surprise or alarm that other interpreters arrive at a different understanding of the texts. From each interpreter much can be learned.

B.   *The Doxology of Judgment*

Hans Walter Wolff accepts the hypothesis of a judgment doxology for the hymn in Amos, and Frank Crüsemann concedes the
possibility that the texts were used in this way. Neither schol-
ar explores the implication of such an interpretation. This was
left for Gerhard von Rad to pursue, although the doxologies of
Amos were merely his point of departure. Von Rad searches for
additional texts to be understood as judgment doxologies, distinguishes individual and communal doxologies, and seeks to il-
luminate the background of the doxology's literary characteristics.

He begins by supplementing Friedrich Horst's initial list
of texts belonging to judgment doxologies. These coincide with
my own additions (Ezr. 9; Neh. 9; Dan. 9; Bar. 1:5-3:8; I Kgs.
8:33ff.), for the most part. Behind these texts, von Rad en-
visions a stable theological tradition complex, if not a single
author.[37] The setting for this tradition, he thinks, was a liturgy of repentance in ancient Israel when a stricken people re-
pented and fasted, acknowledged their sin, and absolved their
God of guilt in sending the calamity prompting such confession
and praise. The impact of the language associated with the liturgy is so powerful that it shapes the vocabulary of literature
after the demise of the special services of repentance and confession. Von Rad observes that Dan. 9 carries us to the schol-
ar's study, and Bar. 1-3 comprises part of a letter.[38] The liturgy's power is especially evident, he writes, in texts where an
individual utters a communal lament (Dan. 9:5,8,11; Neh. 1:6).
Von Rad goes on to inquire whether Neh. 1:5-11 should also be
included in the expanded list of judgment doxologies despite the

---

[37]"Gerichtsdoxologie," 28-29.

[38]*Ibid.*, 30.

absence of an actual declaration of God's righteousness.[39]   He
is inclined to answer his question affirmatively.

Von Rad devotes considerable attention to Tob. 1:3-3:6,
where acknowledgment of God's righteousness is followed by request for death.   In this text one discovers a doxology of judgment, acknowledgment of punishment, request for forgiveness, and
implicit request for an end to punishment.   Von Rad thinks the
form is that of votive stelae (the I-style of calamity, declara-
tive formula, and request for divine deliverance).[40]   He is
troubled, however, by a doxology of judgment to an individual,
and turns to Josh. 7:19 for evidence from the sacral-legal realm.
Achan's actual acknowledgment of guilt is missing, but can be
filled in from the words of the Pharaoh in Ex. 9:27f.   Here one
encounters a confession of sin, a declaration of Yahweh's justice, and a request for prayer in his behalf.   Von Rad writes
that there is hardly any doubt the Yahwist has put in Pharaoh's
mouth a declaration belonging to a doxology of judgment.   A significant conclusion follows: a doxology of judgment does not
necessarily imply execution.[41]

Since Job 5:8ff. is a composite text and thus of doubtful
value in illuminating the judgment doxology, von Rad turns to
Job 33.   He insists, therefore, upon a distinction between a
doxology of judgment to an individual and a communal judgment
doxology.[42]   In the latter case, the form is clear; it includes
a series of popular laments, to which belong doxology, confession of sin and declaration of divine righteousness.   Von Rad
thinks of this liturgy as more than a literary construct; perhaps it was a ceremony of lament in later Israel.

But what of the judgment doxology to the individual?   Must
there always be a sacral-legal procedure and confessional judgment speech?   Does the advice of Job's friends to restore his
relationship with God by doxology and confession belong to actual
procedures in sacral law?   Von Rad suggests that such claims must
be tested by the texts.   He wonders whether these differ substantially from a host of thanksgiving songs of the individual.   He

---

[39]"Gerichtsdoxologie," 31.

[40]*Ibid.*, 31-32.

[41]*Ibid.*, 33.

[42]*Ibid.*, 34-35.

also points to votive stelae as background for autobiographical confession of guilt and punishment, together with a doxology.

In short, von Rad supplies further evidence for the existence of a liturgy best described as judgment doxology, and endeavors to refine our description of that service. In many ways his research coincides with my own,[43] although I do not insist on a distinction between individual and communal doxology of judgment. Both he and I recognize the importance of biblical texts in postulating a judgment doxology, but von Rad probably places more weight on extrabiblical material than I consider appropriate.

Inasmuch as the doxologies of Amos employ various motifs from the theophanic tradition, a few words about Jörg Jeremias' recent monograph are in order. Both components of theophany delineated by Jeremias, a description of Yahweh's coming and an account of nature's response, occur in the doxologies.[44] In addition, two of the three points of contact between the "day of Yahweh" and theophany (darkness, destruction of land and its inhabitants) are present.[45] The doxologies comprise a Yahweh-hymn, but their function is closely related to prophetic announcements of judgment.[46] Thus the two basic forms of theophany combine in the doxologies, and the affinities with material from Israel's larger environment could not be more pronounced.[47] Jeremias' proposed life setting of theophany in battle hymnody[48] receives no support from the doxologies, although it may very well be correct.

---

[43]Apparently von Rad was unaware of my dissertation on the doxologies of Amos, although the essays mentioned in notes 9 and 10 called attention to the prominence of judgment doxology in it.

[44]*Theophanie*, 56-69, 109.

[45]*Ibid.*, 98-100.

[46]Jeremias isolates four forms of theophanic traditions: Yahweh hymn, prophetic announcement of judgment, prophetic proclamation of salvation, and narrative report of a theophany (*ibid.*, 123).

[47]Jeremias emphasizes the common theophanic tradition in the ancient Near East in regard to nature's reaction to God's coming (*ibid.*, 88-90, 151), but insists the idea of Yahweh's coming derives from Israel's own experience, probably the Sinaitic tradition (*ibid.*, 152, 155).

[48]*Ibid.*, 142-44.

C. *Concluding Remarks*

The dissertation devotes considerable space to discussion of the *rîb*. Literature on the covenant lawsuit has exploded since 1964. I have neither time nor inclination to attempt an updating in this area. I shall content myself with an observation, albeit much too succinct: I have read a considerable amount of this material, but have found nothing that negates my essential thesis. I would, however, be somewhat more cautious today in identifying texts that belong to a *rîb*.

Another subject that emerges in the dissertation merits further study, but will have to await a future occasion. I have long been interested in the role of prayer in ancient Israel. Hopefully, I shall return to that topic before too long.

I regret that Werner Berg's recent dissertation on the doxologies of Amos is not available to me.[49] Notice of its appearance reached my desk this week. On the basis of the advertisement, it appears that Berg agrees with me in viewing the refrain, "Yahweh....is his name," as the clue to understanding the doxologies. Time will tell whether the agreement is apparent or real. In any case, I am delighted the doxologies of Amos are finally receiving the attention they deserve. Perchance we may now hear the voice of ancient Israel with greater clarity than before.

---

[49] *Die sogenannten Hymnenfragmente im Amosbuch* (Bern und Frankfurt/M.: Verlag Peter Lang), 1974.

BIBLIOGRAPHY

Books

Anderson, Bernhard W., and Harrelson, Walter (eds.). *Israel's Prophetic Heritage*. New York: Harper and Brothers Publishers, 1962.

Anderson, B. W. *Understanding the Old Testament*. Englewood Cliffs: Prentice-Hall, Inc., 1957.

Arnold, W. R. *The Ephod and the Ark*. Cambridge: Harvard University Press, 1917.

Batten, L. W. *The Books of Ezra and Nehemiah* ("International Critical Commentary"). Edinburgh: T. & T. Clark, 1913.

Baur, Gustav. *Der Prophet Amos*. Giessen: J. Ricker'sche Buchhandlung, 1847.

Bentzen, Aage. *Daniel* ("Handbuch zum Alten Testament"). Tübingen: J.C.B. Mohr [P. Siebeck], 1952.

_____. *Introduction to the Old Testament*, I-II. Copenhagen: G. E. Gad, 1959.

Bewer, Julius. *The Prophets*. New York: Harper and Brothers Publishers, 1957.

Brown, F., Driver, S. R., and Briggs, C. A. (eds.). *A Hebrew and English Lexicon of the Old Testament*. Oxford: Clarendon Press, 1907.

Buber, Martin. *The Prophetic Faith*. Harper and Brothers Publishers, 1949.

Burrows, Eric. *The Oracles of Jacob and Balaam*. London: Burns, Oates and Washbourne, Ltd., 1938.

Černý, Ladislav. *The Day of Yahweh and Some Relevant Problems*. Prague: Sumptibus Facultatis Philosophicae Universitatis Carolinae, 1948.

Colunga, R. P. Alberto, and Turrado, Laurentio (eds.). *Biblia Sacra Iuxta Vulgatam Clementinam*. Matriti: Biblioteca de Autores Christianos, 1959.

Cripps, Richard S. *A Critical and Exegetical Commentary on the Book of Amos*. London: SPCK, 1955.

DeVaux, Roland. *Ancient Israel: Its Life and Institutions*, translated by John McHugh. New York: McGraw Hill Book Company, Inc., 1961.

160

Driver, S. R. *The Books of Joel and Amos* ("Cambridge Bible for Schools and Colleges"). Cambridge: Cambridge University Press, 1934.

Duhm, Bernhard. *Die Theologie der Propheten*. Bonn, 1875.

Edghill, E. A. *The Book of Amos*. London: Methuen & Company, 1926.

Eichrodt, Walter. *Theologie des Alten Testaments*, II. Stuttgart: Ehrenfried Klotz Verlag, 1961.

_____. *Theology of the Old Testament*, I, translated by J. A. Baker. Philadelphia: Westminster Press, 1961.

Eissfeldt, Otto. *Einleitung in das Alte Testament*, 3rd. ed. Tübingen: J.C.B. Mohr [P. Siebeck], 1964.

_____. *Das Lied Moses Deut. 33:1-43 und das Lehrgedicht Asaphs Psalm 78 samt einer Analyse der Umgebung des Mose-Liedes* (Berichte über die Verhandlungen der Sächsichen Akademie der Wissenschaften zu Leipzig), 1958.

Fey, Reinhard. *Amos und Jesaja* ("Wissenschaftliche Monographen zum Alten und Neuen Testament"). Neukirchen-Vluyn: Neukirchener Verlag, 1963.

Frey, Hellmuth. *Das Buch des Ringens Gottes um seine Kirche: Der Prophet Amos*. Stuttgart: Calwer Verlag, 1958.

Galling, Kurt. *Die Bücher der Chronik, Esra, Nehemia* ("Das Alte Testament Deutsch"). Göttingen: Vandenhoeck & Ruprecht, 1954.

Gottwald, Norman K. *A Light to the Nations*. New York: Harper and Brothers Publishers, 1959.

Gray, John. *I and II Kings* ("Old Testament Library"). Philadelphia: Westminster Press, 1963.

Gressmann, Hugo. *Der Ursprung der israelitisch-jüdischen Eschatologie*. Göttingen: Vandenhoeck & Ruprecht, 1905.

Grimm, K. J. *Liturgical Appendixes in the Old Testament*. Leipzig: August Pries, 1901.

Guillaume, A. *Prophecy and Divination among the Hebrews and other Semites*. London: Hodder & Stoughton, 1938.

Gunkel, Hermann, and Begrich, Joachim. *Einleitung in die Psalmen*. Göttingen: Vandenhoeck & Ruprecht, 1933.

Gunneweg, Antonius H. J. *Mündliche und schriftliche Tradition der vorexilischen Prophetenbücher als Problem der neueren Prophetenforschung*. Göttingen: Vandenhoeck & Ruprecht, 1959.

Harper, William R. *Amos and Hosea* ("International Critical Commentary"). New York: Charles Scribner's Sons, 1905.

Heschel, A. *The Prophets*. New York: Harper & Row, 1963.

Holloday, William L. *The Root Šubh in the Old Testament, with Particular Reference to its Usages in Covenantal Contexts*. Leiden: E. J. Brill, 1959.

Holy Bible, The Revised Standard Version. New York: Thomas Nelson & Sons, 1946, 1952.

Hyatt, J. P. *The Heritage of Biblical Faith*. Saint Louis: Bethany Press, 1964.

_____. *Prophetic Religion*. Nashville: Abingdon Press, 1947.

Jacob, Edmund. *Theology of the Old Testament*, translated by A. W. Heathcote and P. J. Allcock. New York: Harper and Brothers Publishers, 1958.

Jeremias, Alfred. *Das Alte Testament im Lichte des alten Orients*. Leipzig: J. C. Hinrichs, 1930 (2nd edition).

Johnson, Norman B. *Prayer in the Apocrypha and Pseudepigrapha*. Philadelphia: Society of Biblical Literature and Exegesis, 1948.

Kapelrud, Arvid S. *Central Ideas in Amos*. Oslo: H. Aschehoug, 1956.

_____. *The Question of Authorship in the Ezra-Narrative: A Lexical Investigation*. Oslo: I Kommisjon Hos Jacob Dybwad, 1944.

Kautzsch, E. and Cowley, A. E. (eds.). *Gesenius' Hebrew Grammar*. Oxford: Clarendon Press, 1910.

Keck, Leander E. *Mandate to Witness: Studies in the Book of Acts*. Valley Forge: Judson Press, 1964.

Kittel, Rudolf (ed.). *Biblia Hebraica*. Stuttgart: Privileg. Württembergische Bibelanstalt, 1937.

Köhler, Ludwig. *Hebrew Man*, translated by Peter Ackroyd. Nashville: Abingdon Press, 1956.

_____. *Old Testament Theology*, translated by A. S. Todd. Philadelphia: Westminster Press, 1957.

Kraus, Hans-Joachim. *Gottesdienst in Israel*. München: Chr. Kaiser Verlag, 1962.

Krause, Gerhard. *Studien zu Luthers Auslegung der Kleinen Propheten*. Tübingen: J.C.B. Mohr [P. Siebeck], 1962.

Kuhl, Curt. *The Prophets of Israel*. Edinburgh: T. & T. Clark, 1960.

Lindblom, Johannes. *Prophecy in Ancient Israel*. Philadelphia: Muhlenberg Press, 1962.

Lods, Adolph. *The Prophets and the Rise of Judaism*. New York: E. P. Dutton & Company, 1937.

Maag, Victor. *Text, Wortschatz und Begriffswelt des Buches Amos*. Leiden: E. J. Brill, 1951.

Mandelkern, Solomon. *Veteris Testamenti Concordentiae Hebraicae atque Chaldaicae*, edited by F. Margolin and M. Goshen-Gottstein. Tel-Aviv: Schocken, 1962.

Marsh, John. *Amos and Micah* ("Torch Bible Commentary"). London: SCM Press, 1959.

Marti, Karl. *Das Dodekapropheton* ("Kurzer Hand-Commentar zum Alten Testament"). Tübingen: J.C.B. Mohr [P. Siebeck], 1904.

Montgomery, J. A. *The Book of Daniel* ("International Critical Commentary"). Edinburgh: T. & T. Clark, 1927.

Morgenstern, Julian. *Amos Studies*. Cincinnati: HUC Press, 1941.

_____. *The Ark, the Ephod, and the 'Tent of Meeting.'* Cincinnati: HUC Press, 1945.

Mowinckel, Sigmund. *He That Cometh*. Oxford: Blackwell, 1959.

_____. *The Psalms in Israel's Worship* I-II, translated by D. R. Ap-Thomas. Nashville: Abingdon Press, 1962.

Neher, A. *Amos. Contribution à l'étude du prophétisme*. Paris: Librairie Philosophique J. Vrin, 1950.

Neugebauer, Otto. *Astronomical Cuneiform Texts*, I-III. London: Lund Humphries, 1955.

Nielsen, E. *Oral Tradition: A Modern Problem in Old Testament Introduction*. London: SCM Press, 1954.

Noth, Martin. *Exodus*, translated by J. S. Bowden ("Old Testament Library"). Philadelphia: Westminster Press, 1962.

_____. *The History of Israel*, translated by Stanley Godman. New York: Harper and Brothers Publishers, 1958.

Nowack, W. *Die Kleinen Propheten übersetzt und erklärt* ("Handkommentar zum Alten Testament"). Göttingen: Vandenhoeck & Ruprecht, 1922.

Oesterley, W. O. E. *Studies in the Greek and Latin Versions of the Book of Amos*. Cambridge: University Press, 1902.

Pedersen, Johannes. *Der Eid bei den Semiten*. Strassburg: Karl J. Trübner, 1914.

_____. *Israel: Its Life and Culture*, I-II,III-IV. London: Oxford University Press, 1926, 1940.

Pfeiffer, Robert H. *Introduction to the Old Testament*. New York: Harper and Brothers Publishers, 1948.

Pritchard, J. B. (ed.). *Ancient Near Eastern Texts Relating to the Old Testament*. Princeton: Princeton University Press, 1955.

Procksch, Otto. *Die Kleinen Propheten*. Stuttgart: Vereinsbuchhandlung, 1910.

Rad, Gerhard von. *Genesis*, translated by John H. Marks ("Old Testament Library"). London: SCM Press, 1961.

_____. *Der heilige Krieg im alten Israel*. Göttingen: Vandenhoeck & Ruprecht, 1958.

_____. *Old Testament Theology*, I, translated by D.M.G. Stalker. London: Oliver & Boyd, 1962.

Rahlfs, Alfred (ed.). *Septuaginta*. Stuttgart: Württembergische Bibelanstalt, 1935.

Reventlow, Henning Graf. *Das Amt des Propheten bei Amos*. Göttingen: Vandenhoeck & Ruprecht, 1962.

Robinson, John A. T. *Honest to God*. Philadelphia: Westminster Press, 1963.

Robinson, Th. H., and Horst, Friedrich. *Die zwölf Kleinen Propheten* ("Handbuch zum Alten Testament"). Tübingen: J.C.B. Mohr [P. Siebeck], 1954.

Rudolph, Wilhelm. *Esra und Nehemia* ("Handbuch zum Alten Testament"). Tübingen: J.C.B. Mohr [P. Siebeck], 1949.

_____. *Jeremia* ("Handbuch zum Alten Testament"). Tübingen: J.C.B. Mohr [P. Siebeck], 1958.

Scharbert, Josef. *Solidarität in Segen und Fluch im Alten Testament und in seiner Umwelt*. Bonn: Peter Hanstein Verlag, 1958.

Schmidt, Hans. *Der Prophet Amos, Sechs Vorlesungen an einem Kriegshochschulkurs*. Tübingen: J.C.B. Mohr [P. Siebeck], 1917.

Sellin, Ernst. *Das Zwölfprophetenbuch übersetzt und erklärt*, I-II. Leipzig: A. Deichertsche Verlag, 1922.

Skinner, John. *The Book of the Prophet Isaiah* ("Cambridge Bible for Schools and Colleges"). Cambridge: University Press, 1898.

Smith, George Adam. *The Book of the Twelve Prophets*, I-II. London: Hodder & Stoughton, 1928.

Smith, J. M. P. *The Day of Yahweh*. Chicago: University Press, 1901.

Smith, W. Robertson. *The Prophets of Israel and Their Place in History*. New York: D. Appleton & Company, 1882.

Snaith, Norman H. *Amos, Hosea and Micah*. London: Epworth Press, 1956.

Torrey, C. C. *Ezra Studies*. Chicago: University of Chicago Press, 1910.

Vriezen, Th. C. *An Outline of Old Testament Theology*. Oxford: Blackwell, 1960.

Vuilleumier-Bessard, René. *La tradition cultuelle d'Israël dans la prophétie d'Amos et d'Osée*. Neuchatel: Editions Delachaux & Niestlé, 1960.

Wambacq, B. N. *L'épithète divine Jahvé $S^eb\bar{a}'\hat{o}t$*. De Brouwer: Desclee, 1947.

Watts, John D. W. *Vision and Prophecy in Amos*. Grand Rapids: Wm. B. Eerdman's Publishing Company, 1958.

Weiser, Artur. *Das Buch des Propheten Jeremia* ("Das Alte Testament Deutsch"). Göttingen: Vandenhoeck & Ruprecht, 1952, 1955.

_____. *Glaube und Geschichte im Alten Testament*. Göttingen: Vandenhoeck & Ruprecht, 1961.

_____. *The Old Testament: Its Formation and Development*, translated by Dorothea M. Barton. New York: Association Press, 1961.

_____. *The Psalms*, translated by H. Hartwell ("Old Testament Library"). London: SCM Press, 1962.

_____, and Elliger, Karl. *Das Buch der zwölf Kleinen Propheten*, I-II ("Das Alte Testament Deutsch"). Göttingen: Vandenhoeck & Ruprecht, 1949.

Wellhausen, Julius. *Geschichte Israels*, I. Berlin: G. Reimer, 1878.

_____. *Die Kleinen Propheten*, unchanged reprint. Berlin: Walter de Gruyter, 1963.

Wendel, Adolf. *Das freie Laiengebet im vorexilischen Israel*. Leipzig: Eduard Pfeiffer Verlag, 1931.

Werner, Eric. *The Sacred Bridge*. New York: Columbia University Press, 1959.

Westermann, Claus. *Grundformen prophetischer Rede*. München: Chr. Kaiser Verlag, 1960.

_____. *Das Loben Gottes in den Psalmen*. Göttingen: Vandenhoeck & Ruprecht, 1961.

Wolff, H. W. *Dodekapropheton I: Hosea* ("Biblischer Kommentar Altes Testament"). Neukirchen Kreis Moers: Neukirchener Verlag, 1961.

Articles

Albright, William Foxwell. "A Catalogue of Early Hebrew Lyric
   Poems (Psalm 68)," *Hebrew Union College Annual*, XXIII
   (1950-51), 1-40.

_____. "The High Place in Ancient Palestine," *Supplement
   Vetus Testamentum*, IV (1956), 242-58.

_____. "The Psalm of Habakkuk," *Studies in Old Testament
   Prophecy*, edited by H. H. Rowley. Edinburgh: T. & T.
   Clark, 1947, 1-18.

_____. "Review of B. N. Wambacq, L'épithète divine Jahvé
   ṣeḇā'ôt," *Journal of Biblical Literature*, LXVII (1948),
   377-81.

Anderson, B. W. "Creation," *Interpreter's Dictionary of the
   Bible*, edited by Buttrick, George Arthur, *et al*. Nashville: Abingdon Press, 1962, 725-32.

_____. "Hosts, Host of Heaven," *The Interpreter's Dic-
   tionary of the Bible*, 654-56.

_____. "Lord of Hosts," *The Interpreter's Dictionary of
   the Bible*, 151.

Andrews, Mary E. "Hesiod and Amos," *Journal of Religion*, XXIII
   (1943), 194-205.

Ap-Thomas, D. R. "Notes on some terms relating to Prayer,"
   Vetus Testamentum, VI (1956), 225-41.

Aptowitzer, V. "Arabisch-jüdische Schöpfungstheorieen," *Hebrew
   Union College Annual*, VI (1929), 205-46.

Bach, Robert. "Gottesrecht und weltliches Recht in der Verkündigung des Propheten Amos," *Festschrift für Günther
   Dehn*. Neukirchen: Verlag der Buchhandlung des Erziehungsvereins, (1957), 23-34.

Bauer, Johannes Baptist. "Der priesterliche Schöpfungshymnus
   in Gen. 1," *Theologische Zeitschrift*, XX (1964), 1-9.

Baumgärtel, Friedrich. "Zu den Gottesnamen in den Büchern
   Jeremia und Ezechiel," *Verbannung und Heimkehr: Festschrift
   für Wilhelm Rudolph*, edited by Arnulf Kuschke. Tübingen:
   J.C.B. Mohr [P. Siebeck], 1961, 1-29.

Baumann, E. "Der Aufbau der Amosreden," *Beihefte zur Zeitschrift für die alttestamentliche Wissenschaft*, VII (1903),
   1-69.

Bayer, P. Edmund. "Danielstudien," *Alttestamentliche Abhandlungen*, III (1912), 1-188.

Begrich, J. "Studien zu Deuterojesaja," *Beiträge zur Wissenschaft vom Alten und Neuen Testament*, LXXVII (1938), 19-42.

166

Bender, A. "Das Lied Exodus 15," *Zeitschrift für die alttestamentliche Wissenschaft*, XXIII (1903), 1-48.

Bentzen, A. "The Ritual Background of Amos 1:2-2:16," *Oudtestamentische Studien*, VIII (1950), 85-99.

_____. "The Weeping of Jacob, Hos. XII:5a," *Vetus Testamentum*, I (1951), 58-59.

Bernhardt, K. H. "Zur Bedeutung der Schöpfungsvorstellung für die Religion Israels in vorexilischer Zeit, *Theologische Literaturzeitung*, LXXXV (1960), 822-23.

Bewer, J. "The Ordeal in Num., Chap. 5," *American Journal of Semitic Languages and Literature*, XXX (1913-14), 36-47.

Blank, Sheldon H. "The Curse, the Blasphemy, the Spell, and the Oath," *Hebrew Union College Annual*, XXIII (1950-51), 73-96.

_____. "Some Observations Concerning Biblical Prayer," *Hebrew Union College Annual*, XXXII (1961), 75-90.

_____. "Studies in Post-Exilic Universalism," *Hebrew Union College Annual*, XI (1936), 159-92.

Bosshard, Everett. "Septuagint Codices V, 62, and 147 in the Book of Amos," *Journal of Biblical Literature*, LVIII (1939), 331-47.

Botterweck, G. Johannes. "Zur Authentizität des Buches Amos," *Biblische Zeitschrift*, Neue Folge II (1958), 176-89.

Bowman, R. A. "The Book of Ezra and the Book of Nehemiah," *The Interpreter's Bible*, edited by Buttrick, G. A., III. (Nashville: Abingdon Press, 1954), 551-819.

Brongers, H. A. "Der Eifer des Herrn Zebaoth," *Vetus Testamentum*, XIII (1963), 269-84.

Browne, L. E. "Ezra and Nehemiah," *Peake's Commentary on the Bible*, edited by Black, Matthew and Rowley, H. H. New York: Thomas Nelson and Sons Ltd., 1962, 370-80.

Budde, Karl. "Zu Text und Auslegung des Buches Amos," *Journal of Biblical Literature*, XLIII (1924), 63-122; XLIV (1925), 46-131.

_____. "Zur Geschichte des Buches Amos," *Beihefte zur Zeitschrift für die alttestamentliche Wissenschaft*, XXVII (1914), 63-77.

Caspari, W. "Wer hat die Aussprüche des Propheten Amos gesammelt?" *Neue Kirchliche Zeitschrift*, XXV (1914), 701-15.

Chapman, William J. "Palestinian Chronological Data, 750-700 B.C.," *Hebrew Union College Annual*, VIII-IX (1931-32), 151-68.

Cohen, Simon. "Amos was a Navi," *Hebrew Union College Annual*, XXXII (1961), 175-78.

Cossmann, W. "Die Entwicklung des Gerichtsgedankens bei den alttestamentlichen Propheten," *Beihefte zur Zeitschrift für die alttestamentliche Wissenschaft*, XIX (1915), 1-231.

Cramer, K. "Amos: Versuch einer theologischen Interpretation," *Beiträge zur Wissenschaft vom Alten und Neuen Testament*, III (1930), 1-215.

Cross, Frank M. Jr., "The Council of Yahweh in Second Isaiah," *Journal of Near Eastern Studies*, XII (1953), 274-77.

_____. "Yahweh and the God of the Patriarchs," *Harvard Theological Review*, LV (1962), 225-59.

_____, and Freedman, David Noel. "The Song of Miriam," *Journal of Near Eastern Studies*, XIV (1955), 237-50.

Deissler, Alfons. "Zur Datierung und Situierung der 'kosmischen Hymnen' Pss. 8,19,29," *Lex Tua Veritas: Festschrift für Hubert Junker*. Trier: Paulinus Verlag, 1961, 47-58.

_____. "Micha 6, 1-8, Der Rechtstreit Jahwes mit Israel um das rechte Bundesverhältnis," *Trierer Theologische Zeitschrift*, LXVII (1959), 229-34.

Driver, G. R., and Miles, J. C. "Ordeal by Oath at Nuzi," *Iraq*, VII (1940), 132-38.

Driver, G. R., and Clarke, Leonard W. "Stars," *Dictionary of the Bible*, James Hastings (ed.), revised by F. C. Grant and H. H. Rowley. New York: Charles Scribner's Sons, 1963, 936-38.

Driver, G. R. "Two Astronomical Passages in the Old Testament," *Journal of Theological Studies*, IV (1953), 208-12.

Duhm, Bernhard. "Anmerkungen zu den zwölf Propheten," *Zeitschrift für die alttestamentliche Wissenschaft*, XXXI (1911), 1-18.

Eissfeldt, Otto. "Der Gott Bethel," *Archiv für Religionswissenschaft*, XXVIII (1930), 1-30.

_____. "Der Gott des Tabor und seine Verbreitung," *Archiv für Religionswissenschaft*, XXXI (1934), 14-41.

_____. "Gott und das Meer in der Bibel," *Studia Orientalia Ioanni Pedersen*. Copenhagen (1953), 76-84.

_____.. "Jahwes Verhältnis zu Elyon und Schadday nach Psalm 91," *Die Welt des Orient*, I (1957), 343-48.

_____. "Jahwe Zebaoth," *Miscellanea Academica Berolinensia*, II (1950), 127-50.

_____. "Lade und Stierbild," *Zeitschrift für die alttestamentliche Wissenschaft*, LVIII (1940-41), 190-215.

_____. "The Prophetic Literature," *The Old Testament and Modern Study*, edited by Rowley, H. H. London: Oxford Press, 1951, 115-61.

Eissfeldt, Otto. "Silo und Jerusalem," *Supplement Vetus Testamentum*, IV (1957), 138-47.

_____. "Zur Überlieferungsgeschichte der Prophetenbücher des Alten Testament," *Theologische Literaturzeitung*, LXXIII (1948), 529-34.

Fischer, T. "Einige neue Beobachtungen zur Septuaginta des Buches Amos," *Anglican Theological Review*, VI (1923-24), 245-47.

Fohrer, Georg. "Neuere Literatur zur alttestamentlichen Prophetie," *Theologische Rundschau*, XIX (1951), 277-345.

_____. "Remarks on Modern Interpretation of the Prophets," *Journal of Biblical Literature*, LXXX (1961), 309-19.

_____. "Zehn Jahre Literatur zur alttestamentlichen Prophetie (1951-1960)," *Theologische Rundschau*, XXVIII (1962), 1-75, 235-374.

Fosbroke, H. E. W. "The Book of Amos," *The Interpreter's Bible*, VI, 763-853.

Freedman, David Noel. "The Name of the God of Moses," *Journal of Biblical Literature*, LXXIX (1960), 151-56.

Frost, Stanley B. "Asseveration by Thanksgiving," *Vetus Testamentum*, VIII (1958), 380-90.

Galling, Kurt. "Bethel und Gilgal," *Zeitschrift der deutschen Morgenländischen Gesellschaft*, XXXVI (1945), 34-43.

_____. "Der Gott Karmel und die Ächtung der fremden Götter," *Geschichte und Altes Testament: Festschrift für A. Alt*. Tübingen: J.C.B. Mohr [P. Siebeck], 1953, 105-25.

Gaster, Th. H. "An Ancient Hymn in the Prophecies of Amos," *Journal of the Manchester Egyptian and Oriental Society*, XIX (1935), 23-26.

_____. "Notes on 'The Song of the Sea'," *Expository Times*, XLVIII (1936-37), 45.

✳ Gemser, B. "The rîb- or Controversy-Pattern in Hebrew Mentality," *Supplement Vetus Testamentum*, III (1955), 120-37.

Gese, Hartmut. "Die hebräischen Bibelhandschriften zum Dodeka-propheton nach der Variantensammlung des Kennicott," *Zeitschrift für die alttestamentliche Wissenschaft*, LXIX (1957), 55-68.

_____. "Kleine Beiträge zum Verständnis des Amosbuch," *Vetus Testamentum*, XII (1962), 417-38.

Goitein, S. D. "YHWH the Passionate: The Monotheistic Meaning and Origin of the Name YHWH," *Vetus Testamentum*, VI (1956), 1-9.

Gordis, Ralph. "The Composition and Structure of Amos," *Harvard Theological Review*, XXXIII (1940), 239-51.

_____. "Some Hitherto Unrecognized Meanings of the Verb Shub," *Journal of Biblical Literature*, LII (1933), 153-62.

Gordon, Cyrus H. "Kir," *Interpreter's Dictionary of the Bible*, 36.

Greenfield, J. C. "Caphtor," *Interpreter's Dictionary of the Bible*, 534.

Grimme, Hubert. "Das Alter des israelitischen Versohnungstages," *Archiv für Religionswissenschaft*, XIV (1911), 130-42.

_____. "Der Begriff von hebräischen הדוה und הדות," *Zeitschrift für die alttestamentliche Wissenschaft*, LVIII (1940-41), 234-39.

Gray, John. "Ashima," *Interpreter's Dictionary of the Bible*, 252.

Guthe, K. "Amos," *Die Heilige Schrift des Alten Testaments*, hrsg. E. Kautsch, II. Tübingen: J.C.B. Mohr [P. Siebeck], 1923, 30-47.

Harper, W. R. "Suggestions concerning the Original Text and Structure of Amos 1:3-2:5," *American Journal of Theology*, I (1897), 140-45.

Harrelson, Walter. "Nonroyal Motifs in the Royal Eschatology," *Israel's Prophetic Heritage*, 147-65.

_____. "Prophecy and Syncretism," *Andover Newton Quarterly*, IV New Series (1964), 6-19.

_____. "Worship in Early Israel," *Biblical Research*, III (1958), 1-14.

Harvéy, Julien. "Le 'rîb-pattern', réquisitoire prophétique sur la rupture de l'alliance," *Biblica*, XLIII (1962), 172-96.

Haupt, Paul. "Moses' Song of Triumph," *American Journal of Semitic Languages and Literature*, XX (1904), 149-72.

Hempel, J. "Die israelitischen Anschauungen von Segen und Fluch im Lichte altorientalischer Parallelen," *Zeitschrift der deutschen Morgenländischen Gesellschaft*, LXXIX (1925), 20-110.

_____. "Ordal," *Die Religion in Geschichte und Gegenwart*, hrsg. Kurt Galling, 3. Auflage. Tübingen: J.C.B. Mohr [P. Siebeck], 1957-, IV, 745-47.

Hentschke, R. "Die Stellung der vorexilischen Schriftpropheten zum Kultus," *Beihefte zur Zeitschrift für die alttestamentliche Wissenschaft*, LXXV (1957), 1-176.

Herrmann, J. "Das Gebet im Alten Testament," *Theologische Wörterbuch*, hrsg. R. Kittel, II (1935), 782-99.

Herrmann, S. "Die Naturlehre des Schöpfungsberichtes," *Theologische Literaturzeitung*, LXXXVI (1961), 413-23.

Hertzberg, H. W. "Die prophetische Kritik am Kult," *Theologische Literaturzeitung*, LXXV (1950), 219-26.

Hesse, Franz. "Amos 5:4-6, 14f.," *Zeitschrift für die alttestamentliche Wissenschaft*, LXVIII (1956), 1-17.

_____. "Das Verstockungsproblem im Alten Testament," *Beihefte zur Zeitschrift für die alttestamentliche Wissenschaft*, LXXIV (1955), 1-107.

_____. "Wurzelt die prophetische Gerichtsrede im israelitischen Kult?" *Zeitschrift für die alttestamentliche Wissenschaft*, LXV (1953), 45-53.

Hoffmann, Georg. "Versuche zu Amos," *Zeitschrift für die alttestamentliche Wissenschaft*, III (1883), 110-11.

Hommel, H. "Das religionsgeschichtliche Problem des 139. Psalms," *Zeitschrift für die alttestamentliche Wissenschaft*, XLVIII (1929), 110-24.

Horst, Friedrich. "Die Doxologien im Amosbuch," *Zeitschrift für die alttestamentliche Wissenschaft*, XLVII (1929), 45-54, reprinted in *Gottes Recht*, München: Chr. Kaiser Verlag, 1961, 155-66.

_____. "Der Eid im Alten Testament" (1957), *Gottes Recht*, 292-314.

_____. "Die Kennzeichen der hebräischen Poesie," *Theologische Rundschau*, XXI (1953), 97-120.

_____. "Zwei Begriffe für Eigentum (Besitz): נַחֲלָה und אֲחֻזָּה," *Verbannung und Heimkehr*, 135-36.

Huffmon, Herbert B. "The Covenant Lawsuit in the Prophets," *Journal of Biblical Literature*, LXXVIII (1959), 285-95.

Humbert, Paul. "Emploi et portée du verbe bārā' (créer) dans l'Ancien Testament," *Theologische Zeitschrift*, III (1947), 401-22.

_____. "'Qānā' en hébreu biblique," *Festschrift für Alfred Bertholet*. Tübingen: J.C.B. Mohr [P. Siebeck], 1950, 259-66.

Hyatt, J. P. "Amos," *Peake's Commentary on the Bible*, 617-25.

_____. "The Deity Bethel and the Old Testament," *Journal of the American Oriental Society*, LIX (1939), 81-98.

_____. "Jeremiah," *The Interpreter's Bible*, V, 777-1142.

Hyatt, J. P. "The Translation and Meaning of Amos 5:23-24," *Zeitschrift für die alttestamentliche Wissenschaft*, LXVIII (1956), 17-24.

_____. "Yahweh as 'the God of my father'," *Vetus Testamentum*, V (1955), 130-36.

Irwin, W. A. "The Thinking of Amos," *American Journal of Semitic Languages and Literature*, XLIX (1932), 102-14.

Jacobsen, Thorkild. "Primitive Democracy in Ancient Mesopotamia," *Journal of Near Eastern Studies*, II (1943), 159-72.

Jeffery, A. "The Book of Daniel," *The Interpreter's Bible*, VI, 341-49.

Jepsen, Alfred. "Kleine Beiträge zum Zwölfprophetenbuch," *Zeitschrift für die alttestamentliche Wissenschaft*, LVI (1938), 85-100; LXI (1945-48), 95-113.

Jones, D. R. "Isaiah--II and III," *Peake's Commentary on the Bible*, 516-36.

Jozaki, Susumu. "The Secondary Passages of the Book of Amos," *Kwansei Gakuin University Annual Studies*, IV (1956), 25-100.

Junker, Hubert. "Amos, der Mann, den Gott mit unwiderstehlicher Gewalt zum Propheten machte," *Trierer Theologische Zeitschrift*, LXV (1956), 321-28.

_____. "Amos und die 'opferlose Mosezeit.' Ein Beitrag zur Erklärung von Amos 5:25-26," *Theologie und Glaube*, XXVII (1935), 686-95.

_____. "Die Entstehungszeit des Ps. 78 und das Deuteronomium," *Biblica*, XXXIV (1953), 487-500.

_____. "Die theologische Behandlung der Chaosvorstellungen in der biblischen Schöpfungsgeschichte," *Mélanges Bibliques en l'honneur de A. Robert*. Paris, 1957, 27-37.

Kapelrud, Arvid S. "Cult and Prophetic Words," *Studia Theologica*, IV (1951-52), 5-12.

_____. "God as Destroyer in the Preaching of Amos and in the Ancient Near East," *Journal of Biblical Literature*, LXXI (1952), 33-38.

Kautzsch, E. "Sebaoth," *Realencyklopädia für protest. Theologie und Kirche*, XXI (1908), 620-27.

Kessler, Werner. "Aus welchen Gründen wird die Bezeichnung 'Jahwe Zebaoth' in der späteren Zeit gemieden?" *Gottes ist der Orient: Festschrift für Otto Eissfeldt*. Berlin: Evangelische Verlagsanstalt, 1959, 79-83.

Kittel, Rudolf. "Der Gott Bet'el," *Journal of Biblical Literature*, XLIV (1925), 123-53.

Kleinschmidt, Otto. "Neues zu dem alten Thema: 'Entwicklungs-gedanke und Schöpfungsglaube,'" *Zeitschrift für Theologie und Kirche*, XLIV (1936), 241-53.

Köhler, Ludwig. "Amos-Forschungen von 1917 bis 1932," *Theologische Rundschau*, IV (1932), 195-213.

_____. "Die Morgenröte im Alten Testament," *Zeitschrift für die alttestamentliche Wissenschaft*, XLIV (1926), 56-59.

Kraus, Hans-Joachim. "Gilgal, ein Beitrag zur Kultusgeschichte Israels," *Vetus Testamentum*, I (1951), 181-99.

Kutsch, E. "Gottesurteil in Israel," *Die Religion in Geschichte und Gegenwart*, II (1958), 1808-09.

Lambert, G. "La creation dans la Bible," *Nouvelle Revue Theologique*, LXXV (1953), 252-81.

Lehming, Sigo. "Erwägungen zu Amos," *Zeitschrift für Theologie und Kirche*, LV (1958), 145-69.

Lempp, W. "Nations in Amos," *South East Asia Journal of Theology*, I (1960), 20-33.

Liebreich, Leon J. "The Impact of Nehemiah 9:5-37 on the Liturgy of the Synagogue," *Hebrew Union College Annual*, XXXII (1961), 217-26.

Lindblom, Johannes. "Theophanies in Holy Places in Hebrew Religion," *Hebrew Union College Annual*, XXXII (1961), 91-106.

Lohr, Max. "Untersuchungen zum Buch Amos," *Beihefte zur Zeitschrift für die alttestamentliche Wissenschaft*, IV (1901), 1-67.

Maag, Victor. "Amosbuch," *Die Religion in Geschichte und Gegenwart*, I (1956), 330-31.

_____. "Jahwäs Heerscharen," *Festschrift für Ludwig Köhler: Schweizerische Theologische Umschau* (1950), 27-52.

_____. "Zur Übersetzung von Maskil in Amos 5:13, Ps. 47:8, und in den Überschriften einiger Psalmen," *Schweizerische Theologische Umschau*, XII (1943), 108ff.

Mauchline, John. "The Book of Hosea," *The Interpreter's Bible*, VI, 553-725.

May, H. G. "Theological Universalism in the Old Testament," *Journal of Bible and Religion*, XVI (1948), 100-07.

Mayer, R. "Der Gottesname Jahwe im Lichte der neuesten Forschung," *Biblische Zeitschrift*, Neue Folge II (1958), 26-53.

Mays, James L. "Words about the Words of Amos," *Interpretation*, XIII (1959), 259-72.

McCullough, W. Stewart. "Some Suggestions about Amos," *Journal of Biblical Literature*, LXXII (1953), 246-54.

⚹ Mendenhall, G. E. "Covenant Forms in Israelite Tradition," *Biblical Archaeologist*, XVII (1954), 50-76.

Morgenstern, Julian. "Amos Studies (Part Four)," *Hebrew Union College Annual*, XXXII (1961), 295-350.

_____. "The Ark, the Ephod, and the 'Tent of Meeting'," *Hebrew Union College Annual*, XVII (1942-43), 153-266; XVIII (1943-44), 1-52.

⚹ _____. "Biblical Theophanies," *Zeitschrift für Assyriologie*, XXV (1911), 139-93; XXVIII (1914), 15-60.

_____. "The Gates of Righteousness," *Hebrew Union College Annual*, VI (1929), 1-38.

_____. "The Historical Antecedents of Amos," *Hebrew Union College Annual*, XV (1940), 59-304.

⚹ _____. "Trial by Ordeal among the Semites and in Ancient Israel," *Hebrew Union College Jubilee Volume*, edited by Philipson, David, *et al.* (Cincinnati: HUC Press, 1925), 113-43.

_____. "The Universalism in Amos," *Essays Presented to Leo Baeck on the Occasion of his Eightieth Birthday*. London: East and West Library, 1954, 106-26.

Mowinckel, Sigmund. "La connaissance de Dieu chez les prophètes de l'Ancien Testament," *Revue d'Histoire et de Philosophie religieuses*, XXII (1942), 69-105.

_____. "The Name of the God of Moses," *Hebrew Union College Annual*, XXXII (1961), 121-34.

_____. "The 'Spirit' and the 'Word' in the Pre-Exilic Reforming Prophets," *Journal of Biblical Literature*, LIII (1934), 199-227.

_____. "Die Sternnamen im Alten Testament," *Norsk Teologisk Tidsskrift*, XXIX (1928), 5-75.

_____. "Zum Psalm des Habakkuk," *Theologische Zeitschrift*, IX (1953), 1-23.

Quell, G. "Der Kultprophet," *Theologische Literaturzeitung*, LXXXI (1956), 402-03.

Müller, Hans-Peter. "Die kultische Darstellung der Theophanie," *Vetus Testamentum*, XIV (1964), 183-91.

⚹ Muilenburg, James. "The Form and Structure of the Covenantal Formulations," *Vetus Testamentum*, IX (1959), 347-65.

_____. "Isaiah 40-66," *The Interpreter's Bible*, V, 381-773.

Muilenburg, James. "The Linguistic and Rhetorical Usages of the Particle יִכ in the Old Testament," *Hebrew Union College Annual*, XXXII (1961), 135-60.

_____. "Old Testament Prophecy," *Peake's Commentary on the Bible*, 475-83.

_____. "The Speech of Theophany," *Harvard Divinity Bulletin*, XXVIII (1964), 35-47.

Nielsen, Eduard. "The Burial of the Foreign Gods," *Studia Theologica*, VIII (1955), 103-22.

Nöldeke, Th. "הָוָצְמַח und םֶלֶצ," *Zeitschrift für die alttestamentliche Wissenschaft*, XVII (1897), 183-87.

Nyberg, H. S. "Studien zum Religionskampf im Alten Testament," *Archiv für Religionswissenschaft*, XXXV (1938), 329-87.

Obermann, J. "The Divine Name YHWH in the Light of Recent Discoveries," *Journal of Biblical Literature*, LXVIII (1949), 309-14.

Paterson, John. "Jeremiah," *Peake's Commentary on the Bible*, 537-62.

Peake, A. S. "Elijah and Jezebel," *Bulletin of John Rylands Library*, II (1927), 296-321.

Pfeiffer, E. "Die Disputationsworte im Buche Maleachi," *Evangelische Theologie*, XII (1959), 546-68.

Pfeiffer, R. H. "The Polemic against Idolatry in the Old Testament," *Journal of Biblical Literature*, XLIII (1924), 229-40.

Pope, Marvin. "Oaths," *Interpreter's Dictionary of the Bible*, 576-77.

Porteous, Norman. "Jerusalem-Zion: The Growth of a Symbol," *Verbannung und Heimkehr*, 235-52.

Prätorius, E. "Zum Texte des Amos," *Zeitschrift für die alttestamentliche Wissenschaft*, XXXIV (1914), 42-44.

Press, R. "Das Ordal im alten Israel," *Zeitschrift für die alttestamentliche Wissenschaft*, X (1933), 121-40, 227-55.

Rad, Gerhard von. "Aspekte alttestamentlichen Weltverständnisses," *Evangelische Theologie*, XXIV (1964), 57-73.

_____. "Das formgeschichtliche Problem des Hexateuchs" (1938), *Gesammelte Studien zum Alten Testament*. München: Chr. Kaiser Verlag, 1961, 9-86.

_____. "Die levitische Predigt in den Büchern der Chronik" (1934), *Gesammelte Studien zum Alten Testament*, 248-61.

Rad, Gerhard von. "The Origin of the Concept of the Day of Yah-weh," *Journal of Semitic Studies*, IV (1959), 97-108.

_____. "Das theologische Problem des alttestamentlichen Schöpfungsglaubens" (1936), *Gesammelte Studien zum Alten Testament*, 136-47.

_____. "Die Stadt auf dem Berge" (1948-49), *Gesammelte Studien zum Alten Testament*, 214-24.

Rendtorff, Rolf. "Priesterliche Kulttheologie und prophetische Kultpolemik," *Theologische Literaturzeitung*, LXXXI (1956), 341-44.

_____. "Die theologische Stellung des Schöpfungsglaubens bei Deuterojesaja," *Zeitschrift für Theologie und Kirche*, LI (1954), 3-13.

Reventlow, Henning Graf. "Prophetenamt und Mittleramt," *Zeitschrift für Theologie und Kirche*, LVIII (1961), 269-84.

Robinson, H. Wheeler. "The Council of Yahweh," *Journal of Theological Studies*, XLV (1944), 151-57.

Robinson, Theodore H. "Neuere Propheten-Forschung," *Theologische Rundschau*, III (1931), 75-103.

Robscheit, H. "Die Thora bei Amos und Hosea," *Evangelische Theologie*, V Neue Folge (1950-51), 26-38.

Rowley, H. H. "Elijah on Mount Carmel," *Bulletin of John Rylands Library*, XLIII (1960-61), 190-219.

_____. "Melchizedek and Zadok," *Festschrift für Alfred Bertholet*, 461-72.

_____. "Ritual and the Hebrew Prophets," *Journal of Semitic Studies*, I (1956), 338-60.

Rozelaar, Marc. "The Song of the Sea," *Vetus Testamentum*, II (1952), 221-28.

Rudolph, Wilhelm. "Gott und Mensch bei Amos," *Imago Dei: Beiträge zur theologischen Anthropologie, Gustav Krüger zum 70. Geburtstag dargebracht*. Giessen, 1932, 19-31.

Sarton, George. "Chaldean Astronomy of the Last Three Centuries, B.C.," *Journal of the American Oriental Society*, LXXV (1955), 166-73.

Schmidt, Hans. "Die Herkunft des Propheten Amos," *Beihefte zur Zeitschrift für die alttestamentliche Wissenschaft*, XXXIV (1920), 158-71.

Schmidt, Nathaniel. "On the Text and Interpretation of Amos V:25-27," *Journal of Biblical Literature*, XIII (1894), 1-15.

Schnutenhaus, Frank. "Das Kommen und Erscheinen Gottes im Alten Testament," *Zeitschrift für die alttestamentliche Wissenschaft*, LXXVI (1964), 1-22.

Schwally, F. "Die biblischen Schöpfungsberichte," *Archiv für Religionswissenschaft*, IX (1906), 159-75.

Scott, R. B. Y. "The Book of Isaiah," *The Interpreter's Bible*, V, 151-381.

Seierstadt, Ivar P. "Erlebnis und Gehorsam beim Propheten Amos," *Zeitschrift für die alttestamentliche Wissenschaft*, XI (1934), 22-41.

Smart, J. D. "Amos," *The Interpreter's Dictionary of the Bible*, 116-21.

Smend, Rudolph. "Das Nein des Amos," *Evangelische Theologie*, VIII (1963), 404-23.

Smith, J. M. P. "The Day of Yahweh," *American Journal of Theology*, V (1901), 505-33.

Smythe, H. R. "Interpretation of Amos 4:13 in St. Athanasius and Didymus," *Journal of Theological Studies*, I New Series (1950), 158-68.

Soper, B. Kingston. "For Three Transgressions and for Four," *Expository Times*, LXXI (1959-1960), 86-87.

Speier, Salomon. "Bemerkungen zu Amos," *Vetus Testamentum*, III (1953), 305-10.

Stamm, J. J. "Die Theodizee in Babylon und Israel," *Jaarbericht...Ex Oriente Lux*, IX (1944), 99-107.

Terrien, Samuel. "Amos and Wisdom," *Israel's Prophetic Heritage*, 108-15.

Torrey, Charles Cutler. "The Composition and Historical Value of Ezra-Nehemiah," *Beihefte zur Zeitschrift für die alttestamentliche Wissenschaft*, II (1896), 1-65.

Vaccari, A. "Hymnus propheticus in Deum Creatorem," *Verbum Domini*, IX (1929), 184-88.

Vriezen, Th. C. "'Ehje 'aser 'ehje," *Festschrift für Alfred Bertholet*, 498-512.

_____. "La tradition de Jacob dans Osee XII," *Oudtestamentische Studien*, I (1942), 64-78.

Waldow, Eberhard von. "Der traditionsgeschichtliche Hintergrund der prophetischen Gerichtsreden," *Beihefte zur Zeitschrift für die alttestamentliche Wissenschaft*, LXXXV (1963), 1-53.

Wambacq, B. N. "Les prières de Baruch (1,15-2,19) et de Daniel (9,5-19)," *Biblica*, XL (1959), 463-75.

Watts, John D. W. "Elements of Old Testament Worship," *Journal of Bible and Religion*, XXVI (1958), 217-21.

_____. "Note on the Text of Amos V:7," *Vetus Testamentum*, IV (1954), 215-16.

_____. "An Old Hymn Preserved in the Book of Amos," *Journal of Near Eastern Studies*, XV (1956), 33-39.

_____. "The Origin of the Book of Amos," *Expository Times*, LXVI (1954-55), 109-12.

_____. "The Song of the Sea--Ex. 15," *Vetus Testamentum*, VII (1957), 371-80.

Weingreen, J. "Rabbinic-Type Glosses in the Old Testament," *Journal of Semitic Studies*, II (1957), 149-62.

Weiser, Artur. "Die Prophetie des Amos," *Beihefte zur Zeitschrift für die alttestamentliche Wissenschaft*, LIII (1929), 1-332.

_____. "Zu Amos 4:6-13," *Zeitschrift für die alttestamentliche Wissenschaft*, V (1928), 49-59.

_____. "Zur Frage nach den Beziehungen der Psalmen zum Kult: Die Darstellung der Theophanie in den Psalmen und im Festkult," *Festschrift für Alfred Bertholet*, 513-31.

_____. "Samuels 'Philister-Sieg,'" *Zeitschrift für Theologie und Kirche*, LVI (1959), 253-72.

Welch, Adam C. "The Source of Nehemiah IX," *Zeitschrift für die alttestamentliche Wissenschaft*, XLVII (1959), 130-37.

Werner, Eric. "The Doxology in Synagogue and Church, A Liturgico-Musical Study," *Hebrew Union College Annual*, XIX (1945-46), 275-352.

Wilson, John. "The Oath in Ancient Egypt," *Journal of Near Eastern Studies*, VII (1948), 129-57.

Winter, Alexander. "Analyse des Buches Amos," *Theologische Studien und Kritiken*, LXXXIII (1910), 323-74.

Wolfe, R. E. "The Editing of the Book of the Twelve," *Zeitschrift für die alttestamentliche Wissenschaft*, LIII (1935), 90-129.

Wolff, H. W. "Die Begründungen der prophetischen Heils- und Unheilssprüche," *Zeitschrift für die alttestamentliche Wissenschaft*, LI (1933), 1-22.

_____. "Hauptprobleme alttestamentlicher Prophetie," *Evangelische Theologie*, XV (1955), 116-68.

_____. "Das Thema 'Umkehr' in der alttestamentlichen Prophetie," *Zeitschrift für Theologie und Kirche*, XLVIII (1951), 129-47.

Wright, G. Ernest. "The Lawsuit of God: A Form-Critical Study of Deuteronomy 32," *Israel's Prophetic Heritage*, 26-67.

Würthwein, Ernst. "Amos-Studien," *Zeitschrift für die alttestamentliche Wissenschaft*, LXII (1949-50), 10-51.

_____. "Die Erzählung vom Gottesurteil auf dem Karmel," *Zeitschrift für Theologie und Kirche*, LIX (1962), 131-44.

_____. "Der Ursprung der prophetischen Gerichtsrede," *Zeitschrift für Theologie und Kirche*, XLIX (1952), 1-16.

Zeigler, Joseph. "Studien zur Verwertung der Septuaginta im Zwölfprophetenbuch," *Zeitschrift für die alttestamentliche Wissenschaft*, LX (1944), 107-31.

Theses and Unpublished Papers

Blechmann, M. *Das Buch Amos im Talmud und Midrasch*. Ph.D. Dissertation, Würzburg, 1937.

Boecker, H. J. *Redeformen des israelitischen Rechtslebens*. Ph.D. Dissertation, Bonn, 1959.

Harrelson, Walter. "Creation and Saving History in Genesis," unpublished paper read to Chicago Society for Biblical Research, April 18, 1964.

Osswald, Eva. *Urform und Auslegung im masoretischen Amostext. Ein Beitrag zur Kritik an der neueren traditionsgeschichtlichen Methode*. Ph.D. Dissertation, Jena, 1951.

Routtenberg, H. J. *Rabbinic Interpretations of Amos*. Ph.D. Dissertation, Boston University, 1943 (*Amos of Tekoa*. New York: Vantage Press, 1971).

Shoot, W. B. Jr. *The Fertility Religions in the Thought of Amos and Micah*. Ph.D. Dissertation, Southern California University, 1951.

SBL DISSERTATIONS

Series Price: $4.20
($3.00 to Society Members)

Payment must accompany order;
orders from individuals cannot be
invoiced. Please send orders, with
check made out to SCHOLARS
PRESS.

SCHOLARS PRESS
UNIVERSITY OF MONTANA
MISSOULA, MONTANA 59801